AP* Student Review Manual

to accompany

Stearns/ Adas/ Schwartz/ Gilbert

World Civilizations

The Global Experience, AP* Edition

Fourth Edition

PEARSON
Longman

New York Boston San Francisco
London Toronto Sydney Tokyo Singapore Madrid
Mexico City Munich Paris Cape Town Hong Kong Montreal

AP Student Review Manual* to accompany Stearns, *World Civilizations: The Global Experience, AP* Edition*

Copyright ©2004 Pearson Education, Inc.

AP and Advanced Placement Program are not registered trademarks of the College Entrance Examination Board, which was not involved in the production of and does not endorse this product.

ISBN: 0-321-20986-9

7 8 9 10

CONTENTS

*"The present state of things is the consequence of the past; and
it is natural to inquire as to the sources of the good we enjoy or the evils we suffer.
If we act only for ourselves, to neglect the study of history is not prudent;
if intrusted with the care of others, it is not just."*

Dr. Samuel Johnson, British essayist, 1709 – 1784

**In memoriam of the victims and heroes
at the World Trade Center, the Pentagon, and in four aircraft,
September 11, 2001**

INTRODUCTION

This *Student Review Manual* is meant to accompany the textbook, *World Civilizations, Advanced Placement Edition* by Stearns, Adas, Schwarz, and Gilbert.

The textbook is divided into six units and thirty-six chapters according to the themes and periodizations developed by the College Board for the Advanced Placement (AP) World History course. This manual follows a similar format. Both text and guide prepare students for success on the May AP exam.

Each of the six broader divisions of the *Student Manual* contains a unit overview and chapters based on the regional themes of the unit. The unit overviews and chapters contain most, if not all, of the following sections: summaries, review questions, vocabulary, map exercises, photo essays and visualizations of the past, statistical analyses, chart and graph analyses, and document analyses. For each of the units and chapters, there are also multiple-choice questions in an Advanced Placement format and numerous essay questions of both a comparative and change over time format. Each unit has a larger geography overview, and there are four document-based questions.

ABOUT THIS GUIDE

Refer to these instructions as often as you need. You should find that materials from the *Student Manual* review what you have studied, but present them in different formats.

There are two ways to use this manual. One involves doing the exercises from each unit or respective chapter after you have read and studied it in the text. This should be in addition to any reading or lecture notes you take. When answering questions and doing the work, you might want to place your answers and responses at the end of your notes or the particular chapter. If you have read well, the exercises should demonstrate your mastery of how well you have understood the text. Another method involves using this manual as a review guide prior to taking the May Advanced Placement exam. You can best accomplish this by reviewing your notes and then doing the exercises in a separate notebook. This second method has the disadvantage of forcing students to review a great deal of material in a short period of time just prior the May exam. Most students cannot study efficiently in this manner. Consequently, it is better to study and review frequently, throughout the course of the year.

UNIT OVERVIEWS
There are six unit overviews that correspond to the program's chronological periods. Each period shares common characteristics, or themes, that delineate and define the period in world history. Use of periodization is a major way in which world history differs from Advanced Placement United States and European histories. As you read the unit, identify themes and learn to recognize them in the chapters within in each unit.

SUMMARIES
Each unit and the main sections of each chapter are summarized in the *Student Manual*. Summaries identify trends, themes, and events within a region or a civilization. And they relate that region to the larger period and unit as a whole. It is helpful if you read and flesh out each main idea with support or elaboration. Additionally, the summaries should place your notes and the subsequent activities in perspective and context.

UNIT AND CHAPTER REVIEW QUESTIONS
The College Board's *Advanced Placement Course Description* and *Teaching Guide* in World History, and the National Standards for World History identified broad questions, themes, and standards to guide students and instructors. Included in the *Student Manual* are unit and chapter review questions to check your understanding of the content materials. The Unit Questions provide an overview for the period and the chapters contained within. They are the broad themes and are critical to uniting geographic civilizations or regions within the broad periods. Chapter Questions review the more important trends and events from a particular region. If you can answer the questions, you probably understand the chapter.

MAP EXERCISES

Several questions on the May exam will test geography knowledge. Do not just skip over the maps within your units or chapters. This Study Manual has two types of map exercises. Examine them and do the exercises in the manual. Each of the six units has an exercise with terms to be identified and located on the maps and provides a geographic overview for the period. The maps and questions in chapters of the *Study Manual* geographically place the region within history, while showing connections between the regions. Maps of this last category will probably be critical to the test. On the test, students will be expected to draw conclusions based on any map provided, or place it in one of the larger historical periods.

VOCABULARY

Not all of the italicized words in your text are critical. History is more than knowing names and memorizing dates. And while it is impossible to understand major events and cultures such as Islam without knowing who the famous historical actors such as Muhammad were, do not spend an inordinate amount of time memorizing names. While few civilizations use a common dating system, historians disagree on which dates are important.

The AP May exam will test for key concepts, themes, and related terms. Define the vocabulary, which is often located either in the chapter or your text's glossary. Students should be able to relate the words to each other and the chapter and region as a whole. One exercise is to write an essay summarizing your chapter by using the key vocabulary.

PHOTO ESSAYS, PHOTO EXERCISES, AND VISUALIZING THE PAST

Students should be able to identify famous locations, cultures, and events depicted in photographs and artwork and to analyze these media. Within a chapter, these visual documents tend to represent a theme common to the civilization or culture. The questions and titles identify the themes. Use the photographs to analyze the theme and subject. If pictures are worth a thousand words, what does the photograph say to you? Additionally, unless a picture is contemporaneous to the time period and civilization, it is a secondary source and may not accurately depict reality.

DOCUMENT ANALYSIS

At the center of any history class is the ability to use and to interpret documents. This is especially true of Advanced Placement history classes, which expect students to interpret primary sources, and to use them in the document-based essay to construct and to support historical essays. While the study of history ideally involves the use of facts and evidence, historians are kind of like detectives of time, who must examine sketchy evidence and draw conclusions to solve a mystery. As writers, historians have to present facts and interpret the data. The conclusions reached are only as valid as the evidence used to support them. Consequently, students must analyze documents according to the following criteria: attribution, point of view, reliability, intent or purpose, audience, and tone. In a document-based essay, you would have to use some of these criteria in order to analyze documents and support your thesis.

Attribution includes knowing who the author is and his or her personal background such as social class, occupation, religion, and education. All are important to understanding the history, relevance, and reliability of the facts and the bias of the author.

Point of view is the result of attribution. It is a neutral way of identifying bias, prejudice, or personal perspective about the topic. Point of view always colors understanding.

Historians must decide how reliable a statement is, or why a person should be believed. Students must question every author's *reliability*. If reliability is strong, the conclusions based on them are more likely to be valid and useful. If an author's reliability is low, his or her statements are suspect and unsupportable, and impair understanding.

Psychologically, there is a motivation behind everything people do. Historians must decide why people do what they do and say what they say. When examining a document, students should identify *the purpose or intent* of the author or motivation behind the document.

Audience is critical to history. And knowing to which group a politician is speaking or the ruler is writing clarifies intent. This is important because famous people slant what they say to fit the audience or purpose. This affects reliability and engenders bias.

Tone is the color of the language and the overall feeling created by the document. Most great leaders and writers know how to use language and words to influence a crowd, make a point, or emphasize an idea. Diplomats, politicians, philosophers, religious leaders, and scholars and courts use choose their words carefully. Understanding and interpreting tone is the hardest thing historians must master.

Take the record by Huang Ma about his 15th century journeys aboard Zheng He's fleets. An example using all forms of analysis would be "*Zheng He, a Chinese Muslim, eunuch, admiral, and explorer,* [attribution] *believed in the superiority of Chinese culture and the supremacy of the Ming emperor* [point of view]. *Zheng He was a chief minister of the emperor and undertook seven missions with his large fleet of warships and trading vessels* [reliability]. *Ma was a chronicler who accompanied the fleet and wrote a log of its journeys for the emperor and court* [intent, reliability, and audience]. *Ma was descriptive of the journeys, recording mundane events, but it is obvious he admired Zheng He.* [tone]."

STATISTICAL ANALYSIS, CHARTS, AND GRAPHS

Historians use visual data to perform statistical analysis and support conclusions. This data may be represented in numerous forms. Pie charts show portions relative to the whole, bar graphs compare different types of data in columns with percentages or relationships over time, and tables display related bits of data in columns and rows.

On the AP exam, students will have to use data in different forms to reach and support conclusions. While the inputs or data are facts, the conclusions we draw or reach based on them may be opinions. Be careful that your facts support your conclusions. And when examining data in any format, students should not refigure the mathematics. Students should look for relationships, make comparisons, interpret the data, and draw conclusions.

MULTIPLE-CHOICE QUESTIONS
AP tests use certain types of questions. Some questions will ask for fact-based responses. Knowledge-based questions will utilize key vocabulary, maps, graphs, major themes, and concepts mentioned in this *Study Manual* and the *AP Course Description*. Some questions will ask you to make comparisons and contrasts amongst cultures, civilizations, or groups, or between time periods. Other questions will expect students to apply knowledge to synthesize data and apply facts to reach conclusions and make judgements.

Each unit or chapter contains multiple-choice questions in an Advanced Placement format. This means five answer choices for each question. All questions in this *Study Manual* are in sequential order to the manner in which data is arranged in the chapters. Remember all test questions not only test knowledge, but can also teach. Use the questions in this manual to learn. None of the answer choices is ridiculous or unintentional. Wrong answers teach as much as the correct ones – look at what is incorrect and decide why they are wrong.

With five choices in a question, one answer is clearly the best answer or most correct. With some questions, one answer choice is the distracter. Distracters are close enough to the answer to be a possible answer. Some are correct and would be the answer if the better answer were not there. In most questions, three answers are clearly wrong. Questions written with "all of these choices EXCEPT" ask for students to identify the four correct answers and choose the one that is incorrect or wrong. Questions phrased with the "BEST" mean four answers are not nearly as useful or as correct as one of the choices. Questions asking for a "FACT" have four statements that are false or opinions.

ESSAYS
Chapters and Unit Overviews in the *Study Manual* reflect the three types of essays students will have to write on the day of the AP World History exam. Two types are called Change over Time and Comparative essays. Also included are four Document-Based Questions (DBQs).

Change Over Time asks students to write an essay, which takes some theme or subject and identifies how it has changed and what has remained the same. Change Over Time will always examine changes or continuities between the six periods.

Comparative asks students to decide how two different subjects are similar and different. It is expected that these questions will only compare within time periods.

The Document-Based Question asks students to use the documents to reach a conclusion about a topic and support it with evidence drawn from the documents in the exercise.

Students can practice writing these essays in preparation for the May exam. The most useful method is not to physically write out the essay. Students should create an outline that answers the question. They should write out hook, thesis, and conclusion sentences, and fill in the outline with all appropriate information necessary to answer the prompt. See *Test-Taking Tips* for essay writing strategies.

TIPS FOR READING YOUR TEXT AND TAKING NOTES

There is a simple formula for success in any class: read the text and take notes. When it comes time to review your notes for tests, use this *Student Manual*.

There is no substitute for reading!
This manual is designed for use with, not instead of, the textbook. If you do not read the text, it is unlikely you will pass any course, and Advanced Placement (AP) World History is no exception to this truism. Professors and teachers frequently have students read from one assigned text, but often lecture from other sources. Consequently, if you do not read the assigned text, you will only have a portion of the material needed for success.

Reading must be supplemented by notetaking.
Few people possess photographic memories. To best prepare to pass your course and the spring AP exam, students should keep a notebook. This should include lecture notes, map work, essays, vocabulary, and the review of all returned work. If you take good notes, reviewing for tests will be easier and should ensure better results.

Notetaking can take many forms.
One superior method is outlining the chapters. While most students do not like to outline, there is no better method to summarize the contents of a book. As you read, take your notes in some organized format. If you opt to outline, each semester, buy a spiral notebook with three sections and around 180 pages. Before your begin, divide the page vertically into two columns. Create a narrower column on the left and a wider one on the right. This is called a T-outline. As you read, *place your reading notes in the larger, right-handed column.* When your teacher lectures, put his or her notes in the left column across from your notes on the same topic.

Do not read and outline simultaneously!
Read each separate section and then go back and outline it. In your text, each chapter is divided into main sections (blue, black, bold letters and numbers) and sub-sections (red, lower-case lettering) within the larger sections. These conditions make it easy to outline.

Do not write everything down.
The titles of each unit, chapter, and section are signposts to the main ideas. Figure out what they mean. Write them down. Summarize the main points of each section or paragraph. Include key vocabulary; it is identified by italics and defined within the text or glossary. Do not copy paragraphs or sentences. Learn to summarize. And use a dictionary. When you read, if you do not understand a word, look it up.

Review your notes prior to a test – do not reread the whole textbook or relative chapters.
When you are ready to study for any exam, review your notes over the relevant sections. If you have read and outlined thoroughly, there is little need to go back to your textbook. Learn to highlight important themes or ideas in one color and vocabulary in another. Or use your notes and the *Student Manual* to test your knowledge in a different format.

TEST-TAKING TIPS

The Advanced Placement World History test consists of two equally weighted sections. Section One is a multiple-choice section with 70 questions that must be completed in 55 minutes. Section Two is a Free Response or an essay portion consisting of three essays. There is one Document-Based Question (DBQ) that must be written in 50 minutes; there are also two shorter essays, Change Over Time and Comparative which must be written in 40 minutes each.

SECTION I: MULTIPLE-CHOICE QUESTIONS

The multiple-choice questions will cover the curriculum, scope, and suggested weight of world history as outlined in the *AP World History Course Description*. This means that 19-20% of the test questions will come from the Foundations period, 8000 B.C.E.—600 C.E., 22% from the Post-Classical period (600– 1450 C.E.), 19-20% from the Early Modern period (1450 – 1750 C.E.), 19-20% from the Modern period (1750 – 1914 C.E.), and 19-20% from the Contemporary period since 1914.

This means that you cannot skip one chronological period and concentrate on another. This also holds true for regions. Do not avoid studying Latin America or Africa in order to concentrate on Southwest Asia, South Asia, or East Asia. *It is also critical that you finish the entire book because the last chapters and periods are as important as the first.* Many of the questions will also be cross period and will compare and contrast different civilizations and cultures, or ask how civilizations have changed or remained the same over time. Ideally, if the last periods are the freshest in your mind, you will probably only have to review the first periods and materials you have studied.

In order to receive a score high enough to earn college credit, *you do not have to answer all of the questions correctly*. Each year the College Board uses a sliding scale and changes the number of correct questions and overall score needed to make each of the five broad scores. This is to reflect the difficulty of the questions and norm reference of the test to get a desired result.

Students are warned not to guess at answers unless they can eliminate two of the choices. You should read the questions, and using your knowledge, try to eliminate two of the choices. If you can, the odds are in your favor to guess. If students cannot eliminate two choices, they should leave the answer blank and go on.

During the test, students should pace themselves. They should not spend too much time thinking over one or more of the choices or questions. If they cannot answer the question, they should move on. Work the other questions, and, time permitting, go back to the questions they did not answer. They should try again, but leave the answer blank unless they can eliminate some of the choices.

SECTION II: THE FREE-RESPONSE QUESTIONS

Before students begin to write any of the three essays, they should access the College Board's Advanced Placement Web site at: http://www.collegeboard.com/student/testing/ap/subjects.html. They should click on World History, then open up the Course Description, where they can find and download the grading rubrics. The rubrics are critical keys to what should be in each of the essays. It is not too strong to say that students should memorize and learn to use the rubrics to structure their essays. Please note that all essays have a basic and an expanded core. *Students cannot earn points from the expanded core unless they have earned all of the points in the basic core.*

All AP essays are graded according to a rubric. All essays should have a comprehensive with an analysis. If students do this, their essays will be stronger.

Students must practice essay writing prior to taking the test. They should begin as early as the school year starts. Ideally students have written essays in class, and the teacher has returned them graded and with comments. Or students can use the appropriate grid in the Appendix section at the end of this guide, plan out an essay, and time permitting, write and grade their own essays.

BASIC ESSAY TECHNIQUES

Essays begin with the prompt. Students should understand what the prompts are asking them to do. *Students may be asked to analyze, assess, evaluate, compare, contrast, describe, discuss, and explain. Know the difference between these words.* Additionally, prompts can be multi-task in that they ask the writer to perform several actions. Students should answer all parts of the prompt.

One helpful guide is to create five paragraph essays. The first should contain a thesis statement. If students have any other sentence, an attention grabber similar to the headlines of a newspaper called a hook could precede their thesis. Students should not waste time and effort on long thesis paragraphs. Students should come to the point – their thesis – immediately, and go on to prove their argument.

One recommendation is to include general examples in the thesis sentence. For example, if the prompt asks about the Mongols, a superior thesis would be "*The Mongols were efficient governors because of their political, economic, and social policies.*" The first portion of the thesis, "*The Mongols were efficient governors,*" is an acceptable, albeit simple, thesis. At the bare minimum, all essays should include this type of thesis. The second part, "*because of their political, economic, and social policies*" turns a simple thesis into a clear, analytical, and comprehensive thesis. The better essays will follow the second format.

The conclusion paragraph need only consist of one sentence. While a conclusion resembles a thesis, students should not copy or paraphrase the thesis. They should write a sentence that sums up what they have learned or proven in their essay.

The other paragraphs form the body of the essay and are critical. Within three of the paragraphs, students prove their argument. *Set up body paragraphs in an order parallel to the structure within the thesis sentence.* Students should organize points in the thesis from the strongest point to weakest point. Strength is based on the amount of evidence presented and the thoroughness of the argument. The weakest point should be last. Based on the above thesis, this means "*political policies*" should be the topic of the first body paragraph, while the second point will be "*economic policies*" and the last paragraph will cover "*social policies.*"

The first sentence in the body paragraphs should expand upon the sub-point from the thesis. An example about the Mongols could be "*Politically, the Mongols were tolerant governors, who insisted upon honesty, efficiency, and equality in their policies.*" Within each paragraph, there should be two or three facts or pieces of historical support material.

While grammar is important, the essay is a rough draft. It does not have to be perfect. Graders know that 50 minutes does not allow students much time to perfect grammar, and syntax. While it is imperative that the essay be readable and intelligible, national graders will not deduct for grammatical mistakes.

THE DOCUMENT-BASED QUESTION (DBQ)

The Document-Based Question consists of a prompt with between four and ten primary source documents. *The question is not primarily designed to test a student's knowledge about world history, but rather the student's ability to use documentary evidence to make and to support an argument.* The graders will be grading by the following criteria:

An *acceptable thesis* requires a simple thesis stating the point of argument. An *expanded thesis* and additional points require a comprehensive thesis statement, such as the preceding example.

Students need to use all or all but one of the documents. Use is defined as citing, quoting, listing, summarizing, mentioning, analyzing, interpreting, or critiquing the documents. *Students must support the thesis with appropriate evidence from the documents.* Students must analyze, interpret, and critique the documents. *Quoting, listing, summarizing, citing, or mentioning a document does not qualify for this criterion*! Basically, students must perform any of the functions used to analyze documents within each chapter of this Study Manual. Students should support their thesis through the use of outside material not mentioned in their documents. If students know of facts and information relevant to the topic but not mentioned in the documents, they should include them.

Students must *understand the basic meaning of the documents cited in the essay*. Students may misinterpret one document but any more will cost one core point. Minor mistakes involving dates and names are not critical but misrepresenting a document can be fatal.

Analyze point of view or bias in at least two or three documents, depending on the essay that year. In order to earn this point, students should attribute and analyze point of view, bias, purpose or intent, tone, audience, or reliability.

Students must analyze documents by grouping them in one, two or three ways, depending on the DBQ prompt. If the DBQ gives students groups in the prompt, they must use the mentioned groups. These groups should be mentioned in their thesis statement. The better writers will create their own groups or categories based on the documents. Nevertheless, students might use the acronym *PERSIAN* to help structure their thoughts. PERSIAN means politics, economics, religion, social (including gender), intellectual, artistic, and near (meaning geography, demography, and environment). Evidence should fit into three of these categories. Other methods of grouping include organizing by gender, social class, occupation, nationality, similar points of view, or religion.

Students will be asked to identify one additional type of document they could have used to support the essay prompt. One useful way to accomplish this is to identify a point of view or group missing from the discussion. For example, an essay on gender rights that does not include a woman's point of view is weak. You should mention this failing. At the same time, if all of the documents in the same easy are from women, a man's point of view might help balance the essay. Students should decide what is missing and mention what type of document or point of view might improve the essay. They should place this sentence in whichever body paragraph will be most effective. This could also include bringing in outside information relevant to the topic.

Students will have 50 minutes to write their essays. They should use 10 minutes to read the documents and to structure or outline their essay. They should spend 40 minutes writing and 10 minutes reviewing what they have written. Students should make sure they have used all the documents, have three groups, and performed all activities they are required to do. They should especially check their prompt to sec that they have addressed all parts required.

CHANGE OVER TIME ESSAY

The Change Over Time essay asks students to access how larger global issues and themes such as gender, trade, technology, and environment changed, and remained the same, over time. If any one essay will give students difficulties, it is likely that this essay will be problematic. *Students will not only have to identify areas of change, but also areas of continuity across chronological periods, and will have to compare two or more chronological periods within one geographic area.*

Unlike other AP history essays, students will not have a choice for the essay. Students will all have the same essay, but within the prompt, students may be able to choose between different geographic regions to answer the question.

The essay must have an acceptable thesis. The remarks about the DBQ thesis, both acceptable and comprehensive, are applicable to the Change Over Time essay.

Students must address all parts of the prompt although not thoroughly or evenly. Students should make sure that the thesis mentions global issues and time periods addressed or implied in the prompt. If the prompt asks for students to assess changing gender relations in a certain geographic region, the student is expected to discuss the changes and continuities over historical time. An example of an appropriate thesis would be: *"In China between 1000 BCE and 2000 CE, until the last few decades of communist rule, women's rights have steadily declined within the political and economic sectors of society, but remained paramount within the family."* The paragraphs would address politics, economics, and the family. Within the paragraphs, students would show a process of decline or erosion of women's rights until the 20th century, except for the paragraph on the family, where Chinese women have always had great influence. Coverage does not have to be even or thorough.

Students must substantiate the thesis with appropriate historical evidence. It is not sufficient to make a statement without use of proof and evidence. Students should use evidence, which is clear and detailed. Key and appropriate vocabulary is critical. For instance, if the prompt is about gender relations in China over time, footbinding, the Five Confucian Relationships subordinating women to men, and the Communist point of view about women in the revolution are all critical points that should be included.

Students must use the historical context effectively to show change and continuity. This requires students to address the topic across *all* relative chronological periods, and show changes and continuities. There must be a discussion and analysis of the beginning, middle, and end of the time frame of the question. Also, they should mention both changes and continuities! Additionally, students should discuss characteristics within the individual time periods. For instance, women in China had considerable rights under the Mongol's Yuan Dynasty, primarily because women had many rights within the nomadic Mongol society. Additionally, many of the leaders of the Chinese Nationalist Revolution in 1911 and the Communist Party between 1928 and 2000 were women.

COMPARATIVE ESSAY

Students will compare (similarities) and contrast (differences) key themes and issues within one chronological period. It will focus on at least two different societies or civilizations, which are probably interacting with each other in some manner.

Again *all essays must have an acceptable thesis, which addresses the similarities and differences between two subjects or themes.* For example, if the prompt asks students to discuss gender issues in China and Western Europe, the thesis will have to show similarities and differences. China and Western Europe both restricted women's rights in patriarchal, aristocratic and militaristic societies, such as during feudal times. But Western culture has always allowed women greater freedoms than China, largely because of Christianity and modern democracy, whereas Confucianism consigns women a clearly inferior role throughout society.

The only other significant difference between the comparative and the Change Over Time essays are that *students must make two or more relevant, direct comparisons between or among societies*. Because of this, students should organize their essays by grouping in a manner similar to the previous examples. The acronym PERSIAN will suffice, and they should use three major groups. It is not wise to have separate paragraphs for similarities and differences. It is best to show similarities and differences about a subject in separate paragraphs, such as women in politics or women in the marketplace.

PROLOGUE

Pages xxix-xxx

I.   SECTION REVIEW

    A. What is world history and when did it emerge as a discipline?

    B. What is the problem with using civilizations as an organizing principle?

    C. How do historians organize chronologies and periods in world history?

II.   VOCABULARY

    A. Periodization, periods

    B. Chronology

    C. World history

    D. Civilization

    E. Ethnocentrism

III.   MULTIPLE-CHOICE QUESTIONS

    1. World history involves the study of
        A. all the world's historical events and historical societies.
        B. the evolution of leading societies and interactions around the globe.
        C. regional histories.
        D. modern history.
        E. the accomplishments of famous people.

    2. The major difference between a civilization and other methods of organizing humans in groups is civilizations
        A. generated surpluses of food beyond mere needs of survival.
        B. invented writing.
        C. traded.
        D. developed institutions.
        E. organized time.

IV.   ESSAY QUESTIONS

    A. Compare and contrast "world history" and other types of history.

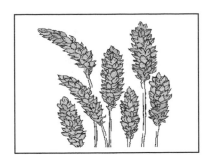

PART I
The Rise of Agriculture and Agricultural Civilizations

Pages 2 - 5

SUMMARY

Because of improvements in technology, our world is becoming smaller, and it is relatively easy for us to travel and communicate all over the world. In some ways, this increased contact makes us more homogeneous than ever before. On the other hand, sometimes societies struggle to cling to their uniqueness. The tension caused by these two contrary trends makes interaction among societies complex. This same tension informs our study of how the world became what it is today. While there are major, long-standing diversities among people, there are also many respects in which humankind has been united and shares certain features. Developments that ultimately shaped much of the world's population can be understood by dividing the past into coherent periods of world history. We will explore patterns of development in the world's seven regions—East Asia, India and Southeast Asia, the Middle East, Eastern Europe, sub-Saharan Africa, Western Europe and North America, and Latin America. Each civilization has had to deal with some common issues and has approached these issues in distinctive ways. In comparing these major civilizations, we will strive to understand these different approaches to common social issues, as well as the extent and effect of interactions among the civilizations.

CHAPTER 1:
From Human Prehistory to the Early Civilizations
Pages 6 – 29

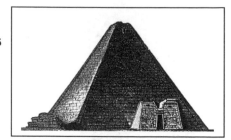

I.   SUMMARY

A. The Neolithic Revolution

In the Neolithic (New Stone) Age, between roughly 8000 and 3500 B.C.E., some human societies in different areas over the globe crossed one of the watersheds in human history. They mastered sedentary agriculture and domesticated animals that would prove critical to human development. These innovations produced the food surpluses and rising populations that made possible the rise of genuine towns and the increasing specialization of occupations within human societies. At the same time pastoral nomadism developed, but these people remained on the periphery of civilizations and sedentary agricultural zones.

B. Civilization

The emergence of civilization occurred in many agricultural societies. It often built on additional changes in technology including the introduction of metal tools. Most civilizations had common features including cities, writing, formal institutions especially government and religion, stratified classes, and trade. Early civilizations included Mesopotamia, Egypt, the Indus River, and China.

C. The Heritage of the River Valley Civilizations

River valley civilizations left a number of durable innovations, but most declined after about 1200 B.C.E. This decline was often due to nomadic migrations across Eurasia by pastoral nomadic chariot peoples from the Central Asian steppe. A number of small centers emerged in Southwest Asia. These civilizations introduced further innovations including the religion of Judaism, the alphabet, iron tools, and extensive trade connections across the Mediterranean basin.

D. The First Civilizations

The river valley civilizations created a basic set of tools, intellectual concepts such as writing and mathematics, and political forms that persisted across three continents. The rise of civilizations reduced local autonomy, as kings and priests tried to spread trade contacts and cultural forms and warred to gain new territory. Civilization itself was an integrating force at a larger regional level, although in Southwest Asia, smaller identities persisted. However, these civilizations had only sporadic contacts with each other. Consequently, they and their leading institutions and cultural forms developed separately. Thus, four distinct centers of civilization developed (five if the emerging Olmec culture in Mesoamerica is included), each with widely varied patterns.

II. CHAPTER REVIEW

A. Describe human migration across the globe.

B. How and where did agricultural societies first emerge?

C. How did sedentary agriculture lead to societal changes?

D. What are the characteristics of civilization and where did the first ones arise?

E. How did geography influence the rise of civilizations?

F. What political, social, economic, and religious institutions emerged?

G. What social hierarchies, gender relationships, and social inequalities arose?

H. How did civilized culture survive the rise and fall of regional states?

I. Describe the contributions of Judaism.

J. How were the first civilizations similar and different?

III. VOCABULARY AND IDENTIFICATIONS

A. Paleolithic (Old Stone) Age

B. Neolithic (New Stone) Age

C. Slash and Burn Agriculture

D. Neolithic Revolution(s)

E. Pastoralism

F. Domestication

G. Sedentary

H. Civilization

I. Institution

J. Patriarchal

K. Animism, Polytheism, Monotheism

IV. MAP EXERCISES

A. Map 1.1: *The Spread of Human Populations, c. 10,000 B.C.E.* (Page 10)
    1. Why does Africa appear to be the home of humans and their near relatives?

    2. What evidence verifies that man migrated to the Americas and Australia?

B. Map 1.2: *The Spread of Agriculture* (Page 12)
    1. What region seems to be the most important core area for agriculture? Why?

    2. What proof exists that agriculture originated in one area but spread to others?

    3. What products seem to have had two areas of first cultivation?

    4. Theorize how bananas, rice, and yams arrived in Africa.

C. Map 1.3: *Egypt, Kush, and Axum* (Page 21)
    1. What geographic features protect Egypt from invasion?

    2. How does the Nile River affect movement?

    3. From what directions would Egypt experience foreign contacts?

    4. How is Kush even more isolated?

    5. Which civilization would have had the greatest influence on Kush? Why?

D. Visualizing the Past: *Mesopotamia in Maps* (Page 17)
   1. Why is Mesopotamia exposed to attack?

   2. What benefit resulted from having larger empires?

   3. Why would this region be a crossroad? With what results?

V. PHOTO ESSAY: *Early Institutions* (Use photos on pages 6, 14, 18, and 22)

   A. How do these photographs depict:
      1. Hierarchy?

      2. Technology?

      3. Complex institutions?

   B. How has technology changed from the Stone Age through the first agricultural civilizations?

VI. DOCUMENT ANALYSIS: *Hammurabi's Law Code* (Page 19)

   A. Analysis
      1. Who wrote it? (Attribution includes biographical references)

      2. What was the author's point of view?

      3. How reliable is the document? Why?

      4. What was the intent or purpose behind the document?

      5. Who was the intended audience?

      6. What is the document's tone?

   B. Drawing Conclusions
      1. What social and familial structures are discussed in the documents?

      2. How does the document reveal information about religious and magical beliefs?

VII. MULTIPLE-CHOICE QUESTIONS

1. The transformation that moved human society toward the current social and cultural society was the
   A. use of fire.
   B. smelting of metals such as copper.
   C. growth of towns and cities.
   D. rise of farming.
   E. rise of specialized classes.

2. Women were probably the first farmers because
   A. men exclusively hunted.
   B. as gatherers they generally knew which seeds to eat and where they grew.
   C. women had ample free time to develop newer techniques and technologies.
   D. in subsequent eras, women and not men in most world societies were farmers.
   E. records from the period indicate women originated farming.

3. The strongest competitor to sedentary agriculture during the Neolithic Age was
   A. pastoralism or a nomadic herding way of life.
   B. continued hunting societies.
   C. slash and burn agriculture.
   D. increased gathering.
   E. fishing and aquatic agriculture.

4. Agricultural surpluses seem to have led most directly to
   A. the rise of cities.
   B. the outbreak of warfare.
   C. monotheistic faiths.
   D. the extinction of Paleolithic peoples and cultures.
   E. specialized services and socially differentiated hierarchies.

5. The start of sedentary agriculture
   A. occurred simultaneously in various places and spread around the world.
   B. began only in the savannas of West Africa.
   C. started in Southwest Asia first but developed independently in other places.
   D. arose in the river valleys of the Huang-he and Yangtze.
   E. began after the abandonment of hunting and gathering.

6. Cities in the ancient agrarian civilizations were
   A. exclusively religious in nature and the center of local worship.
   B. centers of trade, specialized manufacture, and the exchange of ideas.
   C. independent of the local regional economies.
   D. largely military in nature.
   E. rare and scattered.

7. In river valley societies priests developed considerable social power because they
    A. controlled agriculture.
    B. dominated government.
    C. owned the land.
    D. interpreted the gods' wishes and placated the deities.
    E. regulated trade between cities and regional centers.

8. Which of these is an example of patriarchal society in the ancient world?
    A. Young men went to live with their wives' families.
    B. Family descent and property inheritance were traced through the female line.
    C. A woman could have had more than one husband.
    D. Women and men had equal legal rights as written into the first law codes.
    E. After marriage, a woman moved to the residence of her husband's family.

9. Periodic nomadic invasions in the early history of the Middle East
    A. caused disruptions but facilitated innovations and prompted synthesis.
    B. led to the collapse of civilization.
    C. were easily beaten back by the technologically advanced sedentary peoples.
    D. caused mass popular migrations throughout the Middle East.
    E. failed to upset the established political and social patterns of the region.

10. The Fertile Crescent has been called the crossroads of the world because it was
    A. the first center of advanced civilization.
    B. often flooded by the Tigris and Euphrates Rivers.
    C. protected from invasion by the deserts and mountains.
    D. on the routes connecting Europe, Asia, and Africa.
    E. civilization spread outward from the Fertile Crescent to other regions.

11. Unlike Sumer and Egypt, the Indus Valley or Harappan civilization
    A. became a geographic center for a unified, continuous culture lasting millennia.
    B. never had translated writing.
    C. was secure from nomadic incursions and invasions.
    D. never developed a military social class.
    E. developed a monotheistic religion.

12. Compared to river valley cultures in Egypt and Mesopotamia, Chinese civilization
    A. probably developed after civilizations in the Nile Valley and Southwest Asia.
    B. predates the rise of civilization in both Egypt and Mesopotamia.
    C. developed simultaneously with Egypt and Mesopotamia.
    D. did not rely on heavy irrigation as year-round water was plentiful.
    E. has no verifiable historic origins and left no written records.

13. The Aryan invaders of the Indus Valley
    A. were quick to assimilate Harappan culture and abandon their warrior culture.
    B. settled in Indus cities and took over the Harappan farms.
    C. are related to Indo-Europeans and Iranians.
    D. had little use for horses and cattle, as they were vegetarians.
    E. quickly overran the Indian peninsula, eradicating the original inhabitants.

14. In early China, unity and cultural identity were provided by
    A. divine monarchs.
    B. shared religious ceremonies.
    C. a uniform language.
    D. Buddhism.
    E. a common system of writing.

15. Unlike the Harappan civilization, Hindu, Chinese, and Mesopotamian cultures
    A. had little use for writing and written records.
    B. granted women extensive rights and influence.
    C. developed systems and technologies to resist or to assimilate nomadic invaders.
    D. had no contacts with nomadic groups or different cultures.
    E. remained largely pastoral.

VIII. ESSAY QUESTIONS

    A. How did gender roles change from the Paleolithic and Neolithic Ages through the rise of the first sedentary civilizations?

    B. Compare and contrast any two of the river valley civilizations.

    C. Compare and contrast gender roles, social classes, and inequalities in the first river valley civilizations.

    D. Compare and contrast the influences of geography and environment on the rise of civilizations and cultures in Mesopotamia and Egypt.

    E. How did lifestyles, culture, and technologies change from the Paleolithic societies to the first river valley civilizations?

PART I REVIEW

I. PART OVERVIEW

    A. What events mark the beginning and end of this period?

    B. Why was the Neolithic Revolution critical for the rise of civilization?

    C. What challenges did the first civilizations face?

    D. In what ways is the world linked into a global civilization?

    E. What divergences and divisions continue to separate the globe?

    F. What traditions and regional patterns arose in history?

II. VOCABULARY

    A. Institutions

    B. Homogeneous

III. MULTIPLE-CHOICE QUESTIONS

1. The Neolithic Revolutions began around 10,000 B.C.E. with the
   A. first human bands of hunters and gatherers.
   B. adoption of metals for tools instead of stone.
   C. rise of the first human towns and cities.
   D. advent of sedentary agriculture and domestication of animals.
   E. development of complex institutions such as government and religion.

2. The period of the Neolithic Revolutions and river valley civilizations ended when
   A. widespread invasions and new technologies led to the rise of large empires.
   B. various civilizations first established contacts between the regions.
   C. iron was introduced.
   D. the civilizations developed writing.
   E. epidemic diseases destroyed the first civilizations.

3. During the period of river valley civilizations,
   A. technological changes were rapid.
   B. nomadic contacts declined.
   C. hunting and gathering societies disappeared as civilizations arose.
   D. gender and social inequalities decreased.
   E. human trans-regional contacts were limited.

4. Civilizations arose in all these river valley areas during this period EXCEPT the:
   A. Nile River (Egypt).
   B. Tigris and Euphrates Rivers (Mesopotamia).
   C. Niger River (Mali).
   D. Indus River (India).
   E. Huang-He River (China).

IV. ESSAY QUESTIONS

A. How did demographics change from Stone Age to the first urbanized cultures?

PART I: GEOGRAPHY OF THE ANCIENT WORLD

The first civilizations arose in areas of the world that were remarkably similar. All were river valleys located in areas closely bordered by deserts or steppes. The exception was the central valley of Mexico and the modern nation's eastern coast. The climates were often dry and, even if there was rain, a year-round supply of water was problematic. Resources other than soil and water were lacking and natural defensive features were minimal. Civilization may have arisen as a solution to survival and in order to fulfill needs.

I.   LOCATE
    A. Continents
        1. North America
        2. South America
        3. Africa
        4. Eurasia
        5. Australia

    B. Bodies of Water
        1. Atlantic Ocean
        2. Pacific Ocean
        3. Indian Ocean
        4. Mediterranean Sea
        5. Red Sea
        6. Persian Gulf
        7. Arabian Sea
        8. Yellow Sea

    C. Physical Features
        1. Himalayan Mountains
        2. Caucasus Mountains
        3. Hindu Kush Mountains
        4. Sahara
        5. Arabian Desert
        6. Ordos
        7. Thar Desert

    D. Cities
        1. Damascus
        2. Jerusalem
        3. Harappa
        4. Mohenjo Daro
        5. Loyang
        6. Thebes
        7. Babylon

II.   IDENTIFY AND LOCATE
    A. Historical Regions
        1. Fertile Crescent
        2. Mesopotamia
        3. Southwest Asia
        4. Valley of Mexico
        5. Indian Subcontinent
        6. European Subcontinent

    B. River Valley Civilizations
        1. Nile
        2. Tigris and Euphrates
        3. Huang He
        4. Yangtze

MULTIPLE-CHOICE ANSWER KEY

PROLOGUE

1. B
2. A

CHAPTER 1

1. D
2. B
3. A
4. E
5. C
6. B
7. D
8. E
9. A
10. D
11. B
12. A
13. C
14. E
15. C

PART I REVIEW

1. D
2. A
3. E
4. C

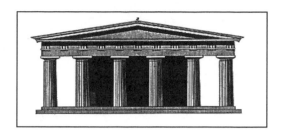

PART II
The Classical Period

1000 B.C.E. – 500 C.E.

Pages 30 – 33

SUMMARY

The remainder of the book covers the last 3,000 years of human experience, drastically slowing down the pace set in Part I, for two important reasons. First, there are many more records to draw from than in the earlier period. Second, civilizations created after about 1000 B.C.E. have direct links to those that exist today. The period after the decline of the river valley civilizations is known as the classical era; it runs from 1000 B.C.E. until the fifth century C.E. The three classical civilizations that will be studied in Part II are China, India, and the Mediterranean civilizations of Greece and Rome. All three were very durable and expanded in many ways even after their decline, contributing to complex syntheses of their respective progeny. Although there was some contact between these classical civilizations, mostly they existed separately. Developments within each of these civilizations, rather than contacts between them, mark this phase of world history.

CHAPTER 2
Classical Civilization: China
Page 34 – 49

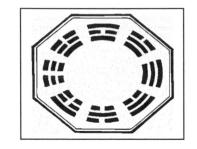

I.   SUMMARY

   A. Patterns in Classical China

   The political rivalries, warfare, and rebellions that arose from the decline of the Zhou dynasty promoted debate over China's political and social ills. In the last centuries of the later Zhou era, some of China's greatest thinkers tried different ways to restore order and social harmony. Central to culture were the family, filial piety, harmony, reciprocal social relationships, and deference to social superiors.

   B. Political Institutions

   Political institutions became one of classical China's hallmarks. Among the most permanent aspects of Chinese culture was the belief in the unity and the desirability of a central government in the hands of an emperor assisted by an educated, professional bureaucracy. Both Legalism and Confucianism became state philosophies under the Qin and Han dynasties.

   C. Religion and Culture

   Chinese culture began coalescing during the last, calamitous centuries of Zhou rule. During this time three critical secular philosophies arose. Daoism taught harmony with the way, and influenced art and science. Confucianism, emphasizing relationships and ethics became the predominant philosophy. Legalism favored the state and harsh rule. All emphasized the role of education to achieve social ends.

   D. Economy and Society

   China's classical economy focused on agriculture. All philosophies extolled the virtues of the peasants and their world. Despite social inequalities based on ownership of land and education, there was respect for the peasant masses. The state also fostered an extensive internal trade, even while maintaining some ambivalence about merchants and commercial values. Socially China was hierarchical, deferential, and patriarchal.

   E. How Chinese Civilization Fits Together

   China's politics and culture meshed readily, especially around the emergence of a Confucian bureaucracy. Economic innovation did not disrupt the emphasis on order and stability, and family structures were closely linked to political and cultural goals. Classical Chinese civilization evolved with very little outside contact. Most Chinese saw the world in terms of a large island of civilization surrounded by barbarians with nothing to offer save periodic invasions.

II. CHAPTER REVIEW

  A. Describe the teachings and institutions of Confucianism, Daoism, and Legalism.

  B. Describe the development of the Chinese state and its political institutions.

  C. How did the dynasties create a unified Chinese society and culture?

  D. How and why did warfare change under classical societies?

  E. Describe the class structure and gender relations in classical China.

  F. What class came to dominate Chinese government and how was it created?

  G. What intellectual and technological advancements did imperial China make?

  H. Describe the influence of merchants and the importance of commerce to China.

III. VOCABULARY

  A. Confucian Five Relationships

  B. Filial Piety

  C. Ancestor worship

  D. Dynasty

  E. Scholar-gentry

  F. Legalism

  G. Daoism; Dao

  H. Secret Societies

  I. Yin-Yang

IV.   MAP EXERCISES

   A. Map 2.1: *China from the Later Zhou Era to the Han Era* (Page 36)
      1. How did physical geography contribute to Chinese isolation?

      2. China calls itself *Chung Kuo* or the Middle Kingdom, the land at the center of the civilized world. How would geography have contributed to this belief?

   B. Extending Knowledge: *Two Chinas and Two Rivers*
      1. There are two distinct regions within China defined by the Yangtze and the Huang-He Rivers. China south of the Yangtze grows rice, while Northern China around the Huang-he grows wheat and grains. How would geography, climate, and foodstuffs lead to two different Chinese cultures and lifestyles?

      2. What policies and technologies would have been necessary to control and to unify the geographically large Chinese state?

V.   DOCUMENT ANALYSIS: *Teachings of the Rival Chinese Schools* (Page 42)

   A. Document Analysis
      1. Who wrote the documents? (Attribution includes biographical references)

      2. What were the authors' points of view?

      3. How reliable are the documents? Why?

      4. What were the intents or purposes behind the documents?

      5. Who were the intended audiences?

      6. What are the documents' tones?

   B. Drawing Conclusions
      1. Which ideas were secular and religious?

      2. Which ideas favored the individual, the state, and the group?

      3. Why would education and social relationships be central to all philosophies?

VI. MULTIPLE-CHOICE QUESTIONS

1. In the influence of geography upon culture, Chinese most closely resembles
   A. India.
   B. Egypt.
   C. Greece.
   D. Mesopotamia.
   E. Rome.

2. Confucianism, Daoism, and Legalism
   A. were officially sanctioned doctrines of the Chin and Han emperors.
   B. are religions, which developed in classical China.
   C. emphasized the needs of the individual over the welfare of the state.
   D. had little influence upon China and Chinese society until the late 900s C.E.
   E. originated as responses to societal problems during times of disruption.

3. Confucian social relationships
   A. established a hierarchy and insisted upon reciprocal duties between people.
   B. taught its practitioners to seek inner harmony with the natural way.
   C. used rewards for correct behavior and punishments for transgressions.
   D. were based on universal love and forgiveness.
   E. stressed the welfare and the interests of the state.

4. The doctrine sponsored by the Qin Dynasty to support its state
   A. encouraged education, new ideas, and tolerated criticism of the state.
   B. broke the power of vassals in order to enhance the power of the emperor.
   C. paid the northern nomadic groups tribute to prevent invasions.
   D. tolerated local lords performing functions for the central government.
   E. used reciprocal social arrangements and scholar-officials as bureaucrats.

5. The Qin Dynasty alienated all of these groups EXCEPT:
   A. Confucian scholars through banning and burning the classical texts.
   B. peasants through conscription and excessive labor projects.
   C. trained bureaucrats who no longer administered government offices.
   D. traditional aristocrats who lost their lands and positions.
   E. Daoist priests.

6. During the Han Dynasty, scholar officials
   A. lost their governmental offices to aristocrats.
   B. came increasingly from the merchant and peasant classes.
   C. utilized Legalism as a ruling doctrine.
   D. insisted on harsh law codes to maintain control.
   E. instituted a system of examination to prepare professional civil servants.

7. Although they varied greatly in wealth and social status in China,
   A. the commoners, especially the peasants, remained the largest group.
   B. the scholar bureaucrats cooperated to limit the influence of the ruler.
   C. aristocrats owned most of the land.
   D. women had many legal rights and protections.
   E. urban artisans and merchants dominated Chinese society.

8. Chinese women in the Classical Age
   A. were free to choose the men they would marry.
   B. could become scholar-gentry provided they passed the state exams.
   C. were legally subordinated to fathers and husbands at all class levels.
   D. dominated the intellectual and artistic activities of China.
   E. varied greatly in status, influence, and rights.

9. Despite their material success and increased wealth,
   A. foreigners were prohibited from settling in China.
   B. Chinese rulers were isolated from the masses and did not intervene in government.
   C. Chinese aristocrats had no influence within the government.
   D. merchants in China ranked below peasants and had little societal influence.
   E. the scholar-gentry were prohibited from owning land.

10. Chinese belief systems differ from single diety religions and polytheism most in
    A. their secular outlooks on the world.
    B. emphasizing correct behavior and performance of rituals and rites.
    C. concentrating on the need for the gods' saving grace.
    D. supporting a relative legally and social equality for women.
    E. deifying nature.

VII. ESSAY QUESTIONS

A. How did Chinese (1) society or (2) government change from the Zhou through the Han dynasties?

B. Compare and contrast Qin and Han government and society with any one of these: (1) Mesopotamia and the Indus Valley civilization; or (2) any other classical civilization in India, Rome, and Greece.

C. Compare and contrast dynastic China and Egypt and account for their longevity.

D. Compare and contrast Daoist, Confucian, and Legalist approaches to solving social disruptions and ineffective and corrupt government.

E. Compare and contrast the rise of the Chinese imperial system with the rise of any one (1) ancient or (2) classical civilization.

CHAPTER 3
Classical Civilization: India
Pages 50 – 67

I. SUMMARY

A. The Framework for Indian History: Geography and a Formative Period

   Geography and climate shaped Indian civilization, which help explain some differences from China. Classical Indian civilization was prepared by cultural and social developments during the centuries of Aryan invasion and consolidation.

B. Patterns in Classical India

   Two major empires formed at the crucial periods in classical Indian history, the Mauryan and, later, the Gupta. The Greek conquest of the Indus and the exchange of ideas with the Mediterranean basin and Southwest Asia influenced the rise of the Mauryan dynasty. The Guptans arose after a period of nomadic invasions.

C. Political Institutions

   Over most of the areas in India where the Aryans settled, religious leaders or Brahmins became the dominant force about 1500 B.C.E. In this era, earlier patterns of social stratification rigidified into a religiously sanctioned hierarchy of social groups, based in part on occupational differences. Brahmans and regional warrior groups dominated shared political power and the highest status.

D. Religion and Culture
   By the last centuries B.C.E., the Indian or Hindu civilization developed a written language, built cities, and produced art and literature, and nurtured two of the great world religions, Hinduism and Buddhism. Artistic patterns linked to religion and a significant scientific tradition developed.

E. Economy and Society
   India developed extensive internal commercial and international maritime trade. Family life combined patriarchy with an emphasis on affection.

F. Indian Influence

   Although Indian civilization after 500 B.C.E. developed several empires, the system of social hierarchy and Hinduism remained the most prominent conservators of Indian culture. Able to withstand the challenge of Buddhism, Hinduism and the caste system was also capable of absorbing and transforming numerous invaders of the Indian subcontinent. Despite its social rigidity, the culture of the Brahmins produced great literary classics and innovated in science and mathematics. India emerged as the center of a Eurasian trade system, a source of great wealth and a means of exporting Indian culture abroad.

G. China and India

China and India offer important contrasts in political emphases, social systems, and cultures. They also resembled each other in seeking to build stable structures over large areas and in using culture to justify social inequality.

II. CHAPTER REVIEW

A. How did geography and environment influence Indian civilization?

B. Describe Aryan society and their social and religious institutions.

C. Explain the beliefs of Hinduism and its evolution from the Aryans to the Guptas.

D. Describe the Hindu political hierarchy, caste structure, and gender relations.

E. What did Buddha teach and how did Buddhism challenge Hinduism?

F. Describe the Maurya and Guptan political and economic institutions.

G. What were the intellectual accomplishments of the Mauryas and Guptas?

H. How and where did Hinduism and Buddhism spread?

I. How did Hinduism respond to the various challenges of Buddhism?

III. VOCABULARY

A. Monsoons

B. Aryans

C. Jatis, castes

D. Untouchables

E. Vedas

F. Brahmin

G. Dharma

H. Karma

I. Nirvana

J. Four Noble Truths

K. Brahma

L. Upanishads

IV. MAP EXERCISES

A. Map 3.1: *India in the Time of Ashoka*; Map 3.2: *The Gupta Empire* (Pages 54-55)
   1. What areas were the cores of Ashoka's state and the Guptan Empire?

   2. Which areas remained outside Mauryan and Guptan control?

   3. What might this have meant for the development of culture? Explain.

B. Visualizing the Past: *Patterns of Trade in the Eurasian World* (Pages 64 – 65)
   1. What physical geographic features would have defined:
      a. The Arab zone?

      b. The Indian zone?

      c. The Chinese zone?

   2. Missing from the map is the Greco-Roman pattern of trade. What physical features defined this area? Use the physical map at the back of the book.

   3. What areas would have been centers of exchange between zones? Why?

   4. If monsoons in the area blow northeast to southwest (November to March) and Southwest to Northeast (April to October) how would this have affected movement?

   5. What products would you have considered luxury goods? Staples, foodstuffs, and raw materials?

   6. Which products would have had the highest profit margins? Why?

   7. Why would trade in foodstuffs have been less profitable?

V. PHOTO ESSAY: *A Civilization's Art* (Pages 50, 58, and 60)
Indian art was largely symbolic, often religious, and had a multiplicity of meanings.

A. How is each of these works of art symbolic? What concept is each intended to represent?

B. We can learn a lot about society from art. Describe Indian social values, material culture, and lifestyles.

VI. MULTIPLE-CHOICE QUESTIONS

1. The highest Hindu caste in India was the
    A. Shudras (workers).
    B. Vaisayas (merchants, herders).
    C. Kshatriya (warriors, rulers).
    D. Brahmans (priests, scholars).
    E. Dasas or the Dravidian peoples.

2. The Indian caste system
    A. differed little from other systems of inequality in the ancient world.
    B. closely resembled the Greco-Roman class structure.
    C. was extremely complex and stratified; a person could not change caste.
    D. had little basis in Hindu religious writings.
    E. integrated non-Aryans into ruling castes as a way of political control.

3. In the famous Hindu story, the *Bhagavad Gita*, Prince Arjuna (Kshatriya caste) questions his caste dharma. In his next incarnation, Arjuna
    A. would likely become a Brahmin.
    B. could expect to be punished for his sins and be denied paradise.
    C. might be reincarnated again as a warrior.
    D. would be denied rebirth.
    E. would incur karma and suffer more rebirths for doubting his dharma.

4. The major difference between Buddhism and Hinduism was
    A. Buddhism denied the need for caste, rites, and sacrifice to achieve nirvana.
    B. Hinduism was monotheistic and Buddhism was polytheistic.
    C. Buddhism denied rebirth, reincarnation and emphasized the real world.
    D. Buddhism encouraged its followers to renounce the political world.
    E. Hinduism taught respect for all living things and prohibited killing.

5. The center of the Buddhist world was
    A. the caste system.
    B. ritualistic sacrifice and the performing of intricate rites flawlessly.
    C. the monastic community of monks and nuns.
    D. the ruler and the worldly realm of power.
    E. the permanence and unavoidability of rebirth.

6. Alexander the Great's invasion of India
   A. led to the spread of Hinduism and Buddhism to the Mediterranean world.
   B. disrupted the existing trade routes between India and the Mediterranean.
   C. had little lasting influence on either region.
   D. led to the rise of the Mauryans and spread of Buddhism to central Asia.
   E. isolated India from contacts with other regions.

7. Buddhism lost its appeal and influence in Guptan India in part because
   A. Hinduism showed its adaptability by emphasizing its mystical side, thus retaining the loyalties of many Indians.
   B. unpopular Guptas supported Buddhism, which led to Buddhism's decline.
   C. Islam was introduced and replaced both Hinduism and Buddhism.
   D. Hindus abandoned the caste system, making Hinduism more attractive.
   E. merchants, the chief patrons of Buddhism, abandoned the religion for Islam.

8. During the Guptan era, all of the following occurred EXCEPT
   A. religious authorities allowed medical researchers to perform dissections in the interest of research.
   B. Indian drama flourished.
   C. the concept of zero was invented.
   D. sculpture and painting moved away from realistic portrayals of the human form to a more stylized representation.
   E. Indians developed an interest in spontaneity and imagination..

9. Over time in classical India, castes
   A. were replaced by simpler social groups.
   B. died out as Buddhism spread throughout India.
   C. intensified and began to differ from region to region.
   D. lost their religious significance.
   E. removed restrictions on gender.

10. In Mesopotamia, the cuneiform culture of the Mesopotamians assimilated invaders and provided continuity. The same role in India was performed by
    A. Buddhism.
    B. the Hindu social hierarchy.
    C. Jain philosophy.
    D. the Greek culture introduced by Alexander the Great.
    E. the culture of the Indus Valley peoples.

VII. ESSAY QUESTIONS

   A. Compare and contrast Buddhism and Hinduism for their views on gender, social hierarchy, and inequalities. (Or an Indian belief with a Chinese philosophy.)

   B. Compare and contrast the classical civilizations of India and China.

C. Compare and contrast gender roles in India and China.

D. How did women's status decline over time in south Asia?

E. Describe the change over time of Hinduism from the Aryans to the Guptas.

F. Compare and contrast the lifestyles of peasants, merchants, and elites in any two classical civilizations.

CHAPTER 4
Classical Civilization in the Mediterranean – Greece And Rome
Pages 68-89

I.   SUMMARY

A. The Persian Tradition

The development of Mediterranean civilization includes the rise of city-states in Greece. This was followed by the Hellenistic expansion. Rome emerged as a separate republic but strongly influenced by Greece. Roman expansion led to a decline of republican forms and the rise of a great empire. Juxtaposed against the three were three Persian empires. Tolerant of local customs, the Persians developed iron technology, organized an effective government and military, developed a new religion and supported a great artistic tradition.

B. Patterns of Greek and Roman History

The rise of the dynamic city-states of classical Greece began around 800 B.C.E., reaching a high point in the 5th century. Then decline set in, but a new pattern of expansion occurred under Alexander the Great. Greek values spread widely in the ensuing Hellenistic period. By the time Hellenism declined, Rome was emerging as an expanding republic, later becoming the Roman Empire. So the pattern was: Greek rise and decline, Hellenism, Roman republic, Roman Empire.

C. Greek and Roman Political Institutions

Greece and Rome featured an important variety of political forms. Both tended to emphasize aristocratic rule. But there were significant democratic elements in some cases, as well as examples of autocracy. Later Rome added emphasis on law and the institutions necessary to run a great yet decentralized empire.

D. Religion and Culture
Greek and Roman culture did not directly generate a major religion, though Christianity arose in the classical Mediterranean context. An emphasis on rationality especially in philosophy, science, and a strong artistic tradition describe the classical Mediterranean culture.

E. Economy and Society in the Mediterranean

Greek and Roman societies mirrored many standard social features of an agricultural economy, including a large peasantry but also a land-owning aristocracy, and dependence on trade and commerce combined with suspicions of it.

Patriarchal family structures predominated. Distinctive features included slavery and a slightly greater ambivalence about women than was true in Classical China.

F. Toward the Fall of Rome

Rome began to decline after about 180 C.E. Symptoms were gradual, including loss of territory and economic reversals. Ultimately, Rome was periodically invaded and the empire finally collapsed.

II. CHAPTER REVIEW

A. How did geography influence the Greek and Roman civilizations?

B. What political institutions were common in the classical Mediterranean?

C. How did warfare and conquest shape classical Mediterranean cultures?

D. What principals motivated Greco-Roman society and culture?

E. Explain the religious and philosophical ideas of classical Greece and Rome.

F. Identify and describe Greek and Roman intellectual accomplishments.

G. Describe the agricultural life and mercantile institutions of the classical Mediterranean.

H. Describe social divisions, gender relationships, and inequalities in the Greco-Roman world.

I. In what ways was Rome the heir to the classical Greek civilization?

J. How did Rome unify its vast empire and diverse peoples?

III. VOCABULARY

A. Zoroastrianism

B. Hellenistic

C. Polis

D. Direct democracy

E. Aristocracy

F. Rationality

G. Tyranny

H. Republic

I. Patrician; plebeian

J. "Balanced and divided government"

K. Clientage

L. Natural law

IV.   MAP EXERCISES

A. Map 4.1: *Greece and Greek Colonies of the World, c. 431 B.C.E.* (Page 72)
   1. What aspects of Greek geography would have divided Greeks?

   2. What aspects of Greek geography would have united Greeks?

   3. Name any influences that the seas had upon Greek life.

   4. Sparta and the Peloponnesian League were land-based Greek states, while Athens and her allies were sea-based. How would this affect warfare and economic perspectives?

B. Map 4.2: *Alexander's Empire, c. 323 B.C.E., and the Hellenistic World* (Page 73)
   1. When Alexander died, his empire fragmented. Look at the physical maps of the same area on pages 349 and 350 of this manual. Where do you think Hellenistic successor states arose? With what boundaries?

   2. Predict how these Greek empires would affect politics, economics, and culture in the area.

C. Map 4.3: *The Roman Empire from Augustus to 180 C.E.* (Page 74)
   1. What advantages did Rome's geographic location give it?

   2. In order to create an empire and defend its borders, what would the Roman Empire need?

   3. How did Rome use geography to define and to defend its borders? (Use the physical map at the back of the book.)

   4. What continents and modern nations did the Roman Empire encompass? (Use the physical map at the end of the book.)

V.   PHOTO ESSAY

    A. Greco-Roman Artistic Values
        1. In what ways did Hellenistic art glorify: (Pages 68, 81, 82, and 83)
            a. Human achievement and striving?

            b. Human form?

            c. Realism?

            d. Everyday life?

        2. In what ways does Greco-Roman architecture emphasize: (Page 82)
            a. Realism?

            b. Symmetry and balance?

            c. Order?

    B. Discuss these statements
        1. Hellenistic art and architecture were designed to be functional and public, while glorifying the state and the gods.

        2. As with the Roman cultural value of *gravitas* or seriousness, Roman art had to reflect not only seriousness, but also *veritas* or realism. How would Roman sculpture look and what might they depict?

VI. DOCUMENT ANALYSIS: *Rome and a Values Crisis* (Page 86)

The Romans believed in *gravitas* (weightiness, seriousness). This quality insisted upon dedication, honesty, perseverance, loyalty, composure, bravery, selflessness, and acceptance of fate.

    A. In what ways does Cicero's speech:
        1. Reflect traditional Roman values?

        2. Depart from traditional Roman values?

    C. Why might traditional Romans see little value in Greek culture as described by Cicero?

    D. Romans were often ambivalent about Greeks and Greek culture, if not distrustful. They also were often jealous of their accomplishments. In what ways does Cicero reflect this dichotomy?

E. Document Analysis
   1. Who wrote it? (Attribution includes biographical references)

   2. What was the author's point of view?

   3. How reliable is the document? Why?

   4. What was the intent or purpose behind the document?

   5. Who was the intended audience?

   6. What is the document's tone?

VII. MULTIPLE-CHOICE QUESTIONS

1. While the types of government in the early Greek poleis (city-states) varied, they were *least* likely to have been
    A. aristocracies.
    B. monarchies
    C. oligarchies.
    D. theocracies.
    E. democracies.

2. Athenian democracy
    A. was limited to males whose parents had both been citizens.
    B. allowed married couples including women to vote
    C. permitted all residents who swore an oath to vote.
    D. distrusted elitism and special interest groups.
    E. created elected representatives to speak and vote for constituents.

3. The result of Greek colonization between 750 and 550 B.C.E. was that it
    A. gave Greek city-states control of Mesopotamia.
    B. brought the Greeks into contact with northern Europe.
    C. established Greek culture throughout the Mediterranean and adjacent seas.
    D. put an end to barbarian and Persian invasions.
    E. led to the conquest of Egypt.

4. The major impact of Alexander the Great's conquests was the
    A. elimination of foreign influences from Greek culture.
    B. establishment of a unified government for the eastern Mediterranean.
    C. birth of mystery religions and the forced migration of the Jews.
    D. spread of Greek culture throughout the eastern Mediterranean.
    E. destruction of regional trade and commerce.

5. In comparison to the Hindus, Persians and Chinese, religiously the Greeks
   A. most resembled Hinduism's polytheism with its caste system.
   B. never developed a major religion.
   C. developed a compassionate system similar to Buddhism.
   D. sought universal harmony in a manner similar to Daoism.
   E. avoided portraying gods with human characteristics.

6. Greco-Roman philosophers attempted to understand human nature through
   A. emotion, especially the desire for love and brotherhood.
   B. its rigid adherence to societal norms with rewards and punishments.
   C. human sin, salvation, and redemption.
   D. human relationships to the state and society at large.
   E. rational observation and deduction.

7. Greco-Roman art and culture emphasized all of these qualities EXCEPT:
   A. human achievement and striving.
   B. public utility and usefulness.
   C. order, symmetry, and balance.
   D. realism.
   E. atheism.

8. While Mediterranean society and economics arose out of a agricultural warrior cultures, it
   A. tolerated trade and merchants but remained suspicious of them.
   B. adopted mercantile cultural values.
   C. relied solely on small independent farmers and few aristocratic estates.
   D. switched to pastoral nomadic ways of life to resolve overpopulation.
   E. encouraged and rewarded trade.

9. Mediterranean agriculture under the Greeks and Romans was
   A. extremely efficient and self-sufficient, supplying large surpluses for trade.
   B. not as dependent on irrigation as were other classical civilizations.
   C. relied heavily on imported grain stuffs and the export of cash crops.
   D. yielded insufficient surpluses to support high urban populations.
   E. favored the small farmers instead of the large, landed estates.

10. In the classical Mediterranean world, gender norms
    A. encouraged equality but only for aristocratic women.
    B. allowed women vital economic roles, but left males in control of the family.
    C. allowed women from agricultural and artisan families influence, but limited the rights of aristocratic women.
    D. allowed women greater economic roles than other classical societies.
    E. gave women no rights.

11. Roman classic culture
    A. owed a great deal of its diversity to trade with China.
    B. developed in relative isolation.
    C. borrowed heavily, especially from the Greek and Hellenistic states.
    D. influenced heavily the cultures of Africa and southwest Asia.
    E. was highly innovative in the arts and science.

12. Unlike most Greek city-states, Republican Rome
    A. developed a balanced government that experienced fewer domestic tensions.
    B. had no aristocratic class.
    C. preferred a monarchical form of government.
    D. granted women and foreigners the right to vote and citizenship.
    E. never allowed the plebeians to participate in government.

13. Rome successfully expanded for all of these reasons EXCEPT:
    A. it possessed a disciplined, trained military.
    B. it had a rich agricultural economy, which supported a large population.
    C. Roman government proved flexible and tolerant.
    D. Roman leaders made citizens out of conquered elites.
    E. it had no organized and powerful rivals to oppose expansion in the area.

14. Unlike Qin legalist philosophy, Roman imperial law
    A. harshly punished mistakes and rewarded success.
    B. was intolerant of innovation.
    C. insisted on centralization of government and absolutist rule.
    D. rested heavily on toleration and local autonomy.
    E. distrusted the military and military rule.

15. What sentence best describes both Roman and Chinese gender relations?
    A. Roman and Chinese women had numerous political rights.
    B. while subordinate to men, Roman women were considerably freer and less oppressed then were their Chinese counterparts.
    C. both cultures were matrilocal – husbands resided with their wives' families.
    D. over the centuries, women's lives improved and their rights increased.
    E. Rome and China were patriarchal societies where elite women had considerable influence.

16. Far more than classical Greece, India, or China, slavery in Rome
    A. was hereditary.
    B. granted no rights or protections to slaves.
    C. was lenient and refused to enslave the young or the elderly.
    D. dominated the labor markets: Rome became dependent on slavery.
    E. encouraged Romans to develop their technology in agriculture and industry.

17. With regard to merchants, classical civilizations in Rome, Greece, China, and India
   A. accorded them high social status.
   B. saw little use for their talents in otherwise largely agricultural societies.
   C. were ambivalent towards merchants despite their vital roles in commerce.
   D. rewarded merchant success through upward social mobility.
   E. made them state bureaucrats.

VIII. ESSAY QUESTIONS

   A. Compare and contrast Greek philosophy and its Hellenistic worldview with Chinese Confucianism or the Aryan religion.

   B. Compare and contrast Mesopotamian and Greek culture, society, and intellectual achievements.

   C. Compare and contrast Hellenistic or Roman and Chinese political heritages and governmental institutions.

   D. Compare and contrast the effect of geography on the classical Mediterranean and any one of these civilizations: (1) Mesopotamia; (2) China; or (3) Egypt.

   E. Compare and contrast classical Mediterranean economical (agricultural and mercantile) practices with other civilizations' institutions.

   F. Compare and contrast gender relations and social systems including societal inequalities with the Hindu social system.

   G. How did Mediterranean political institutions change from the Hellenistic Greeks to Imperial Rome?

   H. Compare and contrast classical Mediterranean attitudes towards the inventions, artisans, and the sciences with their classical Chinese counterparts.

   I. Compare and contrast peasant lifestyles in the classical Mediterranean and Chinese cultures.

   J. Compare and contrast Hellenistic and Han political, social, and economic institutions.

   K. Compare and contrast gender relations and social inequalities in Rome and China.

CHAPTER 5
The Classical Period: Directions,
Diversities, and Declines by 500 C.E.
Pages 90 – 111

I.   SUMMARY

A. Expansion and Integration

Common themes for the classical civilization involve territorial expansion and related efforts to integrate the new territories. Integration included a mixture of central political values and institutions, common cultures and social values, and commercial links.

B. Beyond the Classical Civilization

Outside the centers of civilization important developments occurred. Significant civilizations operated in the Americas and also in Africa outside the immediate classical orbit. Agriculture and other developments spread across northern Europe and northern Asia, where semi-civilized peoples developed extensive contacts with older civilizations. Nomadic societies played a vital role, particularly in Central Asia, in linking and occasionally disrupting classical civilizations. Important popular migrations across Eurasia led to the rise of new cultures.

C. Decline in China and India

A combination of internal weakness and nomadic invasions led to important changes, first in China, and then in India. The central Asian nomadic Huns attacked all three classical civilizations (including Rome).About 100 C.E., the Han dynasty began serious decline. Weakened central government, social unrest led by overtaxed peasants, and epidemics were the most prominent sources of decline, combing to make the government unable to stop invading nomads. However, by 600, China revived, first with the brief Sui dynasty and later (and more gloriously) with the Tang. The decline in India was not as drastic as in China. By 600, Huns destroyed the Gupta Empire. For several centuries, no native Indian led a large state there. Hinduism gained ground as Buddhism, unappealing to the warrior caste, declined in its native land. After 600, Islam entered India and Arab traders took control of Indian Ocean trade routes. What survived was Hinduism (Islam never gained adherence from a majority of the population) and the caste system.

D. Decline and Fall in Rome

Decline in Rome was particularly complex. Although its causes have been much debated, certain issues may have contributed: population declined, leadership faltered, the economy flagged, tax collection became more difficult, and as a result and perhaps most significantly, despondency pervaded much of the citizenry. When Germanic tribes invaded in the 400s, there was little power or will to resist. Developments also varied between the eastern and western portions of the Empire, as the Mediterranean world fell apart.

E. The New Religious Map

The period of classical decline saw the rapid expansion of Buddhism and Christianity. This religious change had wider cultural, social, and political implications. Later, Islam arose, and spread, following the previous spread of Hinduism across South and Southeast Asia.

F. The World around 500 C.E.

Developments around 500 C.E. produced three major themes for world history in subsequent periods. First, there was a collapse of classical civilizations. Societies across Eurasia faced the task of reviving or reworking their key institutions and values after decline and invasion. Second, as new religions arose and older ones spread. These would form the basis of future civilizations. Finally, new developments across the globe, whether through indigenous developments or contacts with older centers led to the rise of new civilizations.

II.   CHAPTER REVIEW

A. What issues and values did classical civilizations stress?

B. Describe the spread of sedentary agriculture outside the older civilized areas.

C. Describe the rise of civilization in the Americas or the spread of civilization to peripheral regions in Africa and Asia.

D. What influences did civilizations have on peoples living near their borders?

E. What roles did pastoral nomads play in world history and commerce?

F. Describe the reasons for the decline and fall of classical civilizations.

G. How were the collapses of classical empires similar and different?

H. How did migrations and nomads threaten classic empires and civilizations?

I.   How and why did new religions develop and spread?

J. What classical traditions and institutions survived despite the fall of states?

III. KEY VOCABULARY

A. Kush; Axum; Ghana

B. Silk routes

C. Shinto

D. Olmecs

E. Huns

F. Rajputs

G. Parthians; Sassanids

H. Syncretism

I. Bodhisattvas

J. Mahayana Buddhism

K. Messiah; Christ

L. Pope

M. Trinity

N. Monasticism

IV. MAP EXERCISES

A. In Depth: *Main African-Eurasian Trade Routes in the Classical Age* (Page 94)
   1. In what ways were land routes affected by geography? (Use the map of physical geography at the back of your book.)

   2. Why might the camel be the preferred beast of burden along these routes?

   3. Using locations on the map, identify the route of the Great Silk Road.

B. Map 5.1: *Civilizations of Central and South America* (Page 97)
   1. Match each civilization with a description of its physical environment and its relative location.
      a. Toltec:
      b. Aztec:
      c. Olmec:
      d. Mayan:
      e. Inca:
      f. The intermediate zone:

2. What elements of geography would have hindered movement and connections between the various civilizations?

C. Map 5.2: *Germanic Kingdoms after the Invasions* (Page 101)
D. Map 5.3: *The Mediterranean, Middle East, Europe, and North Africa* (Page 102)
   1. What geographic features protected the Byzantine (East Roman) Empire from barbarian invasions?

   2. Based on where the Germanic tribes settled, identify the modern states they inhabit (Use the physical map at the end of the book).
     a. Angles, Saxons:
     b. Franks, Burgundians:
     c. Visigoths, Suevi:
     d. Ostrogoths:
     e. Vandals:

V.   VISUALIZING THE PAST: *Religious Geography* (Page 109)

A. Where are the great religions geographically concentrated today?

B. Which religions affect the greatest number of states?

C. Which religions have the greatest populations?

D. How do religious locations today differ from locations during the Classical Era?

E. What might account for the location of religions today?

DOCUMENT ANALYSIS: *Popularization of Buddhism* (Page 104)

A. Analysis
   1. Who wrote it? (Attribution includes biographical references)

   2. What was the author's point of view?

   3. How reliable is the document? Why?

   4. What was the intent or purpose behind the document?

   5. Who was the intended audience?

   6. What is the document's tone?

B. Drawing Conclusions

   1. Why did Buddhism spread in China?

   2. How did Buddhism change as it spread?

   3. What troubles did China face as suggested by this document?

VI.   MULTIPLE-CHOICE QUESTIONS

1. Historically, pastoral nomads
   A. lived interspersed with sedentary farmers.
   B. were rare in Africa and the Americas but common in Central Asia.
   C. lived on the continental plains, where sedentary agriculture was difficult.
   D. prevented contacts between the civilized centers of the world.
   E. had little lasting impact on the development of civilizations.

2. Nomadic peoples
   A. disrupted the transcontinental trade routes such as the Silk Road.
   B. were the greatest threats faced by classical empires.
   C. had few, if any, prolonged contacts with sedentary peoples.
   D. have been agents of contact across the distances between sedentary peoples.
   E. had little on the spread and development of newer technologies.

3. All of these typified contacts between sedentary and nomadic peoples EXCEPT:
   A. trade.
   B. acceptance of each other and each other's ways of life.
   C. tribute payments by weak sedentary societies to strong nomadic groups.
   D. nomads served as mercenaries to some societies.
   E. raids and warfare between both groups.

4. In that the Americas were isolated, the development of civilization involved
   A. convergent development.
   B. contact and exchange.
   C. diffusion.
   D. connections.
   E. independent invention.

5. The two American cultural hearths of civilizations included Central Mexico and the
   A. Mississippi area.
   B. Yucatan Peninsula.
   C. American Southwest (Arizona, New Mexico, and Utah).
   D. Andean river valleys and plateaus of Ecuador and Peru.
   E. Rio Plata and Parana river systems of Argentina.

6. The core or mother civilization for other civilizations in Mesoamerica was the
   A. Olmecs.
   B. Toltecs.
   C. Aztecs.
   D. Mayas.
   E. Chavin peoples.

7. In Ethiopia, trade and contacts
   A. insulated the culture from African influences.
   B. led to the kingdom's conversion to Christianity.
   C. brought the state in contact with Bantu peoples.
   D. led to its conquest by Arabs.
   E. introduced Buddhism and Hinduism from India.

8. Ghana developed as the first great state in western Africa
   A. after Bantu peoples migrated to the area.
   B. as a result of contacts with the Greco-Roman culture on the Mediterranean.
   C. by monopolizing control of the agricultural lands, pastures, and water.
   D. a result of the expansion of agriculture from other areas.
   E. after its conversion to Islam.

9. Early historic Japanese culture
   A. borrowed slavishly from the Chinese and Koreans.
   B. was the product of migrations and constant contacts with other peoples.
   C. remained indigenous.
   D. developed about the same time as Shang China.
   E. was expert in agriculture and fishing.

10. Shinto
    A. is an extremely developed form of animistic nature worship.
    B. arrived in Japan with the first official embassy from China.
    C. is a branch of Buddhism.
    D. is a warrior's religion and glorifies the military way of life.
    E. was pivotal in the transmission of Chinese culture to Japan.

11. All of these must occur for a new period in world history to begin EXCEPT:
    A. nomadic peoples must overrun sedentary civilizations.
    B. the world map must change significantly.
    C. new types of contacts between civilized regions must develop.
    D. new patterns and parallel institutional developments will occur.
    E. new technologies will arise.

12. At the end of the Classical Age
    A. belief systems failed to survive the collapse of classical civilizations.
    B. only the Mediterranean Greco-Roman civilization experienced upheavals.
    C. the Huns (Hsiung-Nu) destroyed all great Eurasian classical civilizations.
    D. there was a religious upsurge as a result of social and economic problems.
    E. trade ceased to be important.

13. As the Han Empire collapsed
    A. Daoists established political control of the various Chinese states.
    B. nomads swept into China replacing the Han with a "barbarian" dynasty.
    C. landowners and warlords dominated the successor governments.
    D. Christianity was introduced to China and began to spread.
    E. internal warfare subsided.

14. In the 5th century C.E., Buddhism spread to China
    A. arriving with nomads from central Asia.
    B. but had little success converting the superstitious peasants.
    C. and was readily accepted by the ruling elites.
    D. which became the center of the Buddhist world.
    E. where the Chinese imposed some of their own cultural values on the religion.

15. In India during the period after the Guptan collapse,
    A. Buddhism reasserted its influence, replacing Hinduism.
    B. the caste system lost its influence.
    C. Hinduism maintained cultural cohesion when the central state collapsed.
    D. invaders rarely assimilated into Hindu culture.
    E. trade and commercial activities collapsed.

16. In comparison to the end of classical civilizations in China and India, the collapse of
    the Roman Empire was
    A. milder and the recovery which followed was quicker.
    B. more severe and extensive than elsewhere.
    C. largely due to internal political, economic, and social decay.
    D. caused exclusively by Germanic and Hunnic invasions.
    E. credited with destroying institutions associated with the Christian Church.

17. Christianity differed from classic Mediterranean culture in all of these ways
    EXCEPT:
    A. it offered salvation to the poor and slaves.
    B. it adapted classical Roman governmental institutions to organize the Church.
    C. it emphasized eternal salvation instead of the pursuits of the secular world.
    D. it granted equal importance to the souls of men and women.
    E. it provided a common culture to unify all classes.

18. All of these contributed to the decline and fall of Rome EXCEPT:
    A. the spread of Christianity.
    B. nomadic invasions.
    C. the collapse of effective government.
    D. plagues which decimated populations.
    E. economic disruptions.

19. The fall of the Roman Empire
    A. left behind a common culture unifying the Mediterranean basin.
    B. left the Persian Empire in control of the eastern Mediterranean.
    C. divided Christianity into Catholic and Orthodox (Greek) sects.
    D. had little effect on artistic and cultural traditions.
    E. divided the Mediterranean into three different cultural zones.

20. Mahayana Buddhism
    A. spread to India and Sri Lanka from China.
    B. emphasizes the original teachings of Buddha.
    C. made little impact on China.
    D. sees Buddha as a savior or god, and stresses the possibility of an afterlife.
    E. found converts only within the elite Chinese scholar-bureaucrats and nobles.

VII. ESSAY QUESTIONS

A. Compare and contrast the role of trade in the development and spread of cultures and civilizations in Africa.

B. How did cultures and civilizations change over time as they spread?

C. Compare and contrast the Olmec and pre-Inca Indian civilizations and one of the river valley civilizations of Mesopotamia, Egypt, China, or India.

D. Compare and contrast the collapses of the Roman Empire and Han China.

E. How did Buddhism change (over time) as it spread from India to China?

F. Compare and contrast the roles any two religious cultures played in mitigating the collapse of classical civilizations.

G. Compare and contrast social classes, social inequality, and gender relations in any two classical religions.

H. Compare and contrast Hinduism and Buddhism; Hinduism and Confucianism; Hinduism and Christianity; or Buddhism and Christianity.

I. Compare and contrast Hinduism's caste system with the Confucian social hierarchy.

Parts II Review

I. PART OVERVIEW

   A. Describe the characteristics and chronology of the classical era.

   B. Describe the changed geographic locations of classical civilizations.

   C. What factors encouraged or limited contacts between the classical cultures?

   D. How did states centralize power and impose unity on vast peoples and regions?

   E. What crises did empires face and what were the consequences of their fall?

   F. What are the ethical and moral teachings of the classical world belief systems?

   G. How did religious and philosophical traditions unify diverse peoples?

   H. How did classical belief systems shape social structures and gender relations?

   I. What role did trade and conquest play in the spread of cultures and religions?

II. VOCABULARY

   A. Classic, classical

   B. Syncretism

III. MULTIPLE-CHOICE QUESTIONS

   1. Classical differed from river valley civilizations in all of these ways EXCEPT:
      A. their societal institutions were more complex.
      B. interregional contacts, especially trade, war, or migration, increased.
      C. government was larger and more complex.
      D. religiously; classic religions were largely monotheistic or atheistic.
      E. large empires and elaborate government institutions arose.

   2. Classical civilizations began with invasions and ended with
      A. the introduction of new religious forms.
      B. a return to smaller, regional states.
      C. dislocations caused by invasions and internal decay.
      D. the disappearance of the last nomadic societies.
      E. the spread to the world of sedentary agriculture or pastoral nomadism.

3. Economically, classical empires and cultures
    A. remained largely agricultural but had considerable commercial contacts.
    B. relied exclusively on slave labor to perform labor.
    C. favored merchants, who became the social elites, and commercial interests.
    D. developed advanced labor-saving technologies.
    E. limited their trans-regional contacts.

4. During classical civilizations, cultures
    A. remained locally based and influenced.
    B. integrated large regions and diverse cultures.
    C. became increasingly matriarchal.
    D. developed increasing rights for women.
    E. avoided innovations, preferring to rely on traditional institutions.

5. Classical cultures
    A. died out shortly after the collapse of their supporting political systems ended.
    B. were based on the beliefs of the imperial ruling elites and rarely spread to other peoples and civilizations.
    C. eventually blended into a unified culture, which stretched from the Atlantic Ocean to the Indus River.
    D. survived the collapse of their supporting empires and continued to influence later generations.
    E. were largely commercial in influence and dependent on trade.

PART II GEOGRAPHY: THE WORLD OF CLASSICAL CIVILIZATIONS

The geographic perspective of the classical world was bigger and more complex than the river valleys of the first civilizations. Classical civilizations spread out. Aspects of physical geography defined the borders of the civilizations. Contacts and sustained communications between the regions arose. Often contacts were across seas, along coasts and rivers, and the plains or steppes between regional centers.

I. LOCATE
    A. BODIES OF WATER
        1. Bay of Bengal
        2. Malaccan Straits
        3. South China Sea
        4. East China Sea
        5. Caspian Sea
        6. Black Sea
        7. Caribbean Sea
        8. Gulf of Mexico

    B. PHYSICAL FEATURES
        1. Andes Mountains
        2. Ethiopian Highlands
        3. Gobi Desert
        4. Eurasian Steppe
        5. North Indian River Plain
        6. Deccan Plateau
        7. Yucatan Peninsula
        8. Sahel

    C. CITIES
        1. Alexandria
        2. Xian (Chang'an)
        3. Rome
        4. Athens
        5. Pataliputra

II. IDENTIFY AND LOCATE
    A. HISTORICAL REGIONS
        1. Polynesia
        2. Bantu Homeland

    B. RIVER VALLEYS
        1. Rhine
        2. Danube
        3. Niger
        4. Amazon
        5. Mississippi

    C. HISTORIC STATES
        1. Roman Empire
        2. Ghana
        3. Nubia
        4. Ethiopia (Axum)
        5. Han China
        6. Maurya, Gupta India
        7. Mayan City-states
        8. Hellenistic Empires

D. OTHER
  1. The Silk Road
  2. Monsoon wind patterns in Indian Ocean

MULTIPLE-CHOICE ANSWER KEY

14. D
15. B
16. D
17. C

CHAPTER 2

1. B
2. E
3. A
4. B
5. C
6. E
7. A
8. C
9. D
10. A

CHAPTER 3

1. D
2. C
3. E
4. A
5. C
6. D
7. A
8. E
9. C
10. B

CHAPTER 4

1. D
2. A
3. C
4. D
5. B
6. E
7. E
8. A
9. C
10. B
11. C
12. A
13. E

CHAPTER 5

1. C
2. D
3. B
4. E
5. D
6. A
7. B
8. D
9. E
10. A
11. A
12. D
13. C
14. E
15. C
16. B
17. B
18. A
19. E
20. D

PART II REVIEW

1. D
2. C
3. A
4. B
5. D

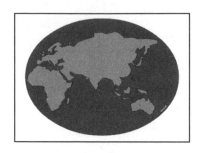

PART III
The Postclassical Era
Pages 112 – 119

SUMMARY

The postclassical period extends from the fifth to the fifteenth centuries C.E. A new international framework emerged to produce a genuine world historical dynamic. Explicit exchange became a standard part of world history.

The Chronology of the Postclassical Period

The stage for the Postclassical Era was set by the same developments that ended its predecessor – the decline and end of classical empires. Capped by invasions of nomadic peoples, the classical decline produced huge changes in the map of the world's civilization. The end of the Postclassical Era was heralded by another set of invasions. Nomadic Mongol invasions poured through much of Asia and eastern Europe. Later the transcontinental epidemic called the Black Death ravaged civilizations again. Both ended governments, realigned institutions, and changed societies.

The Postclassical Millennium and the World Network

Four overreaching developments define the Postclassical centuries. The expanding influence of the Arabs and Islam is one. Another is the spread of civilization to additional regions of the world. A widespread shift in basic belief systems from polytheism to great world religions is the third. Finally, the development of a world network with regular and influential relations among most of the individual civilizations is the fourth general theme.

World History Themes

This period saw no major environmental changes nor were any fundamental new technologies introduced. Change primarily reflected population increases. Nor did basic structures of social or gender inequality shift greatly, although new religions' emphases focused on spiritual equality. Slavery declined in some areas but not all, and several societies introduced new constraints on women. The role of nomads peaked. Trading companies became the leading innovators in formal international relations. Expanding civilizations and new religions provided opportunities for human agency. And international exchanges grew in range and intensity.

Exchange and Imitation in the Postclassical World

Three characteristics of the Postclassical period highlight the importance of imitating established centers. Growing trade intensified contacts between outlying regions and the most populous established civilizations. Missionary activity did the same. Finally, the expansion of civilization as an organized form of life built on the possibility of explicit imitation.

CHAPTER 6
The First Global Civilization:
The Spread of Islam
Page 120 – 145

I. SUMMARY

A. Desert and Town: The Arabian World and the Birth of Islam

Islam appeared first on the Arabian Peninsula, an area occupied by pastoral nomads and on the periphery of the civilized zones. Much of the peninsula is desert, which supported both goat and camel nomadism among peoples called Bedouin. Sedentary agricultural communities were limited to the far south of the peninsula, and trading towns developed along the coasts. The tribal culture of the Bedouin provided a critical backdrop for the emergence of Islam.

B. The Life of Muhammad and the Genesis of Islam

In the 7th century C.E., a new religion arose in the Arabian Peninsula. Built on the revelations received by the prophet Muhammad, a trader from the town of Mecca, the new faith won over many camel-herding tribes of the peninsula within decades. Though initially an Arab religion, Islam, in both beliefs and practices contained a powerful appeal that eventually made it one of the great world religions.

C. The Arab Empire of the Umayyads

Although some Bedouin tribes renounced their allegiance to Islam following Muhammad's death in 632, the Prophet's followers were able to conduct military campaigns restoring the unity of the Islamic community. Once the rebellious tribesmen were brought back into the umma, Muslim armies began to launch attacks on neighboring civilizations outside of Arabia. Within a short period of time, Arab armies captured Mesopotamia, northern Africa, and Persia. A new dynasty, the Umayyads, ruled this Arabic empire.

D. From Arab to Islamic Empire: The Early Abbasid Era

The change of dynasties reflected fundamental transformations within the Islamic civilization. As Islamic civilization spread, regional interests and religious divisions made it difficult to hold together the vast areas the Arabs had conquered. They also gave rise to new divisions within the Islamic community that have divided Islam to the present day. The Abbasids' victory led to bureaucratic expansion, absolutism, and luxury. The Abbasids also championed a policy of conversion. As a result, Islam was transformed from an ethnic religion to a cosmopolitan faith with hundreds of millions of adherents.

II. CHAPTER REVIEW

    A. What conditions influenced the rise of Islam in Arabia?

    B. Describe the development of the Muslim community and the teachings of Islam.

    C. What factors contributed to the rise and success of the Arabic Empire?

    D. How did Islam unite and effectively rule diverse peoples and cultures?

    E. How did Islam and the Arabic empire change during the Abbasid rule?

    F. Describe Islamic society including social classes, gender, and inequalities.

III. VOCABULARY

    A. Islam, Muslim

    B. Quran, Hadith

    C. Bedouin

    D. Umma

    E. Caliph

    F. Sunnis, Shi'is

    G. Mawali, Jizya

    H. Dhimmi (-s)

    I. Harem

    J. Ayan

IV. MAP EXERCISES

    A. Map 6.1: *The Expansion of Islam in the 7th and 8th Centuries* (Page 123)
        1. What states and empires did the Muslims overrun?

        2. Which areas of the Arab Empire are modern Muslim states today? (Use the map at the end of the book.)

3. What parts of Europe did the Muslims overrun? If these regions are not Muslim today, what do you think happened?

4. Locate Damascus and Mecca, the first Muslim capitals. What advantages and disadvantages did these locations present when running the empire?

5. Locate Karbala and Ctesiphon. Between the two cities the Arabs built Baghdad. Why build a capital here? To what cultural influences would this location be exposed?

6. Look at the borders of the Arab Empire. What geographic areas would have contact with non-Muslims?

B. Map 6.2: *Arabia During the Time of Muhammad* (Page 125)
1. Describe the physical environment of the peninsula.

2. Byzantium, the Sassanid Empire, and Aksum are trading states. Why are the locations of Mecca and Medina important?

V. PHOTO ESSAY: *The Five Pillars* (Pages 124, 128, 130, 134, 139, 140, 143, and 144)

A. Islam has Five Pillars of Faith. How do the photos reflect the pillars?
1. Confession of Faith?

2. Prayer Five Times Daily?

3. Fast during the Month of Ramadan?

4. Zakat – tithe and charity?

5. Pilgrimage?

B. Additionally, Muslims have to tolerate the Peoples of the Books – Christians and Jews – and protect the community against attack and the body against impure thoughts. These last two are part of jihad, the Holy War. How do these pictures represent at least one of the acts of faith? Explain.

VI. DOCUMENT ANALYSIS: *The Thousand and One Nights* (Pages 141)

A. Document Analysis
1. Who wrote it? (Attribution includes biographical references)

2. What was the author's point of view?

3. How reliable is the document? Why?

4. What was the intent or purpose behind the document?

5. Who was the intended audience?

6. What is the document's tone?

B. The Lifestyle of the Elites
   1. What symbols of wealth appear in the stories?

   2. Describe the lifestyles in Baghdad.

   3. Describe the lifestyles of men.

   4. What high status occupations are mentioned in the stories?

   5. If literature focuses on the lifestyles of the elites, what problems does this create for historians?

VII. MULTIPLE-CHOICE QUESTIONS

1. Although Islam developed in Mecca and Medina from urban roots, all of these influenced Islam's origins EXCEPT:
   A. the harsh environment of a desert.
   B. clan identity and rivalries.
   C. Greco-Roman culture.
   D. Bedouin culture.
   E. merchants and commerce.

2. In Pre-Islamic times, the status of Mecca was enhanced by
   A. the presence in the city of a Christian bishop.
   B. the Ka'aaba, a religious shrine which attracted pilgrims.
   C. its merchants control of trade throughout the Middle East.
   D. its alliance with the Sasanid Persian Empire.
   E. the freedoms given its slaves and women.

3. The Prophet Muhammad had knowledge of life beyond Mecca because he was
   A. a merchant and had traveled.
   B. well-read and well-educated as an Arab scholar.
   C. exiled to Persia before his conversion.
   D. a judge who frequently arbitrated disputes.
   E. a traveling scholar who moved between cities teaching.

4. Initially the Meccans did not accept Muhammad's message because it
   A. conflicted with the Jewish faith of most Meccans.
   B. was polytheistic and challenged the city's monolithic traditions.
   C. condemned commerce and profit.
   D. threatened to replace Kaaba's gods and disrupt pilgrimages and commerce.
   E. was supported by the Bedouins, enemies of the Meccans.

5. Muslims reenact Muhammad's flight to Medina by which actions of the Five Pillars?
   a. profession of the Faith
   b. charity
   c. fasting during Ramadan
   d. prayer five times daily
   e. pilgrimage to Mecca

6. One of the strengths of Islam which made it a successful universalizing religion similar to Christianity was its
   A. use of a common language, Arabic, to unite all members.
   B. insistence that there was only one God.
   C. support for merchants and commercial values.
   D. egalitarianism that transcended previous loyalties, ethnicities, or allegiances.
   E. condemnation of violence as incompatible with faith.

7. The issue that confronted Muslims following Muhammad's death, and the issue which eventually split Muslims into Shia and Sunni sects involved
   A. toleration or persecution of Christians and Jews.
   B. who was Muhammad's legitimate successor.
   C. conversion of non-Arabs to Islam.
   D. the morality of the holy war (jihad) against enemies of the faith.
   E. the accuracy of different translations and versions of the Quran.

8. The Pillar of Islam which helped created the first global civilization was
   A. profession of faith.
   B. charity and alms giving to help the Muslim community.
   C. the pilgrimage by the faithful to Mecca.
   D. fasting during Ramadan.
   E. the holy war (jihad) against unbelievers.

9. The reasons for the Arab's (Muslim) successful conquest of the Middle East and north Africa was most likely due to
   A. the promise of booty to be won.
   B. overpopulation in the Arabian Peninsula.
   C. desire to convert others to Islam.
   D. the weaknesses caused by their long wars of Islam's two main adversaries, Persia and Byzantine Empire.
   E. the unity provided by their faith in Islam.

10. Initially, Islam with regard to women and gender roles
    A. retained Bedouin matrilineal traditions and greatly strengthened the position of women in society.
    B. adopted Christian attitudes towards women.
    C. secluded women and took away most of their property rights.
    D. introduced a harsh patriarchal system.
    E. greatly strengthened the position of women.

11. The decline of women's position within Islamic civilization was due to
    A. Islamic dogma.
    B. contacts with older sedentary cultures and their highly stratified urban systems.
    C. the necessities of war and holy war.
    D. the high death rates of males; the increased number of women in Islamic society "decreased the value" of women.
    E. Bedouin traditions.

12. As the Muslim empire grew and the Abbasid dynasty came to power
    A. Muslim rulers were increasingly isolated because of advisors and harems.
    B. civil wars destroyed the unity of the empires as provinces broke away.
    C. the Shi'ite doctrines were supported and spread by the Caliphs.
    D. the caliphs increasingly brought distant provinces under central control.
    E. conversions to Islam declined.

13. Unlike merchants in classical civilizations, Muslim traders
    A. had little influence within society.
    B. often ran the governments of the Muslim states.
    C. acquired great wealth and were protected and encouraged by Muslim states.
    D. could not legally change their social status.
    E. were ranked socially behind peasants and farmers.

14. As similarly compared to classical Rome, later Muslim society
    A. granted women extensive rights.
    B. denied merchants high social status.
    C. discouraged toleration of foreigners and conversion to the official religion.
    D. relied on the military to run the government.
    E. used slave labor extensively and had an important landed elite.

15. The first flowering of Islamic civilization
    A. was intolerant towards older civilizations and their learning because these cultures were pagan.
    B. grew largely out of indigenous Arabia and Bedouin traditions.
    C. borrowed exclusively from the Chinese.
    D. borrowed heavily from classical civilizations, but made significant contributions in its own areas.
    E. was mostly imitative rather than creative.

VIII. ESSAY QUESTIONS

    A. How did gender relations change from early Bedouin and Islamic societies to later Islam? (Change over time)

    B. How did Islam change as it aged? (Change over time)

    C. Compare and contrast Bedouin lifestyles, gender relations, and government with those in the Umayyad Age.

    D. Compare and contrast the early Arab imperial institutions with any one of these classical civilizations: (1) Qin China; (2) Rome: (3) Hellenistic; or the (4) Mauryan Empire.

    E. Compare the spread, groups who joined, and universal appeal of Islam with Buddhism or Christianity.

    F. Compare and contrast religious ideas with any one of these universalizing religions: (1) Buddhism or (2) Christianity.

    G. Compare and contrast religious ideas of Islam with any one of these ethnic religions: (1) Shintoism or (2) Hinduism.

    H. Compare and contrast the status of women in the Islamic world with any one of these other civilizations or religions: (1) Indian; (2) China; (3) Christianity; (4) Rome; (5) Greece; (6) Buddhism; (7) nomadic societies; or (8) Japan.

    I. Compare and contrast attitudes about and accomplishments in Islamic sciences, the arts, and learning with the classical Greeks.

    J. Compare and contrast the creation of the Arab empire with the rise of the Qin empire or the empire of Alexander the Great.

CHAPTER 7
Abbasid Decline and the Spread of Islamic Civilization to South and Southeast Asia
Pages 146 – 169

I.   SUMMARY

A. The Islamic Heartlands in the Middle and Late Abbasid Era

The vast Abbasid empire gradually disintegrated between the 9th and 13th centuries. Revolts spread among the peasants, slavery increased, and the position of women was further eroded. Divisions within the empire opened the way for Christian crusaders from western Europe to invade, and for a short time, establish warrior kingdoms in the Muslim heartlands. Political decline and social turmoil were offset for many by the urban affluence, inventiveness, and artistic creativity of the Abbasid Age.

B. An Age of Learning and Artistic Refinement

The avid interest in Muslim ideas and material culture displayed by European knights and merchants in this era cautions us against placing too great an emphasis on the political divisions and struggles that were so prominent in the later Abbasid era. It also invites comparison with neighboring civilizations, such as those in India and western Europe that were much more fragmented and racked by warfare in late Abbasid times. In the midst of the political turmoil and social tensions of the Abbasids, Muslim thinkers and artisans living in kingdoms from Spain to Persia created, refined, and made discoveries in a remarkable range of fields. Their collective accomplishments mark one of the great ages of human ingenuity and creativity. Their thoughts and techniques influenced their counterparts in all the civilized centers of the Eastern Hemisphere from the Sudan of Africa to Iberia and western Europe, and from India to relatively isolated China.

C. The Coming of Islam to South Asia

From the 7th century onward, successive waves of Muslim invaders, traders, and migrants carried the Islamic faith and elements of Islamic civilization to much of the vast south Asian subcontinent. By the 12th and 13th centuries, Muslim dynamics ruled much of north and central India. Muslims conquests and growing numbers of conversions provoked a variety of Hindu responses. They also prompted efforts on the part of followers of both religions to reconcile their differences. Although these measures resulted only in an uneasy standoff between the two communities, Islamic influences had clearly become a major force in south Asian historical development.

They added further layers of richness and complexity to Indian civilization, as well as some of its most enduring linkages to the peoples and cultures of neighboring lands.

D. The Spread of Islam to Southeast Asia

The spread of Islam to India set the stage for its further expansion. Arab traders and sailors regularly visited the ports of southeast Asia long before they converted to Islam. From the 13th century, traders and Sufi mystics spread Islam to Java and the islands of modern Indonesia. As was the case in India, conversion was generally peaceful, and the new believers combined Islamic teachings and rituals with elements of local religions that had spread to the area in preceding centuries.

II. CHAPTER REVIEW

A. What factors led to the decline and collapse of the Abbasid caliphate?

B. What factors served to unite Muslims across continents and diverse cultures?

C. How did women's social status deteriorate during this era?

D. What intellectual movements and divisions arose and how did they affect Islam?

E. Describe the intellectual contributions and achievements of Islamic civilization.

F. What factors contributed to Islam's spread to south and southeast Asia?

G. How did contacts between Hindu society and Islam affect each civilization?

H. What was the impact of Turkish migrations on Islamic civilization?

I. What motivated the crusades and how did they affect the combatants?

J. What Muslim achievements and technologies influenced other civilizations?

III. VOCABULARY

A. Sultan

B. Seljuk Turks

C. Crusades

D. Ulama

E. Sufis

F. Mongols

G. Mameluks

H. Rajas

I. Sati

J. Bhakti

IV. MAP EXERCISES

    A. Map 7.1: *The Abbasid Empire at Its Peak* (Page 148)
       1. Identify the boundaries of the Abbasid Empire.

       2. What cities seem to be centers of trade?

       3. What is the relationship between location and trade during the Abbasid era?

    B. Map 7.2: *The Spread of Islam, 10th – 16th Centuries* (Page 159)
       1. Identify the principal Muslim states depicted on the map.

       2. In what patterns did Islam seem to expand?

V. VISUALIZING THE PAST: *Patterns of Islam's Global Expansions* (Page 157)
    A. What are the three largest Muslim countries in the world today?

    B. What Muslim countries have large non-Muslim minorities?

    C. How did Islam spread?

    D. The traditional view was that Islam was spread by war. How does the information in the chart support or refute this idea?

VI. PHOTO ESSAY: *Islamic Civilization* (Pages 146, 149, 154, 155, 156, and 161)
The Abbasid Empire and their Muslim successor states developed a brilliant civilization, which made many intellectual contributions to the world.

    A. As depicted in the photos, describe Islamic developments in:
       1. the maths and sciences.
       2. the arts including literature and music.
       3. architecture.

    B. How did Islamic achievements blend diverse elements?

C. At the center of Islam is Allah. How do the achievements in the photos support or refute this idea?

D. Describe the lifestyles of the intellectual elites based on the photos.

VII. DOCUMENT ANALYSIS: *Ibn Kaldun* (Page 152)

A. Document Analysis
   1. Who wrote it? (Attribution includes biographical references)

   2. What was the author's point of view?

   3. How reliable is the document? Why?

   4. What was the intent or purpose behind the document?

   5. Who was the intended audience?

   6. What is the document's tone?

B. A Historian at Work
   1. How does the author see nomads and sedentary peoples?

   2. How do dynasties change over time?

   3. How do the Chinese Mandate of Heaven and the cycle of civilizations compare with Ibn Kaldun's cycle?

VIII. MULTIPLE-CHOICE QUESTIONS

1. The decline of the Abbasid power was due to all of these reasons EXCEPT:
   A. the difficulty of governing a widespread empire.
   B. invasions of European crusaders.
   C. regional loyalties.
   D. Shi'ia dissenters and slave revolts.
   E. rebellious governors and new dynasties.

2. During the Abbasid empire, caliphs
   A. exercised strong central control over their distant provinces.
   B. were increasingly isolated by advisors.
   C. avoided the use of mercenaries in their armies.
   D. supported the spread of Shia doctrine and the teachings of the Sufis.
   E. persecuted non-Muslims.

3. Mameluks
   A. were Turkish-speaking slave armies used by Muslims.
   B. were the last great central Asian nomads to disrupt Eurasian civilizations.
   C. broke from the Sunni Muslims over who should be the rightful leader.
   D. overran Spain and established a brilliant Arabo-Hispanic civilization.
   E. were non-Muslim boys forcibly converted to Islam and settled as farmers.

4. During the Abbasid period, women
   A. were at the center of the Shia opposition to Abbasid rule.
   B. frequently became Sufi mystics because of the freedoms allowed them.
   C. acquired rights to own land and engage in business.
   D. became increasingly isolated in the harem and behind the veil.
   E. exercised no influence in palace and harem politics.

5. During the Abbasid period, the use of slaves
   A. began to gradually die out as economically profitless.
   B. spread throughout the region and came to dominate agriculture.
   C. was legally curtailed by the Muslim courts.
   D. was confined to the royal court.
   E. expanded as male and female slaves were valued for their beauty, intelligence and strength.

6. The Seljuks
   A. conquered the Abbasid Caliphate and Byzantine Empire.
   B. favored the Shia sect and became its protector.
   C. settled in the lands of modern Turkey and became the Abbasids' protector.
   D. were unable to stop the Crusades or end Crusader control of Jerusalem.
   E. became a sect of Islam devoted to learning, mysticism, and medicine.

7. The impact of the Crusades
   A. disrupted the Muslim world.
   B. had little effect on the military capabilities of the Europeans.
   C. led to the collapse of the Abbasid caliphate.
   D. was greater on the Europeans because it brought Europe into contact with Muslim civilizations and their accomplishments.
   E. encouraged mass European migrations to the lands of the Eastern Mediterranean.

8. The greatest beneficiaries of the sustained urban prosperity during the rule of the Abbasids were
   A. women, who acquired rights to own property.
   B. slaves, when the caliphs emancipated them and gave them lands to farm.
   C. poor workers, who were freed from taxes.
   D. artisans, artists, architects, and merchants.
   E. foreigners, especially non-Muslims, who ran the empire's bureaucracy.

9. During the Abbasid caliphate, the Arabs lost their dominant influence in governmental affairs and intellectual achievements to the
   A. Christians.
   B. Turks.
   C. Jews.
   D. Armenians.
   E. Persians.

10. The Sufis
   A. condemned scientific and cultural borrowing from non-Muslim sources.
   B. helped spread Islam.
   C. objected to the violence and social strife, which befell the Abbasid world.
   D. led religious wars against Christians in Europe and the Middle East.
   E. attempted to blend Islam with Judaism and Christianity.

11. The Abbasid reign ended when
   A. Mongol soldiers sacked Baghdad.
   B. the Seljuk Turks overran the empire.
   C. Christian Crusaders took Jerusalem.
   D. the Mameluks invaded the empire.
   E. Shia governors and troops revolted and murdered the last caliph.

12. Although India was frequently invaded over the centuries before the arrival of the Muslims,
   A. there was little change to the continual rule of the Guptas.
   B. contacts between invaders and local peoples remained limited.
   C. India was largely isolated from its neighbors.
   D. the Hindu and Buddhist level of material culture assimilated most invaders.
   E. invaders had no impact on the Indians.

13. Muslims were able to initially overcome northern Indians because
   A. there was no strong, unified states or armies to oppose them.
   B. the low caste-segregated Hindus welcomed the Muslims as liberators.
   C. Hindus and Buddhists were engaged in a religious civil war.
   D. their penetration was peaceful, commercial, and welcome.
   E. repeated invasions and diseases had killed off many northern Indians.

14. All of these Indian groups were attracted to Islam and converted EXCEPT:
   A. people who lived in the Indus and Ganges River plains.
   B. Buddhists.
   C. Untouchables.
   D. low caste Hindus.
   E. animistic tribal peoples.

15. Contacts between Hindus and Muslims led to
    A. the seclusion of Hindu women.
    B. constant warfare between the two groups.
    C. the absorption by the Muslims of many Hindu social practices.
    D. mass conversion of Hindus to Islam.
    E. decreased trade opportunities.

IX.   ESSAY QUESTIONS

    A. Compare and contrast spread, conversion, and accommodation in any two of these religions: (1) Islam; (2) Christianity; (3) Buddhism; and (4) Hinduism.

    B. How did the position of women in the Muslim world change from the time of Muhammad through the fall of the Abbasids? (Change over Time)

    C. Compare and contrast the fall of the Abbasids with the fall of any one: (1) the Roman Empire; (2) Han China; or (3) Guptan Empire.

    D. Compare and contrast Arabic intellectual achievements with the classic Greeks.

    E. Compare and contrast the effect of pastoral nomads on Arabic (Islamic) civilization and its relationship with any one other sedentary civilization.

CHAPTER 8
African Civilizations
and the Spread of Islam
Pages 170 – 191

I. SUMMARY

A. African Societies: Diversity and Similarities

African societies developed diverse forms, from large centralized states to stateless societies organized around kinship or age sets rather than central authority. Within this diversity were many shared aspects of language and beliefs. Universalistic faiths penetrated the continent and served as the basis for important cultural developments in Nubia and Ethiopia.

B. Kingdoms of the Grasslands

In the Sahel grasslands, several powerful states emerged that combined Islamic religion and culture with local practices. Mali, Songhay, and the Hausa states were African adaptations of Islam and its fusion with African traditions.

C. The Swahili Coast of East Africa

A string of Islamicized African ports tied to the trade across the Indian Ocean dotted the east African coast. Although these cities were Islamicized, African customs and the Bantu Swahili language remained so strong that they represented a cultural fusion, mostly limited to the coastal areas.

D. Peoples of the Forest and Plains

Across central Africa, kingdoms developed that were supported by complex agrarian societies capable of great artistic achievements. At Benin, in the Kongo, in the Yoruba city-states, and at Great Zimbabwe, royal authority – often considered divinely inspired – led to the creation of powerful states.

II. CHAPTER REVIEW

A. What African political and social institutions predate the arrival of Islam?

B. How did the arrival of Islam and Christianity affect African societies?

C. What internal developments and external contacts spread civilization in Africa?

D. Describe the rise and fall of African states and societies.

E. How did religion and trade connect Africa to a larger world; with what results?

F. Describe the intellectual accomplishments of the African civilizations.

III. VOCABULARY

A. Stateless societies

B. Lineage, secret societies, age sets

C. Animism, diviners

D. Ifriqiya, Maghrib

E. Copts

F. Jihad

G. Conquest states

H. Juula

I. Griots

J. Timbuktu

K. Askia, emir, caliph

L. Sharia

M. Zanj, Swahili

N. Demography

O. Demographic transition

IV. MAP EXERCISES

A. Map 8.1: *Empires of the Western Sudan* (Page 177)
   1. What are the geographic boundaries of the West Sudanic empires?

   2. What city and river are shared by many of these civilizations?

   3. Theorize why the Sahel states did not push southward towards the ocean.

B. Map 8.2: *The Swahili Coast* (Page 182)
   1. What elements of geography and climate would confine the Swahili civilization to the coasts of the Indian Ocean?

   2. With what other Indian Ocean cultures did the Swahili trade?

V.　PHOTO ESSAY 8.4: *Benin Plaque* (Page 187)

Bronzes from Benin have symbolic as well as aesthetic purposes. One purpose is to celebrate the powers and majesty of the royal lineage as well as represent the rituals surrounding kingship. How does the bronze sculpture accomplish these goals?

VI.　DOCUMENT ANALYSIS: *The Great Oral Tradition and the Epic of* (Page 178)

A. Document Analysis
   1. Who wrote it? (Attribution includes biographical references)

   2. What was the author's point of view?

   3. How reliable is the document? Why?

   4. What was the intent or purpose behind the document?

B. Sundiata as the King
   1. Describe the Sudanic qualities of being a king as represented by Sundiata.

   2. What does iron represent and how is iron used in the epic?

   3. Why would Sundiata need a griot?

C. Sundiata and the Outside World
   1. What evidence is there that Sundiata knew of the larger, non-Sudanic world?

   2. What elements of animism and Islam are present in the story?

VII. MULTIPLE-CHOICE QUESTIONS

1. Unlike the Americas, sub-Saharan Africa
    A. never developed a classical civilization.
    B. was never totally isolated from other civilizations.
    C. had little popular migration or trade.
    D. developed its indigenous civilizations later.
    E. had no extensive river systems or grasslands.

2. Sub-Saharan African societies are similar to Latin American Indian societies in that both
    A. built classical civilizations without cultural diffusion from other civilizations.
    B. developed in mountainous environments.
    C. originated complex mathematics and scientific traditions.
    D. were so numerous that it is impossible to generalize about them.
    E. were devastated by contacts with Europeans and Arabs, which led to mass epidemics and the death of whole indigenous populations.

3. Stateless societies in Africa
    A. persisted and predominated until the age of European colonialism.
    B. effectively controlled trade in west Africa.
    C. found it difficult to resist external pressures from more organized states.
    D. lacked the institutions associated with government.
    E. could not maintain stability within the group and often broke up.

4. Common elements in African societies included all of these EXCEPT:
    A. similar languages generally descended from a common proto-language.
    B. animistic religions with a class of diviners.
    C. a belief in a creator god or spirit.
    D. the veneration of ancestors.
    E. settled agriculture as a way of life across most of Africa.

5. While all of these peoples migrated to, settled, and influenced north Africa, the only indigenous inhabitants seem to be the:
    A. Phoenicians (Carthaginians).
    B. Greeks and Romans.
    C. Vandals.
    D. Arabs.
    E. Berbers.

6. Islamic teachings in north and west Africa
   A. served to divide the people.
   B. fostered jihads and crusades between Christians and Muslims.
   C. destroyed the trade between west and north African ports.
   D. introduced a common bond but did not erase social or ethnic stratifications.
   E. put an end to the African slave trade.

7. The first universalist religion to take root in Africa was
   A. Judaism.
   B. Roman Catholicism.
   C. Coptic Christianity.
   D. Islam.
   E. Hinduism.

8. The first black African states and civilizations developed in the
   A. Sahel, the grassland belt south of the Sahara.
   B. in the tropical forests along the coasts of the Atlantic Ocean.
   C. in the Ahaggar and Atlas Mountains around and in the Sahara.
   D. along the coasts of east Africa.
   E. in the highland plateaus of Ethiopia.

9. The Sudanic conquest states
   A. ruled lands through military force and foreign bureaucracies.
   B. monopolized trade in one area.
   C. practiced pastoral nomadism and raided sedentary areas.
   D. exacted taxes and tribute from areas without directly controlling them.
   E. converted to Islam and waged holy wars on non-believers.

10. Islam in west Africa
   A. was popular with most elements of society.
   B. converted the kings and elites first without necessarily affecting the masses.
   C. interested merchants alone.
   D. confronted an entrenched Christian religion, which resisted conversion.
   E. had little lasting effect on the area.

11. A common concern for west African Muslim jurists and clerics was
   A. the persistence of pagan beliefs and practices amongst its population.
   B. control of the trans-Saharan trade.
   C. influence of Christianity on west Africans.
   D. the practice of polygamy by many African families.
   E. puritanical nature of west African society.

12. Islam was spread through west and east Africa as well as Southeast Asia by
   A. Jihad or holy war.
   B. mass conversions ordered by the rulers and monarchs.
   C. wandering Sufi mystics.
   D. merchants who established Muslim families and traditions.
   E. migration to the areas by large groups of Muslims.

13. After the arrival of Islam, societies in west Africa
   A. became largely patrilineal.
   B. implemented Islamic law regarding the seclusion of women.
   C. often continued to recognize traditions granting women extensive rights.
   D. abandoned the tradition of polygamy.
   E. abolished slavery.

14. The slave trade from West Africa to the Muslim world
   A. was abolished once the inhabitants converted to Islam.
   B. existed before the arrival of Islam but was expanded over the centuries.
   C. was introduced by the Muslims.
   D. rivaled the trans-Atlantic slave trade in numbers and brutality.
   E. preferred male slaves for administration and military occupations.

15. In the west African forest states, the king's power
   A. was considered divine but limited by the aristocrats.
   B. was absolute and similar to the power of the Japanese leaders.
   C. rested on his relationship to Islam and his authority as an Islamic judge.
   D. varied based on the amount of trade he controlled.
   E. was symbolic; the priests and the diviners ran the state.

VIII. ESSAY QUESTIONS

   A. Compare the spread of Islam in west Africa with the spread of Buddhism to China and Japan.

   B. How did Islam change as it spread across Africa? (Change over time)

   C. Compare and contrast animism and Islam.

   D. Compare and contrast the African civilizations of the forest and savannas.

   E. Compare and contrast African and Muslim views of gender.

   F. Compare and contrast the rise and fall of west African savanna civilizations with the cycle of civilizations in Mesopotamia.

G. Compare and contrast African institutions before and after contacts with Christianity and Islam.

H. Compare the impact of trade on Africa with the impact of trade in southeast Asia.

I. Compare and contrast one of the African sahel states with any other postclassical state.

CHAPTER 9
Civilization in Eastern Europe:
Byzantium and Orthodox Europe
Page 192 – 211

I.   SUMMARY

A. The Byzantine Empire

The Byzantine Empire unfolded as part of the larger and older Roman Empire. As this classical framework shattered with Roman decline, the eastern provinces that became the Byzantine Empire took on a life of their own, particularly from the reign of the Emperor Justinian onward. It centered on a territory different from and smaller than the eastern Mediterranean as Rome had defined it. This was the result of pressures, particularly the surge of Islam throughout north Africa and the Middle East, and popular migrations throughout the Balkans. Despite many invasions and domestic trends, the empire flourished until the 11th century invasion by the Seljuk Turks. The collapse of the empire in Anatolia led to repeated conflicts with Turkish border states and spurred the Byzantines to ask the Pope for help. The Western Crusaders reconquered some old imperial lands but eventually sacked Constantinople.

B. The Spread of Civilization in Eastern Europe

Christian missionaries, Byzantine conquests in the Balkans, and trade routes running through western Russia and Ukraine created abundant contacts with portions of eastern Europe. Regional states formed. After the creation of a state by the Varangian Swedes and its conversion to Orthodox Christianity, Kiev developed some of the formative features of Russian culture and politics. Mongol invasions ended this period of Russian history, cutting parts of the region off from western contacts. A Turkish tribe migrated into the Balkans, intermarried with local Slavs, warred with Byzantium but converted to Orthodox Christianity; the Bulgars became the empire's chief Balkan rival and threat.

II.   CHAPTER REVIEW

A. How did Byzantium originate?

B. Which peoples threatened the empire? How did the state survive 1,000 years?

C. How did Byzantium combine classical traditions to create a new civilization?

D. What were the significant Byzantine political, social, and religious institutions?

E. What led to the split between the Orthodox and the Roman Catholic churches?

F. How did Orthodoxy spread throughout eastern Europe and with what results?

G. How did Christianity influence society in Byzantium and eastern Europe?

H. What contributions did the Byzantines make to the development of Europe?

I. What considerations and influences led to the rise of a Russian state in Kiev?

J. What were the significant Russian political, social, and religious institutions?

III.   VOCABULARY

A. Byzantine

B. Orthodoxy: Greek and Russian

C. Byzantine Empire

D. Tsar

E. Icon, Iconoclasm

F. Cyril and Methodius

G. Kievan Rus

H. Boyars

I. Tartars

J. Schism

IV.   MAP EXERCISES (Use maps on pages 101 and 102 in addition to the pages listed)

A. Map 9.1: *The Byzantine Empire* (Page 197)
    1. What Germanic kingdoms did Justinian destroy?

    2. What defensive problems would this larger empire create?

    3. If someone seized Egypt, how would it affect the Empire?

B. Map 9.2: *The Byzantine Empire 1000 – 1100* (Page 203)

1. Why are the borders of the empire during this period easier to defend than the borders of Map 9.1?

2. What happened that would reduce the Byzantine Empire to a minor power?

C. Map 9.3: *East European Kingdoms and Slavic Expansion* (Page 205)
   1. Identify the Slavic states on the map. [It would help if you read the first few paragraphs on pages 204 – 206].

   2. What peoples probably played a key role in the rise of Russia? Why?

   3. Why did not the Slavs (Russians) control the area immediately north of the Black Sea?

V.   DOCUMENT ANALYSIS: *RussiaTurns to Christianity* (Page 207)

A. Document Analysis
   1. Who wrote it? (Attribution includes biographical references)

   2. What was the author's point of view?

   3. How reliable is the document? Why?

   4. What was the intent or purpose behind the document?

B. Understanding the Reasons for Conversion
   1. According to the account, why did the Russians convert?

   2. Describe the relationship between church and state.

VI. PHOTO ESSAY: *Heir to Three Traditions* (Pages 192, 196, 198, 199, 201, and 202)

Orthodox Christianity and the Byzantine Empire were heirs to three traditions, Caesar and Rome, Christ and Christianity, and Greek civilization. How does their art confirm this belief?

VII. MULTIPLE-CHOICE QUESTIONS

1. Unlike the Romans in the western part of the empire, the Eastern Roman Empire or Byzantine Empire,
   A. was never invaded or threatened by pastoral nomads.
   B. recognized the political influence of the Pope and Catholic Church.
   C. continued to use Latin as its chief language until its fall.
   D. became Muslim.
   E. did not succumb to Germanic invasions in the 5th century.

2. As had Hammurabi's Code (Mesopotamia), Justinian's Code (Byzantine)
   A. dealt primarily with church law and religious issues.
   B. became the basic law and unified code for states, which existed after its original creator.
   C. led to internal disruptions and faced harsh opposition.
   D. greatly influenced the laws of Islam.
   E. deviated sharply from previous legal traditions when it sought to create a new tradition.

3. Under the emperors after Justinian, the chief concern of the Byzantine state was
   A. religious heresy and controversy.
   B. the overtaxation of the peasants and frequent peasant rebellions.
   C. defense against Slavs, Russians, and Arab invaders.
   D. the conversion of the Slavs to Christianity.
   E. support of the arts, including new building projects such as the Hagia Sophia.

4. Within the Byzantine state, as had been the case with government in most of the dynasties of China, the chief power and influence was
   A. emperors and their trained bureaucrats.
   B. the Church and clergy.
   C. large aristocratic landowners.
   D. the military.
   E. merchants and artisans.

5. Unlike monarchs in Catholic western Europe but like the Muslim caliphs, the Byzantine emperor
   A. held political but not religious power.
   B. headed both church and state; there was no separation of power.
   C. was considered divine.
   D. was uninterested in running the daily affairs of government and left all but ceremonial duties to his advisors.
   E. was the head of the military, but not the government.

6. Intellectually and culturally, Byzantine life often
   A. centered on the secular aspects of classical Hellenism.
   B. produced great innovations in literature.
   C. borrowed heavily from the Muslims.
   D. slavishly copied Roman secular traditions in art and architecture.
   E. was censored and controlled by the Church.

7. Contacts with Islam and the Muslims led the Byzantines to
   A. blend Islam and Christianity.
   B. restrict trade and contacts in order to protect the empire.
   C. attack the use of icons as graven images.
   D. adopt Islamic government policies and institutions.
   E. conclude a peace treaty and stop their wars with the Muslims.

8. Although Byzantine society was patriarchal, elite and educated women enjoyed considerable influence because
   A. Greek traditions accorded women great freedom and influence.
   B. Roman traditions granted women extensive legal rights.
   C. contacts with Islam led the Byzantines to protect women's rights.
   D. women could inherit the imperial throne and own aristocratic estates.
   E. wars kept men and husbands away from their traditional societal functions.

9. The schism between the Catholic and Orthodox churches was due to all of these issues EXCEPT:
   A. papal interference in Byzantine political and religious affairs.
   B. clerical celibacy; Catholic priests could not marry but the Orthodox could.
   C. the Pope's support for a rival, revived Catholic empire in the west.
   D. the Byzantine state controlled the church in the eastern lands.
   E. Muslim influence on the Orthodox branch of Christianity.

10. All of these peoples and states contributed to the destruction of the Byzantine Empire EXCEPT the:
   A. Kievan Rus.
   B. Seljuk Turks.
   C. independent Slavic states in the Balkans such as Bulgaria and Serbia.
   D. Western crusaders and the Roman Catholic Church.
   E. Italian trading city-states such as Venice and Genoa.

11. The Byzantine's greatest contribution to postclassical (Medieval) civilization was
   A. its centuries-long economic stability and opportunities for trade.
   B. its development of a uniquely Christian tradition in art and architecture.
   C. the defeat of the Arabs and its reconquest of the Middle East.
   D. to protect eastern Europe from the Muslims before the Europeans were strong and developed enough to resist.
   E. the preservation of the classical, Greco-Roman Mediterranean civilization.

12. Christianity spread to the Balkans and Russia through
   A. mass migration by Greeks to these regions.
   B. forced conversions of the Slavs by the victorious Byzantine armies.
   C. military conquest.
   D. Christian merchants who intermarried and settled amongst non-Christians.
   E. missionary activities, which converted the ruling elites of regional states.

13. Unlike the Roman Catholic Church, Byzantine Orthodox missionaries
    A. were frequently merchants and traded while they preached.
    B. permitted people to use local languages in religious services and literature.
    C. were sent out by the religious, not political, authorities.
    D. never intermarried into the local populations.
    E. rarely established monasteries, hospitals, and convents to further conversions.

14. The first state in Russia arose due to
    A. nomadic pastoralists who established a sedentary Jewish state.
    B. Byzantine missionaries.
    C. Viking traders and warriors who set up a state to protect trade routes.
    D. Arabs who conquered the area and established a province of the Muslim empire.
    E. Catholic influences from western Europe.

15. All of these influences served to differentiate western Slavs (Poles and Czechs) from eastern and southern Slavs (Russians, Serbs, and Bulgars) EXCEPT:
    A. different sects of Christianity.
    B. Mongols and Turks ruled eastern and southern Europe for centuries.
    C. the Western Slavs were subjected to German culture and influences.
    D. Western Europe escaped violence and wars, which the East suffered.
    E. different alphabets.

VIII. ESSAY QUESTIONS

    A. Compare and contrast Byzantine and Chinese imperial institutions.

    B. Compare and contrast Roman Catholicism and Eastern Orthodoxy.

    C. Compare and contrast the decline and fall of the Byzantines or Kievan Rus with (1) the Arab caliphate or (2) any classical civilization.

    D. Compare and contrast the spread of civilization to Russia with the spread of Islam and civilization to sub-Saharan Africa.

    E. Compare and contrast Byzantine and Muslim religious and political institutions.

**CHAPTER 10
A New Civilization Emerges
in Western Europe**
Pages 212 – 237

I.   SUMMARY

A. Stages of Postclassical Development

Medieval European development unfolded in two subperiods up to about 1300. Between the 6th and 10th centuries, chaotic conditions prevailed, despite gains made by the church and Charlemagne's brief empire. Then, improvements in trade and agriculture brought new strength and diversity. Feudal monarchy developed as a stronger political form. During this period, western Europe also developed expansionist tendencies, particularly in the Crusades.

B. Western Culture in the Post-Classical Era

Christian culture formed the clearest unifying element in western Europe during the Post-Classical centuries, although it changed as European society matured. Theologians and artists developed distinctive expressions, although there were other philosophical and artistic currents as Europe's cultural creativity increased.

C. Changing Economic and Social Forms in the Post-Classical Centuries

With the revival of trade and agriculture, commercial ties spread through most of western Europe. Urban merchants gained unusual power, but early capitalism was disputed by the different economic values of the guilds.

D. The Decline of the Medieval Synthesis

Amid problems of overpopulation and disease, post-classical Western civilization declined after 1300. The decline was evident in feudalism and the church.

II.   CHAPTER REVIEW

A. What characteristics define medieval west European civilization?

B. How did manorialism affect the legal, social, and economic position of the serfs?

C. What economic and demographic developments changed Western society?

D. How did feudal monarchies organize power? How was their power limited?

E. Why did Europeans support the Crusades and how did they impact Europe?

F. What problems did the medieval church face and how did it solve them?

G. How did the rise of universities affect religion, society, and learning?

H. What changes occurred in agriculture, towns, and commerce after 1000 C.E.?

I. What social, economic, religious and political changes ended this era?

J. How did Christianity affect the social, legal, and economic status of women?

K. What roles did upper class women play in the feudal and religious institutions?

III.   VOCABULARY

A. Medieval, Middle Ages

B. Manorialism

C. Serfs

D. 3-Field System

E. (Holy Roman) emperors

F. Feudal monarch; vassals

G. Feudalism

H. Parliaments (Three estates)

I. Crusades

J. Papacy

K. Investiture

L. Scholasticism

M. Hanseatic League

N. Guilds

O. Black Death

IV.   MAP EXERCISES

    A. Map 10.1: *Charlemagne's Empire* (Page 218)
      1. What modern nations did Charlemagne rule?

      2. What modern nations did each division of the Frankish empire become:
        a. West Franks?
        b. East Franks?
        c. Kingdom of Lothair?

      3. What is the relationship between Charlemagne's borders and Europe's religious groups?

    B. Map 10.2: *West Europe toward the end of the Medieval Era, 1360 C.E.* (Page 233)
      1. What medieval states have already established their modern borders?

      2. What areas have not yet united into modern states?

      3. Why would the Holy Roman Empire be difficult to govern?

V.   DOCUMENT ANALYSIS: *Changing Roles for Women* (Page 231)

    A. Who wrote it? (Attribution includes biographical references)

    B. What was the author's point of view?

    C. How reliable is the document? Why?

    D. What was the intent or purpose behind the document?

    E. Who was the intended audience?

    F. What is the document's tone?

    G. How have roles for women changed?

VI.   PHOTO ESSAYS: *The Rise and Fall of Medieval Europe*

    A. *The Age of Faith* (Pages 216, 217, 222, 226)
    The Middle Ages in Europe was called an Age of Faith. In what ways do the photos represent this title?

B. *Feudalism* (Pages 212, 217, 221, 228)
Politically, many regions in medieval Europe utilized a feudal system to restore and maintain stability. How do the photographs depict aspects of feudalism?

C. *The Death of Feudalism and the Age of Faith* (Pages 230, 234, and 235)
How would towns, commerce, war, and the Black Death destroy medieval institutions?

VII.   MULTIPLE-CHOICE QUESTIONS

1. The period known as the Middle Ages in Europe
    A. was an era in which European culture and civilization dominated the Mediterranean region.
    B. was a period of isolation and stagnation for European society.
    C. began with feudal kings in control and ended with the Roman Catholic Church the dominant power in Europe.
    D. began with the fall of Rome and ended with the decline of the feudal and religious institutions.
    E. saw Christianity confined to a few lands in western Europe.

2. During much of the early Middle Ages, the literate population
    A. generally lived in the cities around the universities.
    B. tended to be merchants rich enough to afford an education.
    C. included the rulers and aristocracy.
    D. was confined to the clergy and monasteries of the Catholic Church.
    E. had all but vanished leaving Europe in a Dark Age.

3. During the Middle Ages, effective political and military power in Europe was
    A. wielded by the Roman Catholic Church.
    B. the domain of the national monarch such as the King of France.
    C. local in nature with regional aristocrats holding the greatest influence.
    D. furnished by mercenary armies supported by the rich towns and cities.
    E. shared by the peasants, urban dwellers, and the Church.

4. Manorialism was characterized by all of these conditions EXCEPT:
    A. most peasants were serfs.
    B. manors and peasants depended on merchants for most necessities.
    C. peasants were obligated to give their lord a portion of their produce.
    D. the lords protected the peasants.
    E. levels of production and technology were low and limited.

5. Serfs differed from slaves in that
   A. serfs were largely commercialized artisans while slaves were agricultural.
   B. serfs were ethnically Europeans while slaves were Muslims, pagans, and Africans.
   C. they could not be bought or sold, and owned some of the land they farmed.
   D. serfs could serve in the military, while slaves could not.
   E. slaves frequently were better educated and lived in towns.

6. After the collapse of Charlemagne's empire, the pattern of political life in western Europe
   A. was dominated by the strong empire, that his sons and heirs established.
   B. was modeled on the Byzantine Empire.
   C. returned to small tribes and clans with regional or local loyalties.
   D. focused on religious control of states and politics.
   E. consisted of regional monarchies with strong aristocracies.

7. New agricultural techniques and technologies introduced during the Middle Ages included all of these EXCEPT:
   A. more nutritious foods from the Americas such as potatoes and corn.
   B. moldboard plows.
   C. horse collars.
   D. clearing forestland and draining swamps.
   E. three field rotation system.

8. The growth of towns in Europe after the 10th century C.E.
   A. failed to stimulate new trade or commercial opportunities.
   B. was greater than similar developments in China.
   C. was due largely to support from the Church.
   D. occurred in northern France and England.
   E. weakened the feudal system as towns were outside the feudal system.

9. Medieval universities and schools
   A. were established to train bureaucrats to run the government.
   B. were hesitant to study the Greek classics and Arab sciences.
   C. trained middle class townspeople largely in theology, medicine, and law.
   D. arose in rural settings around the larger, more famous monasteries.
   E. welcomed members of all classes including women, provided they passed the entrance exams.

10. West European feudalism
    A. inhibited the development of strong central monarchies, but did reduce local warfare.
    B. encouraged the growth of strong kingdoms.
    C. failed to end invasions by the Arabs, Magyars, and Vikings.
    D. was largely economic in practice.
    E. did not include the church and religion in feudal contracts.

11. To circumvent or counteract the power of feudal lords, national monarchs used all of these tools EXCEPT:
    A. alliances with the middle classes.
    B. taxes on towns and cities.
    C. professional armies loyal only to the monarchs.
    D. confiscation of church lands and a tax on the clergy.
    E. royal officials and professional bureaucrats.

12. The major lasting result of the Crusades was the
    A. conversion of eastern Europe to Roman Catholicism.
    B. establishment of cultural and economic contacts between western Europe and the Middle East.
    C. conquest of the Holy Land and Jerusalem.
    D. destruction of the European nobility and military class.
    E. creation of a new Holy Roman Empire ruling many Mediterranean lands.

13. Most religious reforms during the Middle Ages
    A. were attempts to combat widespread heresies.
    B. failed because of royal and aristocratic opposition.
    C. failed to increase papal control and influence.
    D. fought secularism in the clergy and feudal interference in church affairs.
    E. were directed by secular lords against a corrupt church.

14. When scholars began to study Greek classics, most early west European intellectuals and scholastics
    A. rejected Christianity when it conflicted with classical learning.
    B. found that Aristotle and Plato stressed the importance of faith and God.
    C. doubted the accuracy and validity of classical learning.
    D. readily accepted Greek ideas and integrated them into Christian theology.
    E. found the Greek notion of reason troubling because it questions faith.

15. Increased attempts by nobles in the late Middle Ages to assert their control over serfs led to
    A. the expansion of serfdom.
    B. increased revolts and resistance by the peasants and serfs.
    C. the decline of agricultural output.
    D. increased conflict with the Church, which protected the serfs.
    E. a rise in slavery in order to replace the lost labor of the serfs.

16. The Commercial Revolution in late medieval western Europe
    A. met with little resistance from the Church.
    B. preceded the first Crusades.
    C. encouraged the growth of trade, banking, and trading alliances.
    D. arose in Italy.
    E. was dominated by Jews, Muslims, and foreigners.

17. Although western society was not as tolerant of merchants as were Muslim and Indian societies
    A. weak governments allowed merchants to assert considerable power in semi-independent trading cities.
    B. the Roman Catholic Church encouraged profits.
    C. western merchants amassed greater wealth than their Muslim and Hindu counterparts.
    D. western rulers rarely interfered in or regulated trade or commerce.
    E. Christian merchants married easily into the aristocratic elites.

VIII.   ESSAY QUESTIONS

    A. Compare and contrast west European and Japanese feudalisms.

    B. How did political institutions in western Europe change from the fall of the Roman Empire to the end of the Middle East? (Change over time)

    C. Compare and contrast the roles of women in medieval western Europe with their counterparts in India and the Islamic world.

    D. Compare and contrast western European medieval commercialism with its Indian and Muslim equivalents.

    E. Compare and contrast Roman Catholic and Orthodox institutions.

    F. Compare and contrast the roles of religion and faith in western Europe and the Muslim world.

    G. Compare and contrast the Hanseatic League and the Swahili trading cities.

H. Compare and contrast medieval scholasticism with Muslim or Hindu intellectual achievements.

I. Compare and contrast the treatment of Jews and minorities in western Europe and Muslim lands.

J. Compare and contrast western European crusades with Muslim jihads.

CHAPTER 11
The Americas on the Eve of the Invasion
Pages 238 – 261

I. SUMMARY

A. Post-Classical Mesoamerica, 1000 – 1500 C.E.

Among the civilizations that followed abandonment of the Maya cities in the 8th century C.E. and the collapse of Teotihuacan were the Toltecs and the Aztecs, who built on the achievement of their predecessors but rarely surpassed them except in political and military achievement. The Toltecs created an empire whose influence extended beyond central Mexico. In the 15th century, the Aztecs rose to create an empire organized for war, motivated by religion, and based on farming.

B. Aztec Society in Transition

Aztec society became more hierarchical as the empire grew and differentiated social classes developed, although the older organization based on the calpulli never disappeared. Tribute was drawn from subject peoples, but Aztec society confronted barriers that made it difficult to maintain a large population.

C. Twantinsuyu: World of the Incas

After about 1300 C.E. in the Andean cultural hearth, a civilization emerged and spread its control over the whole region. The Inca empire was a highly centralized system that integrated different ethnic groups into an imperial state. Extensive agriculture supported a state religion and a royal ancestor cult. With notable achievements in architecture and metallurgy, the Incas, like the Aztecs, incorporated many elements of the civilizations that preceded them.

D. The Other Indians

The civilizations of Mesoamerica and the Andes were high points of an Indian cultural achievement cut short by contact and conquest. However, the Americas continued to be occupied by peoples who lived in different ways, ranging from sedentary agricultural civilizations to kin-based bands of hunters and gatherers.

II. CHAPTER REVIEW

A. What institutions did the Aztecs and Incas inherit from their predecessors?

B. What was the relationship between war and religion in the rise of the Aztecs?

C. How did the Aztecs organize their agriculture?

D. What social, political, and technological problems did the Aztecs face?

E. What is a tribute empire and what was its relationship to trade?

F. How did the Inca overcome geographic problems to unite their large empire?

G. How did the Inca use institutions and policies to unify their empire?

H. How did Inca trade and tribute differ from that of other civilizations?

I. How did contacts affect cultures bordering the classical civilizations?

J. What characteristics did American Indians share? How were they different?

III.   VOCBULARY

A. Indian

B. Toltec

C. Aztec

D. Tlaloc and Huitzilopochtli

E. Calpulli

F. Pipiltin

G. Chinampas

H. Pochteca

I. Inca socialism

J. Ayullu

K. Inca

L. Split inheritance

M. Curacas

N. Mita

O. Mitmag

P. Tambos

Q. Yanas

R. "Orejones"

S. Quipu

IV. MAP EXERCISES

A. Map 11.1: *Central Mexico* (Page 241)
1. Describe the physical world of the Aztecs.

2. How might environment have influenced Aztec civilization?

B. Map 11.2: *Inca Expansion*; Map 11.3: *Ancient Cities of Peru* (Pages 252 and 254)
1. How did geography influence Inca expansion?

2. What problems would distance create for the Incas?

V. DOCUMENT ANALYSIS: *Aztec Men and Women* (Pages 248-249)

A. Learning from Documents
1. In what ways do men and women differ in Aztec society?

2. How do expectations for proper behavior for men and women differ?

3. What social, political, and economic divisions does this create?

B. Writing a Document Based Essay
These documents form a superior document based essay question. Consider writing a DBQ. In 15 minutes, read the documents and plan your essay; use 45 minutes to write the essay.

Prompt: How did occupations and expectations of proper behavior create gender differences within Aztec society?

VI. PHOTO ESSAY

A. *The Aztecs* (Pages 243, 245, and 247)
In the Aztec state there was a strong connection between war, agriculture, and religion. It was the central relationship of Aztec society. How do the photographs depict:

1. War?

2. Agriculture?

3. Religion?

4. How would these institutions have led to the creation of an empire?

B. *Daily Life* (Pages 245, 247, 253, and 255)
   1. How do the photographs depict:
      a. Social classes?

      b. Work?

      c. Architecture?

   2. What conclusions can you draw about daily life in the Americas?

VII.   STATISTICAL EXERCISE: *Population Estimates* (Page 257-258)

A. Data
   1. Around 1500 C.E. what countries are the most populated? Least?

   2. How does Europe, including Russia, compare to the rest of the world?

   3. How do the Americas compare to Europe and the rest of the world?

B. Interpretations
   1. What might account for the large American population?

   2. How would the sizes of Indian and Chinese populations affect invaders?

   3. Why might it be difficult to assimilate the Indians and Chinese?

   4. If the Europeans were to eventually conquer the world, why would their population base be a disadvantage and how might the Europeans have overcome their small populations?

VIII. MULTIPLE-CHOICE QUESTIONS

1. Although later civilizations in Mesoamerica borrowed and built on the previous accomplishments of the Olmecs and Maya, later civilizations
   A. were not as war-like as their predecessors had been.
   B. rarely surpassed previous intellectual predecessors.
   C. failed to improve on the political institutions and types of Olmec and Maya states.
   D. abandoned polytheism in favor of monotheism.
   E. abandoned trade.

2. As happened in the Fertile Crescent, India, and China, the fall of civilizations in the Americas was often due to
   A. migrating nomadic invaders.
   B. crop collapse.
   C. famine and diseases.
   D. civil war.
   E. environmental disasters.

3. The Aztecs rose to power through all of the following means EXCEPT:
   A. control of water and irrigation.
   B. political alliances with neighboring cities.
   C. marriage alliances.
   D. warfare.
   E. trade.

4. In the Aztec state, the military, monarchs, and aristocrats
   A. owned the artisans, who were slaves and produced their goods for the gods.
   B. taxed the food trade between the various city-states to raise revenues.
   C. manipulated human sacrifice and used terror as a means to maintain power.
   D. were socially and politically inferior to the priests.
   E. were constantly at odds over policies and offices of the state.

5. For the Mesoamericans of the Aztec period, religion
   A. was increasingly monotheistic.
   B. developed into idealistic philosophies and intellectual discussions.
   C. taught that humans should live ethical, moral lives.
   D. declined and atheism began to spread widely.
   E. was oppressive and made little distinction between the sacred and secular.

6. In order to supply food to Tenochtitlan, the Aztecs
   A. obtained food through tribute from conquered city-states.
   B. relied largely on trade for foodstuffs.
   C. used slave labor.
   D. built floating agricultural islands on the lake.
   E. filled in Lake Texcoco to obtain agricultural lands.

7. Aztec merchants
   A. administered and collected the tribute from allies and defeated enemies.
   B. rarely journeyed far from their homes.
   C. worked part-time in trade and part-time in fields producing food.
   D. were traditionally priests and temple employees.
   E. were nobles.

8. Around 1500 C.E., membership in Aztec society was hierarchically defined by all of these methods EXCEPT:
   A. social classes.
   B. gender.
   C. clans or tribes.
   D. ethnicity.
   E. occupational groups.

9. Because of their level of technological development, Aztec work and production
   A. relied heavily on tools and machines.
   B. relied heavily on the physical labor of humans.
   C. utilized domesticated beasts of burden extensively.
   D. richly rewarded intellectual invention and innovation.
   E. were performed by slaves and conquered or tributary states.

10. Demographic evidence of the Aztec empire around 1500 C.E. indicates
    A. a falling population base when the Europeans arrived.
    B. decreasing birthrates.
    C. women outnumbered men due to the loses during the frequent wars.
    D. most Aztecs lived in cities.
    E. an extremely high population density.

11. One reason offered for the expansion of the Inca state was
    A. need for humans to sacrifice to the state gods.
    B. overpopulation and the need for new crop land.
    C. each new Inca ruler had to secure new land and wealth for himself.
    D. changing environment and climate drove the Incas from their homeland.
    E. superior technologies made it easy for the Incas to conquer other peoples.

12. Religious practices of the Incas included all of these attributes EXCEPT:
    A. animism.
    B. ancestor worship.
    C. monotheism.
    D. sun worship.
    E. theocratic government.

13. The methods the Incas used to rule their empire most resembled the
    A. Aryan caste system of religious castes.
    B. Roman's practices of citizenship, colonies, and local autonomy.
    C. Zhou system of feudalism.
    D. Greek city-states.
    E. Ghanaian practice of controlling trade in salt and gold.

14. All land in the Inca state
    A. belonged to the priests.
    B. was owned by merchants and traders.
    C. belonged to the oldest woman of the family.
    D. was owned by those who worked the land.
    E. was owned by the state but assigned and redistributed to others.

15. Notably absent in Inca society was a class of
    A. warriors.
    B. priests.
    C. nobles.
    D. merchants.
    E. slaves.

IX. ESSAY QUESTIONS

    A. Compare and contrast the debts the Aztecs owed the Toltecs with either of these relationships: Romans to the Greeks and Etruscans, or the Mayans to the Teotihuacáns.

    B. Compare and contrast the Aztec and Inca cultures.

    C. Compare and contrast the Aztec or Inca to any classical or post-classical civilization.

    D. Compare and contrast the Aztec religion to any one of these: Hinduism, Mesopotamian, or Egyptian religion.

    E. Compare and contrast Inca methods of ruling with Roman practices.

F. Compare and contrast Mesoamerican technological developments with similar developments in peripheral regions of the world such as Japan, southeast Asia, West Africa, or Polynesia.

CHAPTER 12
Reunification and Renaissance in Chinese Civilization: The Era of the Tang and Song Dynasties
Pages 262 – 285

I.   SUMMARY

A. Rebuilding the Imperial Edifice in the Sui-Tang Era

The emergence of the Sui dynasty at the end of the 6th century C.E. from the patchwork of warring states that had predominated for nearly four centuries signaled a return to strong dynastic control. In the Tang era that followed, the bureaucratic institutions begun under the Han were restored, improved, and expanded. A Confucian revival enhanced the position of the scholar-gentry and provided the basis for a return to highly centralized rule under an imperial dynasty.

B. Tang Decline and the Rise of the Song

After several centuries of rule, the Tang fell on hard times. Beset by internal rebellions and nomadic incursions, the Tang gave way to the Song in the early 10th century C.E. Although the Song domains were smaller than the Tang, a Confucian revival flourished under the successor dynasty. Following new waves of nomadic invasions, in the mid-12th century the Song lost control of north China. A century and a half later, their empire in south China fell to the Mongols.

C. Tang and Song Prosperity: The Basis of a Golden Age

The Tang and Song period was a time of major transitions. Shifts in the population balance within China, new patterns of trade and commerce, urban expansion, novel forms of artistic and literary expression, and a series of technological breakthroughs contributed to new directions in Chinese civilization. These shifts became pronounced in the late Tang period and the Song dynasty. The China that emerged from this era was wealthy and market-oriented and more bureaucratized, urbanized, and more cosmopolitan than the Han civilization.

II.   CHAPTER REVIEW

A. How did the Sui and Tang reestablish a centralized empire in China?

B. What institutions did the Tang use to govern their empires?

C. What problems did religion cause in this period and how did the state resolve them?

D. Identify Neo-Confucianism; how did it influence Chinese culture and the state?

E. What problems plagued the Song state and how did it attempt to solve them?

F. Describe the Chinese commercial revolution.

G. How did the Chinese expand agricultural production?

H. Describe family life and society during the Tang-Song era.

I. How did gender relations change during the Tang-Song era?

J. Describe Chinese intellectual accomplishments during this period.

III.   VOCABULARY

A. Ministry of Rites

B. Jinski

C. Pureland Mahayana Buddhism

D. Chan (Zen) Buddhism

E. Sinified

F. Neo-Confucians

G. Jurchens

H. Junks

I. Flying Money

J. Hangzhou

K. Footbinding

IV.   MAP EXERCISES

A. Map 12.1: *China during the Era of Divisions, the Sui, and the Tang* (Page 265)
    1. What modern countries did the Tang rule? (Use a modern atlas.)

    2. How did Tang borders conform to natural geography?

    3. Why would China want to control the Tarim Basin?

B. Map 12.2: *China in the Southern Song Dynastic Periods* (Page 273)

1. How do the two maps differ?

2. What has happened to change the two maps?

3. Why would the Southern Song's existence be precarious?

4. During this period, why might the south develop differently from the north?

V.   PHOTO ESSAY: *Art Imitates Life* (Pages 262, 267, 269, 271, 277, 278, and 283)

Irrespective of the subject, Chinese art is known for its simplicity of composition, empty space, emphasis on nature, and muted colors.

A. Look at the colors, composition, space, and symmetry. What rules does Chinese art seem to follow?

B. Chinese art is realistic and mirrors life. What does the art tell you about:
1. Gender issues?

2. Social hierarchies?

3. Work?

4. Leisure activities?

5. Dress?

6. Religion?

7. Technology?

8. Intellectual pursuits?

VI.   DOCUMENT ANALYSIS: *Ties that Bind: Paths to Power* (Page 268)

A. Analysis
1. Who wrote it? (Attribution includes biographical references)

2. What was the author's point of view?

3. How reliable is the document? Why?

4. What was the intent or purpose behind the document?

5. Who was the intended audience?

6. What is the document's tone?

B. Learning from Documents
1. What does the document tell us about favoritism and patronage in China?

2. Comment: "It is not what you know or how much but who you know."

3. Would you want to hire Wu Bao? Why or why not?

VII. MULTIPLE-CHOICE QUESTIONS

1. The era of Tang and Song rule in China was known as a(n)
   A. golden age of Chinese culture and accomplishments.
   B. period of Buddhist dominance.
   C. time where Christianity and Islam spread widely in China.
   D. time of technological and commercial stagnation.
   E. era where nomadic dynasties ruled most of China.

2. Between the collapse of the Han and the rise of the Tang dynasties, China experienced all of these events EXCEPT:
   A. non-Chinese nomadic dynasties ruled China.
   B. Buddhism eclipsed Confucian teachings.
   C. Chinese classical culture and institutions died out.
   D. China was divided into competing states and dynasties.
   E. trade expanded and cities grew.

3. The Tang rulers were able to control potential nomadic threats to China by
   A. bribery.
   B. playing one nomadic group against another.
   C. settling the nomads within the Chinese borders on land to farm.
   D. intermarriage between the nomadic and Chinese ruling families.
   E. diverting the nomads and sending them westward, away from China.

4. To administer China, the Tang and Song dynasties relied on
   A. Turkish administrators.
   B. the aristocracy.
   C. merchants.
   D. scholar-gentry.
   E. Buddhist monks.

5. In Tang China, the exam system to become a scholar-bureaucrat
   A. was open only to the sons of the aristocrats.
   B. denied intelligent peasants the right to take the exam.
   C. was open to all, but family connections better prepared the elite to take the tests.
   D. favored army officers.
   E. was closed to Buddhists and Muslims.

6. Buddhist successes in China during the Tang era
   A. were opposed by the merchants and farmers.
   B. provided the state with tax revenues and conscripted labor.
   C. were counterbalanced by the introduction of Islam into China.
   D. encouraged the scholar-officials, who were largely Buddhist.
   E. led to persecutions and seizures of Buddhist monastic lands.

7. Although the Song Dynasty existed for 300 years, it
   A. could not afford a well-run or well-policed government.
   B. was a period of intellectual and economic stagnation.
   C. rarely trusted merchants or supported commercial interests.
   D. never possessed an army or navy.
   E. existed at the mercy of nomadic peoples from the northern steppes.

8. Neo-Confucianism
   A. emphasized tradition, authority, and harmony at the expense of innovation.
   B. blended Buddhism and Daoism with traditional Confucian doctrine.
   C. abandoned the emphasis on classical learning and test-taking.
   D. warmly encouraged the merchant and commercial activities.
   E. borrowed and utilized legalist ideas to run the Song state.

9. The major demographic change in China between 500 and 1000 C.E. was the
   A. decline of cities as populations moved to the countryside.
   B. widespread migration of Chinese to foreign lands.
   C. population decrease in the north due to frequent nomadic raids.
   D. large population increase in the south around the Yangtze.
   E. internal migration of the populace from rural to urban areas.

10. Tang military expansion into central Asia
    A. led to constant warfare between the Chinese and the Muslims.
    B. promoted renewed commercial contacts between China and west Asia.
    C. eliminated nomadic invasions.
    D. obtained land to settle large Chinese population surpluses.
    E. was easily defeated by the Turks and other pastoral nomads.

11. The technological advance they facilitated Chinese overseas trade was
    A. the Grand Canal.
    B. sericulture or the production of silk.
    C. the manufacture of paper.
    D. the introduction of gunpowder.
    E. maritime tools such as the junk.

12. In order to facilitate the Chinese commercial revolution during the Tang and Song dynasties, all of these institutions were first developed EXCEPT:
    A. deposit shops (banks).
    B. the abacus.
    C. coins.
    D. paper money.
    E. credit vouchers.

13. In order to lessen the influence of the aristocrats and bolster the position of the peasants, the Tang and Song monarchs
    A. broke up large landed estates and gave the land to the peasants.
    B. established courts and rural police to protect the peasants.
    C. set a percentage of governmental occupations and positions reserved for peasant applicants.
    D. set up free, government sponsored-schools for the peasants.
    E. recruited the military officers from the peasant class.

14. Women in Tang and Song China
    A. had many outlets for social and intellectual advancement.
    B. increasingly copied or borrowed Hindu practices.
    C. legally acquired rights independently of their fathers, husbands, or brothers.
    D. improved their social position under the Tang, but increasingly lost their rights under the Song.
    E. often became Confucian scholars or increasingly ran family businesses.

15. Both footbinding in China and the harem and veil in Islam
    A. ended with the spread of Buddhism to Confucian and Muslim areas.
    B. were condemned by the Confucian scholar-gentry.
    C. were rejected by their societies' religious establishments.
    D. originated in Hindu lands and spread to Chinese and Muslim lands.
    E. symbolized the increasing subordination of women to men.

16. The invention of explosive powder (gunpowder) in China
    A. was borrowed by the Chinese from the nomads.
    B. allowed the Song to defeat the northern nomads.
    C. led to the Arab conquest of China.
    D. had little initial impact on warfare.
    E. had no uses in Song society except for fireworks.

17. The high level of Chinese literacy was due to
    A. free schooling for all classes of society.
    B. the introduction of an alphabet during the Song dynasty.
    C. the invention of movable-type printing and cheap paper.
    D. the simplicity of the Chinese system of writing.
    E. priests and Confucian theology, which insisted that Heaven wanted all people to be able to read and to write the Confucian classics.

VIII. ESSAY QUESTIONS

   A. Compare and contrast Hindu resurgence in India against Buddhism with the Confucian reaction to Buddhism.

   B. Compare and contrast Buddhist wealth and influence in China between the Han and Song dynasties with Roman Catholic institutions in western Europe.

   C. Compare gender relations in the Chinese, Hindu, and Muslim Post-Classical civilizations with women in western or eastern Europe.

   D. Compare and contrast Tang and Song intellectual and technical achievements with the Muslim achievements during the Abbasid era.

   E. Compare demographic shifts during the post-classical eras in China and western Europe.

   F. Compare and contrast Tang and Song commercial revolutions with the revival of trade and commerce in medieval western Europe.

   G. Compare and contrast styles and motivations of art, artistic endeavors, and architecture of any two: Tang/Song China, Abbasid Islam, medieval western Europe, and Classical Greece.

   H. How had Confucianism changed from the era of Confucius to the Neo-Confucians? (Change over time)

CHAPTER 13
The Spread of Chinese Civilization: Japan, Korea, and Vietnam
Pages 286 – 311

I.   SUMMARY

A. Japan: The Imperial Age

Chinese influence on Japan peaked in the 7th and 8th centuries as Japanese rulers and their courtiers tried to build a Chinese-style bureaucracy and army and to emulate Chinese culture. But the isolated and civilized court centers lost political control to aristocratic families and local warlords. Intensifying rivalries between regional military leaders eventually plunged Japan into a long series of civil wars.

B. The Era of Warrior Dominance

From the 12th century onward, Japanese history was increasingly dominated by civil wars between shifting factions of the court aristocracy and local warlords. Chinese influence declined steadily in the centuries that followed. But in the midst of strife and social dislocation, the warrior elite and the artisan classes that served them managed to develop a distinctly Japanese intellectual tradition. This creativity was obscured by continuing civil strife, which ended in the 16th century.

C. Korea: Between China and Japan

Korea was the east Asian state most profoundly influenced for the longest period of time by the Chinese culture. Because the Korean peninsula is an extension of the Chinese mainland, historical Korean kingdoms were dwarfed by their giant neighbor to the west. Nevertheless, Korea has been ruled by native dynasties throughout most of its history, and developed a distinctly Korean civilization.

D. Between China and Southeast Asia: The Making of Vietnam

From the Chinese point of view, the Red River, which became the heart of Vietnam, was just another rice-growing river valley to be annexed. But the Viets differed in critical ways from the other "southern" barbarians the Chinese had encountered. Their homeland was farther away from the centers of Chinese political power. For another, the Viets developed a sophisticated and resilient culture, which, while it might have borrowed from China, successfully resisted political incorporation.

II.   CHAPTER REVIEW

A. Describe the influence of Chinese culture on Heian Japan.

B. Describe court life during the Heian period.

C. What led to the decline of imperial power within Japan?

D. How did the rise of provincial warrior elites change Japanese institutions?

E. Describe social, political, and economic institutions during the Bakufu Age.

F. To what extent did Vietnam and Korea accept and reject Chinese influences?

G. Which classes and institutions were largely Sinified in Korea and Vietnam?

H. How did Korea and Vietnam maintain political independence from China?

III. VOCABULARY

A. Taika Reforms

B. Heian Period

C. Kami

D. Bushi (Bushido)

E. Samurai

F. Seppuku (Hara-kiri)

G. Bakufu

H. Shogun

I. Daimyos

J. "Gatekeepers"

K. Sinification

L. Tribute states

M. Kowtow

IV. MAP EXERCISES

A. Map 13.1: *Japan in the Imperial and Warlord Periods* (Page 289)

The Japanese home islands resemble very closely the physical geography of ancient Greece (except that Japan is wetter). How might physical geography affect movement and political developments within Japan?

    B. Map 13.2: *The Korean Peninsula* (Page 299)
       1. Which part of Korea would be most heavily influenced by Chinese culture?

       2. Which part would be least affected?

       3. Looking at the map on page 865 of the book (Map 35.1), why is the 20th-century division into North and South Korea not a new development?

    C. Map 13.3: *South China and Vietnam* (Page 303)
       1. Why is travel and communication within the area difficult?

       2. What routes would permit the easiest geographic movement in the area?

       3. Why would Chinese influence on Vietnam be greater than Hindu or Buddhist from the Khmer and Mekong River area?

V.   DOCUMENT ANALYSIS: *Literature as a Mirror of the Exchanges* (Page 308)

    A. What ideas in the documents are:
       1. Chinese?

       2. Buddhist (Indian)?

       3. Japanese?

       4. Vietnamese?

    B. How are the documents similar? Different?

    C. What would account for the differences?

    D. How would you summarize the degree of Sinification of neighboring cultures?

    E. How have the Vietnamese and Japanese maintained their cultural identities?

VI.   PHOTO ESSAYS

    A. *Indigenous Cultures* (Pages 286, 290, 291, 298, and 301)

Japanese, Korean, and Vietnamese cultures are syncretic blends of foreign and indigenous cultural elements. Identify these elements in the above photos:

1. Chinese.

2. Buddhist.

3. Indigenous elements.

B. *Feudal Militaristic Societies*
Compare and contrast western European and Japanese (page 295) feudal military societies.

C. *Religious Architectures*
Compare and contrast the religious architectures of the Christians, Shinto (page 298), Buddhists (pages 290), and Muslims. What elements are universal and transcendental, and which are local, ethnic, or particular to an individual society?

VII. VISUALIZING THE PAST: *Gatekeeper Elites* (Pages 304)

A. Who are gatekeepers?

B. Who were the gatekeepers in:
   1. Japan?

   2. Aztec society?

   3. Western Europe?

   4. China?

C. With which other elites did each gatekeeper share their respective society?

D. What does the type of gatekeeper tell us about important values in societies?

VIII. MULTIPLE-CHOICE QUESTIONS

1. The only indigenous aspect of Japanese culture during the Heian era was
   A. Mahayana Buddhism.
   B. the imperial administration.
   C. written characters.
   D. Shinto.
   E. court etiquette and protocol.

2. The group which most directly challenged Chinese influences in Japan and Vietnam during the Post-Classical era was
   A. the merchants.
   B. Buddhist monks and priests.
   C. the emperor.
   D. the imperial bureaucracy.
   E. aristocrats and local provincial administrators.

3. Aristocratic women during the Heian period
   A. directed court protocols in the imperial capital.
   B. had incredible artistic and intellectual freedom often denied the women of other cultures.
   C. were restricted to the father's, husband's, or family household.
   D. encouraged the court to embrace Shintoism and abandon Buddhism.
   E. studied and wrote about the worlds of the common Japanese people.

4. As the power of the Heian emperors declined,
   A. Chinese trained scholar officials assumed control of the government.
   B. civil war broke out between branches of the imperial family.
   C. local nobles carved out estates and reduced Japanese peasants to serfdom.
   D. China conquered Japan.
   E. religious groups and the clergy became the effective government.

5. Real government in Japan after the 11th century rested with
   A. the emperor's immediate family.
   B. women.
   C. Confucian scholar-gentry.
   D. shoguns or military governors.
   E. Buddhist monks.

6. Japan's form of government during the Bakufu period most resembles a
   A. feudal state.
   B. Gerontocracy or rule by the elderly.
   C. democracy.
   D. theocracy.
   E. government by rich merchants.

7. The key link for the conduit of Chinese culture to Japan and Korea was
   A. Buddhism.
   B. commercial contacts such as trade.
   C. migration by the Chinese to Korea and Japan.
   D. diplomatic missions.
   E. war.

8. During the Bakufu periods, Japanese women exercised the most influence and had the most freedom within
   A. peasant communities.
   B. aristocratic families.
   C. religious establishments.
   D. the courts of the emperors.
   E. the rising merchant and artisan classes.

9. The typical pattern for relations between China and its neighbors during the Post-Classical period was
   A. military occupation by the Chinese armies.
   B. for these states to acknowledge Chinese superiority and pay tribute but remain independent.
   C. incorporation of these states as provinces in the Chinese empire.
   D. to form equal alliances as partners against nomadic invaders.
   E. to maintain no formal relations or treaties with neighboring states.

10. Historical Vietnamese society differed from traditional Chinese society in all these ways EXCEPT:
    A. a tradition of village autonomy was strong in Vietnam.
    B. the major language of both was Chinese.
    C. the Vietnamese preferred nuclear families.
    D. the Vietnamese had no strong clans.
    E. Women had greater freedom and influence in Vietnam than China.

11. The French in the 1950s and the Americans in the 1960s could have predicted the Vietnamese would resist foreign invasions and defeat invaders because
    A. the majority of Vietnamese literature and art depicted Vietnam's history and mocked foreign influences.
    B. Vietnam had maintained its distinct Vietnamese identity despite centuries of Chinese rule.
    C. Vietnam's war of independence against China and the Mongols lasted 1,000 years in order to achieve freedom.
    D. the Vietnamese constantly invaded and defeated their neighbors including China.
    E. Vietnam had conquered and ruled its neighbors in Indo-China.

12. Local Vietnamese officials favored and imitated the styles and culture of
    A. Confucian scholar officials.
    B. Hindu rulers.
    C. the imperial court and high administrators.
    D. the peasants and local village culture.
    E. merchants.

13. After their independence from China, the Vietnamese
    A. slavishly copied Chinese culture and ruling styles.
    B. degenerated into constantly feuding clans and villages.
    C. were conquered by the Khmers and Thais.
    D. became a largely commercial society in southeast Asia.
    E. conquered the highlands and coasts between the Mekong River and South China Sea.

14. Geography, environment, and movement in Vietnam
    A. successfully fostered the growth of a uniform Vietnamese culture.
    B. have increasingly isolated Vietnam from its neighbors.
    C. divided the nation into two cultural divisions – one in the south along the Mekong River and the other in the north along the Red River.
    D. have made it difficult to ignore the influence of China in history.
    E. led to the spread of Christianity and Islam throughout the country.

15. In Japan, Korea, and Vietnam, the class that most welcomed Chinese influence and culture was
    A. the local aristocrats.
    B. the court bureaucrats (scholar-gentry).
    C. peasants.
    D. Buddhist monks.
    E. the merchants.

IX. ESSAY QUESTIONS

A. How did the role of women change in Japan during the first millennium?

B. Compare and contrast the north and south divisions in China, Vietnam, and Korea with the east-west divisions in Europe.

C. Compare and contrast how smaller states and societies on the periphery of a greater or larger civilization are affected by the larger, more influential society: Korea, Japan, sub-Saharan Africa, southeast Asia with Islam or China. How widespread is acculturation and how much of a society's culture is indigenous?

D. Compare and contrast Japanese and western European feudalisms.

CHAPTER 14
The Last Great Nomadic Challenges: From Chinggis Khan To Timur
Pages 312 – 333

I. SUMMARY

A. The Mongol Empire of Chinggis Khan

The Mongols intervened periodically in Chinese history. But tribal divisions and rivalries with neighboring ethnic groups, particularly Turkic peoples, had long blunted the expansive potential of Mongol warrior culture. Within the first decades of the 13th century, because of the political strategies and military accomplishments of Chinggis Khan, the Mongols and allies nomadic groups built an empire that stretched from the Middle East to the East China Sea.

B. The Mongol Drive to the West

While pursuing a fleeing Persian ruler, the Mongols made their first contacts with the kingdoms to the west of Chinggis Khan's Empire. Subjugating these regions became the projects of the armies of the Golden Horde, the Mongol khanate, which ruled the western lands. After the death of Chinggis Khan, the empire was divided into four khanates. The khanate to the south, called the Ilkhan Empire, attempted to conquer the Muslim world. Although neither Europe nor the Islamic lands were subdued, Mongol successes affected the regions' history.

C. The Mongol Interlude in Chinese History

Of all the areas the Mongols conquered, perhaps none was more closely administered than China. The Mongol interlude in Chinese history lasted only about a century. Although the Chinese attempted to assimilate the Mongols from the start, the Mongols managed to retain a distinct culture and social separateness until they were driven back beyond the Great Wall in the late 1360s. They also opened China to influences from Arab and Persian lands, and even to contacts with Europe, which came to full fruition in the centuries of indigenous Chinese revival that followed under the Ming Dynasty.

II. CHAPTER REVIEW

A. How did Chinggis Khan create the Mongolian war machine and empire?

B. How did the Mongols govern their empire and its peoples?

C. How did Mongol rule allow religion and commerce to flourish?

D. How did Mongol rule influence Europe, the Muslim world, and China?

E. Why did nomads cease to be a threat to civilizations after the Mongols?

III. VOCABULARY

A. Khanate

B. Khan

C. Tumens

D. Shamanistic

E. Tartars

F. White Lotus Society

G. Nestorians

H. Mameluks

I. Kuriltai

J. Metropolitan

IV. VISUALIZING THE PAST: *The Mongol Empire as a Bridge Between Civilizations* (Page 321)

A. Identify the movement of goods and ideas.
from east to west
from west to east

B. How did the Mongols facilitate exchanges and interactions?

C. What factors limited the ability of the Mongols to trade with some regions?

V. MAP EXERCISES

A. Map 14.1: *The Mongol Empire of Chinggis Khan* (Page 314)
1. What are the physical geographical boundaries of the empire?

2. What geographic feature limited the Mongols':
a. Northern borders?
b. Southern borders?

B. Map 14.2: *The Four Khanates of the Divided Mongol Empire* (Page 322)
1. What modern states did the Ilkhan rule?
2. The Djagatai empire?
3. The Golden Horde?
4. The Empire of Kubilai Khan?
5. Using the map at the back of the book, can you determine what physical limits and geographic elements create the boundaries of the Empire?

VI. PHOTO ESSAY: *The Mongols Through Other Eyes*

A. How did the conquered civilizations portray the Mongols?
1. Persians (Page 316)?
2. Arabs (Page 324)?
3. Chinese (Pages 326 and 327)?
4. west European Christian (Page 328)?

B. Mongol Technologies
1. Describe the Mongol military technologies.

2. Describe the Mongol communications technologies.

3. Why is the Mongol level of technology suited to their way of life?

VII. DOCUMENT ANALYSIS: *A European Assessment of the Mongols* (Page 317)

A. What can a document tell us about the values of the writer?

B. Why is the writer so complimentary to the Mongols?

C. How does the document conform to typical nomadic values?

D. What bias does the author exhibit?

E. How does it affect your understanding of the documents?

VIII. MULTIPLE-CHOICE QUESTIONS

1. One problem facing historians who study the Mongols is
    A. lack of primary sources.
    B. inability to translate the Mongolian language and its literature.
    C. all contemporary chroniclers used exaggeration and hyperbole to describe the Mongols.
    D. the bias of historical accounts, written by those whom the Mongols defeated.
    E. the Mongols never wrote anything down, leaving no written records.

2. Although the Mongols were often brutal, they were
   A. no less violent than Europeans, Muslims, or the Chinese of the day.
   B. tolerant of religious differences and encouraged trade.
   C. unwilling to destroy art works and buildings.
   D. devoted to nonviolence.
   E. apt to leave enemies alive and revolting cities unpunished.

3. Pastoral nomads from the central Asian steppe who had threatened sedentary civilizations throughout world history included all of these EXCEPT:
   A. Indo-Europeans.
   B. Hsiung-nu (Huns).
   C. Scythians.
   D. Turks.
   E. Bantu.

4. If peoples surrendered or were subdued without resistance, the Mongols
   A. exacted tribute but generally left the inhabitants alone.
   B. sold only the men into slavery.
   C. destroyed the towns and resettled the people on farmlands.
   D. settled amongst the sedentary peoples.
   E. forced the inhabitants to migrate to new lands.

5. In general, Mongol rule, like Roman rule, was
   A. intolerant.
   B. brutal.
   C. very disruptive to societies and their values.
   D. peaceful and prosperous.
   E. welcomed by sedentary peoples.

6. When the Mongols divided their empire, the only region which did not become a center for one of their khanates was
   A. Iran and Mesopotamia.
   B. Central Asia.
   C. India.
   D. East Asia.
   E. the steppes of Russia, the Ukraine, and Siberia.

7. Russia's defeat by the Mongols
   A. had little effect on Russian development.
   B. led to 250 years of Mongol dominance.
   C. was avoided by the willingness of Russian princes to pay tribute.
   D. was meaningless because the Mongols abandoned the area for their homeland.
   E. left Poland and Sweden the dominant powers in eastern Europe.

8. Mongol policies in Russia
    A. led to the rise of serfdom.
    B. left Moscow and Kiev weak and unimportant.
    C. led to the rise of Novgorod as the chief Russian town.
    D. weakened Orthodox Christianity in Russia and allowed Islam to spread.
    E. permitted a free exchange of ideas with eastern Europe through increased trade.

9. The Mongol assault on the Middle East
    A. led to the conversion of the Mongols in the area to Nestorian Christianity.
    B. strengthened Muslim armies to effectively resist the Mongols.
    C. capture and devastation of Baghdad.
    D. was supported by Muslims living in the area.
    E. extended the life of the Abbasid Caliphate.

10. The only power to successfully defeat the Mongols before 1300 C.E. was the
    A. Song China.
    B. Russian principality of Moscow.
    C. Turks of Asia Minor.
    D. Turks of central Asia and Persia.
    E. Mameluks of Egypt.

11. The greatest long term impact of the Mongol unification of much of central Eurasia was the
    A. new technologies introduced.
    B. facilitation of trade.
    C. conversion of the Mongols to Christianity.
    D. destruction of old states and the rise of new ones.
    E. spread of the Black Death from China to Europe and the Muslim world.

12. Kublai Khan's major concern in governing China was
    A. creating integrated Chinese and military units.
    B. to avoid the Mongols being assimilated by Chinese culture and practices.
    C. educating Mongol leaders and elites in Chinese Confucian culture.
    D. the conversion of the Chinese to Islam.
    E. reestablishing the Confucian civil service exams and scholar-bureaucrats.

13. The most favored non-Mongolian people to be included in high social groups and inner circles of the Mongol khans were
    A. Muslims especially Persians and Turks.
    B. the Chinese.
    C. the Nestorian Christians.
    D. Italian merchants.
    E. Buddhists.

14. Mongolian favoritism towards all of these groups would have angered Confucian scholars EXCEPT:
    A. artisans.
    B. peasants.
    C. foreigners.
    D. Muslims.
    E. merchants.

15. The transformation that most immediately weakened the power and influence of pastoral nomads over sedentary civilization was due to
    A. introduction of better organized sedentary states.
    B. increased centralization of sedentary governments.
    C. the devastation to nomadic populations caused by the Black Death.
    D. newer technologies, especially weapons, used by sedentary civilizations.
    E. settling of farmers on the traditional lands of the nomads.

IX.   ESSAY QUESTIONS

A. Compare and contrast the lifestyles and accomplishments of the Mongols with one of these peoples: Aztecs, Turks, or Aryans.

B. Compare and contrast gender roles in the Mongolian society with the Muslims or Chinese societies.

C. Compare and contrast the destruction brought by the Huns with the Mongol invasions.

D. Compare and contrast the Roman Peace and their style of rule with that of the Mongols.

E. Compare the Roman and Mongol war machines and military tactics.

CHAPTER 15
The West and the Changing World Balance
Pages 334 – 349

I. SUMMARY

   A. The Decline of the Old Order

   The first step in the new world order that was beginning to emerge by 1400 involved reshuffling in the Middle East and north Africa. Following the destruction brought by the Mongols, who destroyed the Abbasid Empire, the Ottomans rose to power, conquered the Byzantine Empire and overran most of the region.

   B. The Rise of the West

   Western Europe began to undergo important changes in the 14th and 15th centuries. Some involved new problems such as trade and the rise of the Ottoman Empire; others like the Renaissance and maritime expeditions created new opportunities. Examining of the various strengths and weaknesses of this once backward region sets the stage for Europe's new ventures in world trade.

   C. Western Expansion: The Experimental Phase

   Specific European attempts to explore the Atlantic beyond the earlier Viking voyages in the North Atlantic began in the later 13th century. Early discoveries increased Europeans' interest in setting up a colonial system.

   D. Outside the World Network

   The international framework that had developed during the postclassical period embraced most of Asia, Europe, and Africa. This network left out important groups such as the Polynesians and American Indians and regions, Mesoamerican and the Andean civilizations, that had their own vigorous histories in their centuries.

II. CHAPTER REVIEW

   A. What led to the decline of the Muslim world and its empires?

   B. How did the Mongols disrupt international relations?

   C. Why were post-Mongol states unwilling to reestablish contacts?

   D. What institutions and situations gave Europe an advantage?

E. How did the Renaissance affect and benefit European society?

F. What advantages did Spain and Portugal have when expansion began?

G. Which regions were outside the world network and why were they vulnerable?

III. VOCABULARY

    A. Renaissance

    B. Secularization

    C. Humanism

    D. Ethnocentrism

IV. DOCUMENT ANALYSIS: *Italian Renaissance Culture* (Page342)

    A. Analysis
1. Who wrote it?
2. What was the author's point of view?
3. How reliable is the document? Why?
4. What was the intent or purpose behind the document?
5. Who was the intended audience?
6. What is the document's tone?

    B. Interpreting
1. What values does Petrarch emphasize?

2. In what ways is Petrarch's work secular and religious?

3. Why might this new outlook threaten the medieval, sacred emphases?

4. What values does Petrarch exhibit that help European maritime expansion?

5. How does Petrarch emphasize individuality?

V. PHOTO EXERCISES: *Europe's New Spirit Amid Old Values* (Pages 341)

The European Renaissance broke with traditional medieval values associated with religion and the influence of the sacred and began to emphasize increasingly secular, everyday themes.

    A. How does the painting represent religious themes?

B. How does the painting represent secular themes?

VI. VISUALIZING THE PAST: *Population Trends* (Page 339)

A. Finding Relationships
   1. Which continents have the largest and smallest populations?

   2. Which continent has had the greatest population growth?

B. Trends
   1. Which populations show the greatest change from 1000 – 1700?

   2. What might account for the decline in Asian and African populations?

   3. When did the population increase the most?

   4. What might account for the decline in Europe and Asia's populations between 1900 – 1975?

   5. What information is missing that might make your analysis easier?

VII. MULTIPLE-CHOICE QUESTIONS

1. The medieval state, which originated in the Classical Era, and whose fall in 1453 signed the end of the Postclassical era was
   A. Song China
   B. Abbasid Caliphate
   C. Kievan Rus
   D. Byzantine Empire
   E. Mameluk Caliphate in Egypt

2. What change in Islam ended the postclassical age and began a new era?
   A. Islamic faith and piety won out over rationalism and secular themes.
   B. Mass conversions of Muslims to Christianity began.
   C. The secularization of Islamic society began.
   D. Islamic lands in Central Asia and the Middle East fell to Hindu conquerors.
   E. Muslims began to speak of a messiah and await his coming.

3. As the Postclassical Era ended, within Muslim society
   A. Christian and Jewish merchants began to dominate trade and commerce.
   B. secularized schools opened.
   C. landlords seized power over the peasants and agricultural productivity fell.
   D. slavery was abolished.
   E. women were granted rights to own property and work outside the home.

4. In comparison to the fall of the Roman Empire, the fall of the Arab caliphate
   A. had few repercussions on its inhabitants.
   B. was not due to outside invasions by pastoral nomads.
   C. produced prolonged economic and political confusion in the Middle East.
   D. left no religious institutions to support the Islamic faith.
   E. was not dramatic or sudden but occurred gradually over several centuries.

5. The resulting power vacuum in international affairs following the collapse of the Arab caliphate was
   A. further disrupted by the rise of the Mongols.
   B. not restored until the west European nations emerged as great powers.
   C. restored by the rise of the Ottoman Empire in the Middle East.
   D. restored by the Ming Dynasty in China.
   E. not restored until the 19th century C.E. when Great Britain created an empire that spanned all continents.

6. The Ming Chinese naval expeditions of the early 15th century C.E.
   A. ended because they challenged Confucian values and typical expenditures.
   B. were followed by the Chinese conquest of Southeast Asia.
   C. were stopped by Muslim navies in the Indian Ocean.
   D. led to a renewed Chinese interest in scientific and geographic exploration.
   E. stimulated trade between China and Africa.

7. The Ming Dynasty in China valued all of the policies and traditions EXCEPT:
   A. reviving foreign relations and the tribute system with its neighbors.
   B. military expenditures to eliminate nomadic threats in northern China.
   C. explorations and overseas adventures.
   D. agricultural interests over commercial opportunities.
   E. internal economic development instead of trade.

8. All of these events led to the weakening or end of medieval western European institutions EXCEPT the:
   A. Bubonic Plague.
   B. political and theological attacks on the Roman Catholic church.
   C. rise of national monarchies.
   D. Ottoman Turk invasion of western Europe.
   E. rise of non-aristocratic armies loyal to national monarchs.

9. The Renaissance in Europe
   A. rejected medieval values.
   B. was largely a cultural and intellectual movement.
   C. was a political revolution against the power of the pope.
   D. was not a rebirth of classical cultures as it borrowed little from Greek, Roman or Islamic achievements.
   E. avoided challenging medieval values.

10. The Renaissance spirit of west Europe is BEST characterized as
    A. religious and sacred.
    B. imitative.
    C. innovative and ambitious.
    D. deferential towards elites and traditions.
    E. fearful and fatalistic.

11. Besides the Italian city-states, the geographic region or state in west Europe MOST supportive of change at the end of the post-classical era was
    A. the Holy Roman Empire (Germany and Low Countries).
    B. France.
    C. England.
    D. the Iberian Peninsula (Spain and Portugal).
    E. Russia.

12. The major barrier to west European expansion prior to the 15th century C.E. was
    A. the low level of European technology.
    B. the lack of interest by west European rulers for acquiring territory.
    C. the overwhelming power of Muslim and Mongol states.
    D. religious civil wars divided western Europe and made overseas expansion impossible.
    E. lack of popular interest and public funds to support expansion.

13. The first west European nation to establish an overseas empire in the 15th century C.E. was
    A. the Netherlands.
    B. Sweden.
    C. Portugal.
    D. Spain.
    E. France.

14. The first European colonial estates were set up to
    A. export foodstuffs back to Europe.
    B. receive excess populations and alleviate overpopulation at home.
    C. were unsuccessful and failed.
    D. produce cash crops like sugar to supply European markets.
    E. caused very few ecological, environmental, and demographic disruptions in the Atlantic islands.

15. Later developments that brought the Post-classical Age 1000 – 1450 C.E. to an end would have influenced and affected all of these regions EXCEPT:
    A. the Middle East and North Africa.
    B. East Asia.
    C. South Asia.
    D. Western Europe.
    E. Polynesia and the Americas.

VIII. ESSAYS

A. Compare and contrast the intellectual Renaissances of 12th and 15th century Europe.

B. Compare and contrast 13th century Muslim fundamentalist reaction to the increasing secularization of western Europe.

C. Compare and contrast Chinese and Portuguese naval expeditions in the Indian Ocean during the 15th century.

D. Compare and contrast the end of the Postclassical Era with the collapse of the Classical Era.

PART III REVIEW

I.   PART OVERVIEW

    1. What events began and ended this period in world history?

    2. What developments define the Postclassical Era?

    3. What new civilization arose and how did it influence other, older cultures?

    4. To what new geographic areas did civilizations and world religions spread?

    5. What allowed civilizations to expand?

    6. What features created a unified zone of exchange in Eurasia and Africa?

II.   VOCABULARY

    A. Postclassical

III.   MAP EXERCISE: *The Postclassical World*

    A. Changes over Time Comparisons
       1. What states are represented on both maps? What could this mean?

       2. To what areas has civilization spread?

    B. Locations of Civilizations
       1. If the green represents states with a sophisticated level of civilization, what conclusions can you make about the beige (empty) areas on the maps?

       2. Why could you argue that the empty areas such as India and Northern Europe were likely civilized, while open areas of North and South America were still without urbanized cultures?

       3. Around which bodies of water (seas and oceans) did civilizations exist? How might bodies of water help civilizations?

IV.   TIMELINES: *Chronologies*

    A. What three civilizations are noted at the beginning and end of the timelines?

    B. What cultures seem to be great powers during this era?

V.   MULTIPLE-CHOICE QUESTIONS

1. During the Postclassical Age, 450 – 1450 C.E.
    A. Europe achieved its domination of the world.
    B. the Americas established contacts with Africa and Asia.
    C. nomadic peoples dominated the great civilizations of the world.
    D. the first international, as opposed to regional, connections arose.
    E. trade was limited.

2. The era from 450 – 1450 C.E. began with the
    A. collapse of most classical civilizations.
    B. rise of Islam.
    C. technological revolution in shipping and communication.
    D. invasion of Europe, the Middle East, and India by the Mongols.
    E. discovery of the Americas by the Europeans.

3. The postclassical world ended when the
    A. Black Death devastated civilizations on three continents.
    B. Ming in China, Mughals in India, and Russian tsars overthrew the Mongols.
    C. Portuguese ships rounded Africa and reached India.
    D. Mongol, Mameluk, and Turkish invasions devastated three continents.
    E. Spanish discovered the Americas.

4. All of these developments characterize the Postclassical Age EXCEPT the:
    A. expanding influence of the Arabs and Islam.
    B. domination of the Atlantic and Mediterranean by Christian Europeans.
    C. spread of civilization to new regions such as west Africa and southeast Asia.
    D. widespread shift in basic belief systems such as Christianity and Islam.
    E. development of a world network for trade, ideas, and diseases.

5. The leading civilization during the Postclassical Era (450 – 1450 C.E.) was
    A. the Christian West.
    B. the Byzantine Empire.
    C. India.
    D. sea-based trading states such as Venice and the Swahili states.
    E. Islam.

6. During the Post classical Era, all of these regions joined the civilized geographic cores EXCEPT:
    A. Japan.
    B. Northern Europe.
    C. Australia.
    D. Southeast Asia.
    E. Sub-Saharan Africa.

7. During the Postclassical Era, religions
   A. had few contacts with other world faiths.
   B. remained geographically and culturally restricted.
   C. developed rivalries with other faiths.
   D. rejected missionary activities.
   E. ended their traditional alliances with political authorities.

8. The growing world network of the Postclassical period possessed all of these characteristics EXCEPT:
   A. exchanges of ideas including mathematics and sciences.
   B. destructive threats to the environment due to increased populations.
   C. the expansion of trade and commerce, especially in luxuries.
   D. the spread of epidemics such as the Bubonic Plague.
   E. the spread of key technologies.

9. The Postclassical Era cannot be called "global" because
   A. the Americas, Polynesia, and Australia were not included in the world network.
   B. the Japanese and Europeans isolated their lands and cultures from contacts.
   C. China was excluded from the world system.
   D. only Muslim areas of the world interacted in the world system.
   E. civilization had not yet arisen in Sub-Saharan Africa.

10. During this era, politics and related institutions
    A. were dominated by religious institutions.
    B. favored aristocratic, patriarchal rule.
    C. were dominated by commercial interests.
    D. had one predominant form of type or state or government – empire.
    E. favored smaller states especially city-states.

VI.   ESSAY QUESTIONS

   A. Compare and contrast western Europe or one of the major medieval European monarchies and one of the African empires.

   B. Contrast the economic, social, cultural and political roles of Postclassical cities such as Guangzhou, Hangzhou, Heian, Angkor Wat, Samarkand, Timbuktu, Baghdad, Cairo, Constantinople, Venice, and Cordoba.

   C. Compare and contrast gender systems and inequalities and their changes over time.

   D. Compare and contrast the Aztec and Inca empires.

   E. Compare and contrast west European and Japanese feudalism.

PART III: GEOGRAPHY OF THE POSTCLASSICAL GEOGRAPHY

During the Postclassical Era the areas of civilization spread to all continents except Australia and the Antarctic. Areas, which had never known civilization, especially the lands and islands on the periphery of older civilizations, were settled and brought into contact with the core centers of civilizations.

I.   LOCATE
    A. RIVERS AND BODIES OF WATER
    1. North Sea
    2. Baltic Sea
    3. Adriatic Sea
    4. Sea of Japan
    5. Java Sea
    6. Lake Victoria
    7. Congo River
    8. Mekong River
    9. Volga
    10. Dnieper

    B. PHYSICAL GEOGRAPHY
    1. Rift Valley
    2. Namibian, Kalahari Deserts
    3. Alps
    4. Urals
    5. Italian Peninsula
    6. Iberian Peninsula
    7. Northern European Plain
    8. Madagascar
    9. Java
    10. Sumatra
    11. Hawaiian Islands
    12. North, South Zealand
    13. Bosporus, Dardanelles

II.   IDENTIFY AND LOCATE
    A. HISTORICAL REGIONS
    1. Deccan
    2. Sudan (West Africa)
    3. El-Zanj (East Africa)
    4. Catholic West Europe
    5. Orthodox Europe
    6. Muslim world

    B. HISTORICAL STATES
    1. Song China
    2. Mongol Empire
    3. Zimbabwe
    4. Frankish Empire
    5. Holy Roman Empire
    6. Kievan Rus
    7. Byzantine Empire
    8. Mali, Songhay
    9. Aztec Empire
    10. Incan Empire
    11. Khmer Empire
    12. Srivijava
    13. Chinese Empires
    14. Arabic Caliphates

C. CITIES
1. Constantinople
2. Cairo
3. Venice
4. Cordoba
5. Timbuktu
6. Guangzhou
7. Samarkand
8. Baghdad
9. Hangzhou
10. Tenochtitlan
11. Heian

MULTIPLE-CHOICE ANSWERS

CHAPTER 6

1. C
2. B
3. A
4. D
5. E
6. D
7. B
8. C
9. D
10. E
11. B
12. A
13. C
14. E
15. D

CHAPTER 7

1. B
2. B
3. A
4. D
5. E
6. C
7. D
8. D
9. E
10. B
11. A
12. D
13. A
14. E
15. C

CHAPTER 8

1. B
2. D
3. C
4. E
5. E
6. D
7. C
8. A
9. D
10. B
11. A
12. D
13. C
14. B
15. A

CHAPTER 9

1. E
2. B
3. C
4. A
5. B
6. A
7. C
8. D
9. E
10. A
11. D
12. E
13. B
14. C
15. D

CHAPTER 10

1. D
2. D
3. C
4. B
5. C
6. E
7. A
8. E
9. C
10. A
11. D
12. B
13. D
14. E
15. B
16. C
17. A

CHAPTER 11

1. B
2. A
3. E
4. C
5. E
6. D
7. A
8. D
9. B
10. E
11. C
12. C
13. B
14. E
15. D

CHAPTER 12

1. A
2. C
3. B
4. D

5. C
6. E
7. E
8. A
9. D
10. B
11. E
12. C
13. A
14. D
15. E
16. D
17. C

CHAPTER 13

1. D
2. E
3. B
4. C
5. D
6. A
7. A
8. E
9. B
10. B
11. C
12. D
13. E
14. C
15. B

CHAPTER 14

1. D
2. B
3. E
4. A
5. D
6. C
7. B
8. A
9. C
10. E

11. E
12. B
13. A
14. B
15. C

CHAPTER 15

1. D
2. A
3. C
4. E
5. B
6. A
7. C
8. D
9. B
10. C
11. D
12. A
13. C
14. D
15. E

PART III REVIEW

1. D
2. A
3. A
4. B
5. E
6. C
7. C
8. B
9. A
10. B

DOCUMENT-BASED QUESTION:
TWO TRADING ALLIANCES

DIRECTIONS

The following question is based on the accompanying documents. (The documents have been edited for the purpose of this exercise). The question is designed to test your ability to work with and understand historical documents. Write an essay that:

- Has relevant thesis and supports that thesis with evidence from the documents.

- Uses all or all but one of the documents.

- Analyzes the documents by grouping them in as many appropriate ways as possible and does not simply summarize the documents individually.

- Takes into account both the sources of the documents and the authors' points of view.

ESSAY PROMPT

While the Hansa and Swahili shared many similarities, their differences were equally important. What differences in the two trading alliances were critical to the cultural, economic, and political development of the two alliances?

Based on the following documents, discuss Postclassical merchant alliances. What types of additional documentation would help explain the different cultural, economic, and political paths taken and institutions developed by the Hansa and the Swahili?

HISTORICAL BACKGROUND

During the Postclassical Era from 1000 to 1450 C.E., cities, which relied heavily on trade, arose and flourished. Some of the most notable were Venice and Genoa in Italy, Hangzhow in China, Malacca on the Malaccan Straits, Hormuz in Persia, and Cambay and Quilon in India. At the same time, many smaller trading cities formed trading alliances and associations. Two of the most successful and famous were the German Hansa in Northern Europe and the Swahili cities along the coast of East Africa.

DOCUMENT 1

FOREIGN GOLD & SILVER COINS DISCOVERED AT SWAHILI CITIES: From Classical and Post-Classical Era Trading Civilizations to 1450 C.E.							
	Kilwa	Mafia	Zanzibar	Pemba	Kenya	Somalia	Total
Hellenistic		1		2		22	25
Persian			5				5
Roman				2	1	6	9
Byzantine				2		46	48
Umayyad				2			2
Abbasid				7		1	8
Seljuk				1			1
Mameluk	2			4		6	12
Mongol	2	4		1			7
Muslim, misc.		20	3	15			38
Tang China			4			1	5
Sung China		9	185		2	16	212
Ming China						6	6
Ceylon						4	4
Vietnam						4	4
South India						2	2

Kenyan Swahili cities are Mombasa and Lamu; Somalia includes Mogadishu

DOCUMENT 2

The Hansa reply to a memorandum from the English Privy Council, after the English arrested Hansa merchants and confiscated their property, 1469

"The Hansa came into being through agreement and alliance of different towns; But the German Hansa is a firm confederation of many cities, towns, and communities for the purpose of ensuring that business enterprises by land and sea should have a desired and favorable outcome and that there should be effective protection against pirates and highwaymen, so that their ambushes should not rob merchants of their goods and valuables. The Hansa is not controlled by the merchants; on the contrary each city and each town has its own lords and its own magistracy by whom its affairs are directed. For the Hansa is nothing other than a kind of alliance between towns, which does not release the towns from the jurisdiction of those lords who ruled over them. The Hansa has no common council; but each town sends delegates, with instructions. The towns of the Hansa assemble whenever there are questions to be discussed and decide amongst themselves what they consider necessary for the good of their merchants."

DOCUMENT 3

Joao de Barros, Portuguese merchant and soldier from his book, *Decadas da Asia* completed in 1520s about his travels along East Africa's coast

"It was part of the agreement between the pagans [of Sofala] and the Muslims of Mogadishu that they should bring every year some young Muslims so that there might always be in town certain [Muslim merchants]. When the King of Kilwa learned from the fishermen of this part of the contract, he gave orders that a ship should be sent so as to arrange to enter into commerce with the blacks. With regard to the young Muslims for whom they asked, or if they wanted these Muslims so far as to have a race of them there, some of the inhabitants of Kilwa would agree to go and live there in a factory for merchandise and they would be glad to take the pagans' daughters as wives, by which means the people [Muslim merchants] would be multiplied. By means of this entry, the Muslims of Kilwa got possession of the trade. In course of time by means of trade which the Muslims had with the blacks, the kings of Kilwa became absolute masters of the trade in gold. From this time onwards the kings of Kilwa sent their governors to Sofala, so that everything might be transacted through [Muslim] merchants."

DOCUMENT 4

Declaration of the Hanseatic League for the prosecution of the war against Denmark and Norway, their meeting in Koln, Holy Roman Empire, 1367

"We declare that we have agreed, firstly, that because of the manifold wrongs and injuries which the kings of Denmark and Norway have inflicted and do still inflict upon Hanseatic merchants, we have become their enemies and that we shall loyally support one another in the following manner: namely, that the Wendish towns together with the Livonian towns and with those towns which are associated with them, will fit out ten ships, manned with able men-at-arms, that is, 100 men to each ship, and that two supply ships shall accompany each larger ship. The Prussian towns, that is, seaports, shall equip five ships of a like kind. And when all ships [from Holland and Zealand and the Baltic cities] are assembled in the Danish Sound, the whole fleet from both districts is to remain with the warships and to do as the commanders bid them. Further, to cover the costs, every merchant shall pay poundage on his goods. And similarly captains shall pay poundage on their ships. This poundage shall be levied in every town of the Confederation and is to be kept at the disposal of all those towns, which have fitted out ships of war. The above mentioned Confederation with all its rules and regulations shall remain in full force for a further three years."

DOCUMENT 5

Abdul Hassan ibn Ali al Mas'udi, Arab traveler, merchant and geographer, from Cairo and Baghdad, late 10th century C.E. about his trips to the East African coastal area of el-Zanj, the Swahili peoples between Somalia and Mozambique

"The sea of Zanj reaches down to the country of Sofala and the Wak-Wak, which produces gold in abundance and other marvels; its climate is warm and its soil fertile. It is there that the Zanj built their capital; then they elected a king whom they called [Swahili]. The king has under him all the other Zanj kings, and commands three hundred thousand men. Although constantly employed in hunting elephants and gathering ivory for domestic purposes, they wear iron instead of gold and silver. Tusks form the country of the Zanj go generally to Oman, and from there are sent on to China and India. That is the route they follow, and were it otherwise, ivory would be very abundant in Muslim countries. In China the kings and their military and civilian officers use carrying-chairs of ivory; no official or person of rank would dare to visit the king in an iron chair, and ivory alone is used for this purpose. Ivory is much prized in India; there it is made into handles for the daggers or swords or in the manufacture of chessmen and other gaming pieces."

DOCUMENT 6

Renewal of the contract for the supply of foodstuffs and materials to and exports from Bruges, Flanders by the Hanseatic diet [Parliament] in Lubeck, 1470

"And nobody, whoever he may be, whether he is a merchant in the Hansa, as a burgess [citizen] or inhabitant, or whether he does not belong to the Hansa, shall take cloth made in Flanders, Brabant or Holland into any Hansa town or its territory, which has not passed through the market at Bruges or was not bought or offered for sale in Antwerp or Bergen-op-Zoom at the fair held there. Similarly all eastern Hanseatic towns, and all other Hansa towns, shall refrain from supplying anyone, whether he belongs to the Hansa or not, with any staple goods for passage through [the seas between the North and Baltic Seas], unless he swears an oath beforehand or gives surety that he intends to take those goods to the markets in Flanders and Holland."

DOCUMENT 7

Ibn Battuta, Muslim traveler and qadi (religious judge), from the chronicles of his visit to the coasts of East Africa, 1331 C.E.

"We sailed for fifteen nights and came to Mogadishu, which is a town of enormous size. Its inhabitants are merchants possessed of vast resources. In this place is manufactured the woven fabrics called after it, which are unequalled and exported from it to Egypt and elsewhere. It is the custom that whenever there comes a jurist or a sharif or a man of religion, he must first see the sultan before taking a lodging. So I went to the sultan, as they asked. The sultan of Mogadishu is Abu Bakr, son of Sultan Omar; he is by origin from [Northern Somalia] and he speaks the language of Mogadishu, but knows the Arabic language. After we had eaten, we went to the congregational mosque and made our prayers. When the sultan came out, he said in Arabic, 'You are welcome, and you have honored our land and given us pleasure.' On Saturday, the population comes to the Sultan's gate, and the qadi, with the viziers (chief ministers), the private secretary, and four of the principal amirs, sits for deciding cases among the population and petitioners. Every case that is concerned with the rulings of the Divine Law is decided by the qadi, and all cases other than those are decided by the members of the council. If any case calls for consultation with the sultan, he sends out the reply to them immediately."

DOCUMENT 8

Contingents of armed men, which Rostock (Hansa city in Northern Germany) guilds had to furnish for the defense of the town, from official list of 1483		
Porters (150)	Butchers (20)	Pewterers (16)
Shoemakers (40)	Coopers (20)	Linen weavers (16)
Blacksmiths (40)	Bridlemakers (20)	Hoopers (10)
Bakers (30)	Tailors (20)	Masons (10)
Retailers (30)	Tanners (20)	Carpenters (10)
Haberdashers (20)	Wool Weavers (20)	Old Tailors (10)
Furriers (20)	Fishermen (20)	Barbers (6)
Plus an additional 40 guilds with 2 to 3 armed men each		
Total: 622 armed guildsmen		

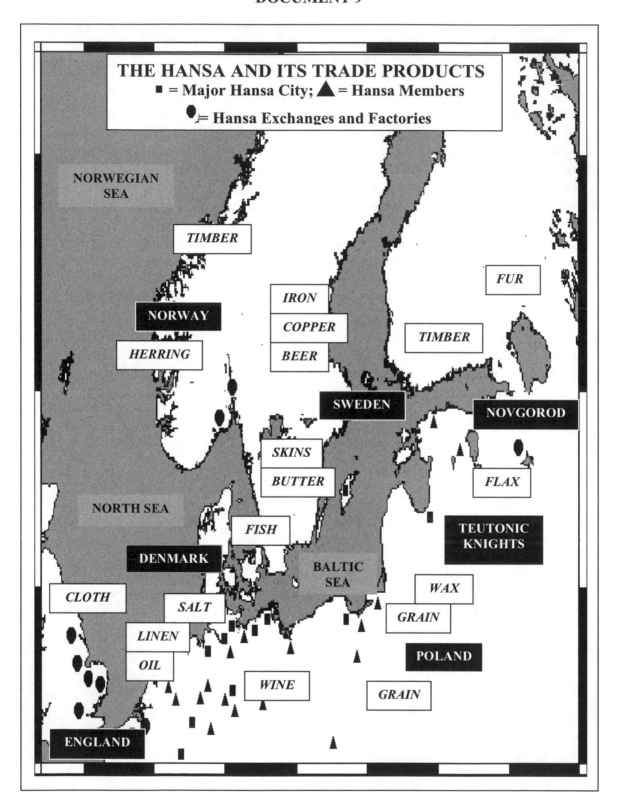

THE HANSA AND ITS TRADE PRODUCTS
■ = Major Hansa City; ▲ = Hansa Members
● = Hansa Exchanges and Factories

NORWEGIAN SEA

TIMBER

FUR

NORWAY

IRON

COPPER

TIMBER

BEER

HERRING

SWEDEN

NOVGOROD

SKINS

BUTTER

FLAX

NORTH SEA

TEUTONIC KNIGHTS

FISH

DENMARK

BALTIC SEA

CLOTH

WAX

SALT

GRAIN

LINEN

POLAND

OIL

WINE

GRAIN

ENGLAND

FOOTNOTES: TWO TRADING ALLIANCES

1. Basil Davidson, *Africa: Civilization Revisited – From Antiquity to Modern Times* (Trenton, New Jersey: Africa World Press, Inc., 1991), 138 – 139.

2. Philippe Dollinger, *The German Hansa*, trans. and edited by D. S. Ault and S. H. Steinberg (Stanford, California: Stanford University Press, 1970) , 412 – 413.

3. Zoe Marsh, *East Africa through Contemporary Records* (Cambridge, England: University Press, 1961), 9.

4. Dollinger, *The German Hansa*, 385 – 387.

5. Davidson, *Africa: Civilization Revisited*, 132 – 134.

6. Dollinger, *The German Hansa*, 413 – 414.

7. Robert O. Collins, ed. with introductions, *African History: Text and Readings* (New York: Random House, Inc., 1971), 269 – 272.

8. Johannes Schildhauer, *The Hansa: History and Culture*, translated from German by Katherine Vanovitch (Leipzig, Germany: Edition Leipzig, 1985), 163.

9. Johannes Schildhauer, *The Hansa: History and Culture*, 10 – 11.

PART IV
The World Shrinks
1450 – 1750

Pages 350 – 355

SUMMARY

Many developments highlighted world history between 1450 and 1750, which marked a major new period – the early modern – in the global experience. The balance of power among major civilizations shifted; western Europe became the most dramatic force worldwide. Contacts among the civilizations intensified. The world became smaller as trade affected diverse societies and the speed and size of ships increased. The growth of commerce affected all continents but its greatest impact was in western Europe. New empires based on technology and new forms of organization arose. Two types were land-based and maritime commercial empires.

On the Eve of the Early Modern Period: The World around 1450

When this period began, no one civilization predominated in world affairs; a power vacuum existed. A number of powerful societies arose during the post-classical period. A Russian empire expanded across the steppes and forests of Eurasia. Western European regional kingdoms, attempting to expand in Europe, turned to overseas colonial empires. Gunpowder empires with strong governments arose on the Sahel of Africa, across the Middle East and India, and in China, yet by the end of the period, all were powerless to oppose the growing political, economic, and military power of many European states.

The Rise of the West

Between 1450 and 1750, Western Europe – headed initially by Spain and Portugal, and then by Holland, France, and England – gained control of the key international trade routes and established colonies across the globe. At the same time, the West itself changed rapidly and by the end of the period had assumed a position similar to the role of Islam from 1000 to 1450.

The World Economy and Global Contacts

Fed by new naval technologies, the world network intensified and took on new dimensions. The Europeans came to dominate international trade. The world network expanded to global proportions as all continents were brought into contacts. The new globalism led to many exchanges including flora and fauna, humans, diseases, goods, and ideas. Unequal relationships arose, as slavery and serfdom spread. For the first time, humans began to have an adverse effect on the environment as migrating settlers cleared forests; overworked the soil; and transplanted plants, animals, and foodstuffs across the globe.

World Boundaries

From 1450 to 1750, the world saw an unusually high number of boundary changes. The spread of Western colonies was the most obvious, but the establishment or extension of several large land-based empires was almost as significant.

The Gunpowder Empires

The evolution of new weaponry, such as cannon and muskets, on land and sea, spurred imperial expansion by the West and the Ottoman Turks. The Russian, Persian Safavid, Mughal Indian, and Qing Chinese empires relied on the new technology. Guns were almost important in Japan and Africa.

Themes

Key themes of world history changed. The effect of nomadic societies declined after the Mongol invasions. New gunpowder states conquered many of their lands. The nomads' role as intermediaries was replaced by relations between states and merchants. Gender relations remained mostly unchanged, but labor systems were transformed by a great expansion of slavery and serfdom. The accumulating wealth and increasing cultural contacts created new opportunities in all fields for a few individuals. Drastic environmental change occurred because of the movement of foods, animals, and diseases.

Civilizations and Larger Trends

Three international trends – Western expansion, intensification and globalization of the world commercial network, and the military and political results of gunpowder – influenced all civilizations. Differing responses spurred different courses of evolution in separate cultures.

CHAPTER 16
The World Economy
Pages 358-379

I. SUMMARY

A. The West's First Outreach: Maritime Power

Between 1450 and 1650, various Western European nations gained unprecedented mastery of the world's oceans. Trading patterns and colonial expansion focused on Europe's maritime power and maritime technologies, which gave the Europeans their first advantage on the world scene. Pioneering efforts by Spain and Portugal were followed by the surge of England, Holland, and France.

B. Toward a World Economy

Europe's maritime dominance and the opening of the Atlantic and Pacific Oceans had three major consequences in world history. They created a new international pool for basic exchanges of foods, diseases, and a few manufacturing products. They created a new, world economy, involving the first embrace of the Americas in international trade but setting a different framework even for Europe and Asia. And they created the conditions for direct Western penetration of some parts of the world through colony formation.

C. Colonial Expansion

Along with the larger world economic system, a new wave of colonialism took shape after the early Spanish and Portuguese explorations. Key European nations developed direct overseas empires. Two sets of American colonies developed, one in Latin America and the Caribbean, one in parts of North America. The Americas hosted the largest colonies, but colonialism also spread to Africa and Asia, where European states maintained smaller but extremely valuable possessions dedicated largely to trade in spices, luxuries, and slaves.

II. CHAPTER REVIEW

A. What advantages allowed Spain and Portugal to expand overseas first?

B. After the 16th century, to whom did the lead in European colonial expansion pass and with what results?

C. What were the Colombian Exchanges and how did they affect the world?

D. What global labor and commercial structures, patterns, and relationships arose?

E. Why would it be incorrect to call the system of world contacts, which arose during this period, a "global system"?

F. How did European nations acquire and govern their American colonies?

G. How did European colonial possessions and practices in Asia and Africa differ from practices in the Americas?

H. How did contacts affect Europe and European settlers in the Americas?

III. MAP EXERCISES

A. Map 17.1: Spain and Portugal – Explorations and Colonies, c. 1600 C.E. (Page 362)

1. Colonies and Geography

a. Where are Spain's colonies located?

b. Where are Portugal's colonies located?

2. Routes

a. Identify the explorers who sailed for Spain and Portugal.

b. Describe their routes using compass directions and seas sailed.

B. Map 17.2: France, Britain, and Dutch Holdings, c. 1700 (Page 364)

1. Identify the colonial holdings of each European power.

a. France

b. Britain

c. The Dutch

2. Why would Europe be able to settle the interiors of the American continents but not Africa?

3. Why might European possessions be very limited on the continental coasts of Asia (as opposed to the islands off shore)?

IV. PHOTO ESSAY: *World Exchanges* (Pages 361, 363, 366, 371, 372, 375 and 377)

Columbus' discoveries began centuries of exchanges between the continents. Few areas escaped the influences and effects of these Columbian Exchanges.

A. Identify European influences on other regions and cultures in each photo and explain each exchange.

1. Political

2. Economic

3. Religious

4. Social

5. Intellectual and Artistic

6. Demographic and Environmental

B. How might contacts and exchanges have affected Europe and the Europeans?

V. VISUALIZING THE PAST: *West Indian Slaveholding* (Page 368)

A. Interpreting Statistics

On an Advanced Placement test, never refigure data in a table because it will take too long; look instead for trends and relationships.

1. In 1688, how many taxable plantations and businesses did Antigua have?

2. How many were slaveholders?

3. What is the ratio of slaveholders to total businesses in 1706? 1767?

4. Who owns slaves in Antigua?

5. How does this change over time?

6. What other changes do you notice?

B. Drawing Conclusions from Data

While data and statistics are factual, your conclusions can be opinions. Whatever conclusions you reach, back it up with evidence.

1. What social and economic trends do the figures suggest?

2. Is the Antiguan economy more or less labor intensive? Why?

3. What does the data suggest about the social class of Europeans in Antigua?

VI. DOCUMENT ANALYSIS: Western Conquerors – Tactics and Motives (Page 373-374)

A. Document Analysis

1. Who wrote each? (Attribution includes biographical references)

2. What were the authors' points of view?

3. How reliable are the documents? Why?

4. What were the intents or purposes behind the documents?

5. Who were the intended audiences?

6. What are the documents' tones?

B. Comparison

   1. How do the two documents agree? Disagree?

   2. What might account for these differences?

   3. What biases do you detect?

   4. How do they affect your understanding or the reliabilities of the authors?

   5. What would account for changes in perspectives?

C. Conclusions

   1. What are the motives of the Spanish conquerors?

   2. How do they achieve their goals?

   3. How might non-Europeans view the same incidents and judge Europeans?

VII. MULTIPLE-CHOICE QUESTIONS

   1. What types of technologies allowed the Europeans to expand overseas?
      A. superior weaponry
      B. agricultural techniques
      C. superior institutions of government, especially the bureaucracy
      D. maritime technologies
      E. manufacturing and industrial systems

   2. All of these influenced or encouraged Europe to expand EXCEPT:
      A. fear of the states and peoples Europe might encounter.
      B. desire for gold and monetary gain.
      C. rivalries with other European states to acquire new lands.
      D. hope for personal glory by explorers and conquerors.
      E. desire to spread Christianity abroad.

   3. The main reason European conquerors and navigators were able to sail and continue to explore, and the reason the Ming Chinese fleets in the Indian Ocean failed was
      A. Europeans had superior military technologies and the Chinese did not.
      B. Europe encountered no opposition, while the Chinese did.
      C. European governments supported and encouraged overseas expeditions; the Ming did not.
      D. European nations were wealthier than the Chinese.
      E. China had a smaller population base than Europe and could not afford to send people abroad

4. Spain established colonies in
   A. the Persian Gulf and West Africa.
   B. Southern India and the Caribbean Sea.
   C. the Philippine Islands and the Spice Islands.
   D. Brazil and India.
   E. Mexico and Peru.

5. In comparison to Spain and Portugal, the Northern European states and their expeditions
   A. began earlier, but conquered fewer lands.
   B. were more successful.
   C. had superior technologies and commercial practices but were uninterested in acquiring colonies.
   D. began later and initially acquired only limited holdings outside Europe.
   E. were more motivated by religion than had been Portugal or Spain.

6. In order to facilitate colonization, settlement, and exploration, the British, French, and Dutch
   A. chartered companies and created commercial monopolies in a given region.
   B. paid mercenaries to conquer desired lands.
   C. negotiated with peoples and states to peacefully acquire holdings and trade concessions abroad.
   D. encouraged private initiative because national governments were uninterested in overseas expeditions.
   E. relied on missionaries to establish markets and colonies.

7. All of these were examples of the Columbian Exchanges EXCEPT:
   A. the spread of smallpox and measles in the Americas.
   B. New World crops such as corn and potatoes spread around the world.
   C. domesticated animals such as the horse spread to the Americas.
   D. Muslim and Chinese merchants came to monopolize Atlantic trade.
   E. Africans and Europeans migrated or were forcibly settled in the Americas.

8. During the Early Modern Period in world history, laborers were
   A. generally paid a fair wage but worked long hours.
   B. largely coerced in work, which was often unfree.
   C. moved to where there was a demand for their work.
   D. mostly skilled.
   E. universally slaves.

9. During the Early Modern Era, the world economy and trade
   A. spread to and linked all countries and continents except Antarctica.
   B. was dominated by Muslim merchants.
   C. did not include areas such as China, Japan, and many Muslim regions.
   D. relied heavily on the slave trade to generate capital and profits.
   E. shipped primarily agricultural products.

10. All of these regions were included in the Early Modern Era's first world economy EXCEPT:
    A. South America.
    B. the West Indies.
    C. the Atlantic coast of North America.
    D. islands and coasts of West Africa and the East Indies.
    E. the Middle East.

11. European nations acquired their first colonies in the Americas
    A. following the conquests by military, gold-seeking adventurers.
    B. when merchants bought islands and landholdings from the inhabitants.
    C. through missionary activities to convert the inhabitants.
    D. through intermarriage between reigning royal families.
    E. peacefully.

12. The Dutch, French, and English North American colonies
    A. received few colonists.
    B. remained largely unsettled and unclaimed.
    C. attracted little attention because they were so vast.
    D. were not as financially important as the income from colonies in the West and East Indies.
    E. eventually were conquered by the Spanish.

13. In their American colonies, the British and French settlers
    A. arrived largely for religious reasons.
    B. encountered little organized Indian resistance and created European-like societies.
    C. established institutions radically different from their home countries' cultures.
    D. relied heavily on manufacturing to make a living.
    E. received no support from their respective mother countries.

14. In Africa during the Early Modern Period, Europeans
    A. controlled the slave trade.
    B. had to negotiate with African kings, who controlled the slave trade.
    C. settled widely in West Africa.
    D. exported gold and raw minerals.
    E. started the slave trade.

15. The only area of Africa colonized by Europeans prior to the mid-1700s was
    A. North Africa especially Algeria, which was settled by the French.
    B. West Africa settled by the French.
    C. Congo and Angola settled by the Spanish.
    D. South Africa settled by the Dutch.
    E. Brazil settled by the Portuguese.

16. Europeans in India during the 17th and 18th centuries
    A. cooperated peacefully to share the lucrative trade.
    B. traded only when permitted to do so by the Mughal rulers.
    C. lost their rights to trade in India to local Muslims.
    D. had no interest in missionary work.
    E. increased their presence and control as Mughal power declined.

17. The most important basic commodity traded in the early modern period was
    A. grain.
    B. gold.
    C. tobacco.
    D. cotton.
    E. sugar.

VIII. ESSAY QUESTIONS

    A. Compare and contrast European colonial empires with the imperial institutions of any one: Roman Empire, Muslim Abbasid state, Tang China, or the Mongols.

    B. Compare and contrast a maritime with a land-based empire.

    C. Compare and contrast the Spanish or Portuguese with any North European colonial empire.

    D. Compare and contrast Columbian Exchanges with Mongol exchanges across the steppes.

    E. How has trade changed from the Classical to the Early Modern period?

    F. Compare and contrast colonial empires in the Americas with European colonial possessions in Africa and Asia during this period.

CHAPTER 17
The Transformation of the West, 1450-1750

Pages 380 – 401

I.   SUMMARY

A. The First Big Changes: Culture and Commerce

During the 15th century the Renaissance emphasized new styles and beliefs. This was followed by even more sweeping cultural and political changes in the 16th century, with the Protestant and Catholic Reformations, and the political changes both engendered. During the Commercial Revolution, a new commercial and social structure grew as well, creating new opportunities and new grievances.

B. Science and Politics: The Net Phase of Change

As the impact of the Reformation and commercialization continued, new scientific discoveries and political forms took shape from 1600 onward. These two forces shaped a new round of change that continued into the 18th century. The revolution in science set the seal on the cultural reorientation of the West. After the political upheavals of the Reformation, a more decisive set of new government forms arose in the West centering on the emergence of the nation-state. Simultaneously, the functions of the state expanded.

C. The West by 1750

The three great currents of change – commercialization, cultural reorientation, and the rise of the nation-state – continued to operate in the West after 1700, along with the growing international influence of the West. These flowered simultaneously during the Enlightenment. Each current produced new changes that furthered the overall transformation of the West. Even as absolutism gave way to enlightened despotism in states, parliamentary government expanded and a new school of economics, capitalism, and new forms of commerce arose.

II. CHAPTER REVIEW

A. How did the two Reformations change European culture and society?

B. What new economic and commercial structures arose during the period and how did they fundamentally redefine the European institutions?

C. How did the Renaissance and Scientific Revolution affect intellectual life and promote changes in popular outlook?

D. What new ideas arose during this period and how did they change European society?

E. How did European governments, attitudes towards government, and state structures change during this period?

F. What was the relationship between the Enlightenment and changes in popular culture and government?

G. What changes occurred in social structures, families, and gender relations?

III.   VOCABULARY

A. Renaissance

B. Humanism

C. European family style

D. Protestant, Catholic Reformations

E. Indulgences

F. Anglican Church

G. Predestination

H. Jesuits

I. Commercial Revolution

J. Proletariat

K. Witchcraft persecution

L. Scientific Revolution

M. Heliocentric universe

N. Deism

O. Absolute monarchy

P. Mercantilism

Q. Parliamentary monarchy

R. Enlightenment

S. Classical Economics

T. Socialists

U. Capitalism

IV.   MAP EXERCISES

A. Map 16.1: Western Europe during the Renaissance and Reformation (Page 387)

1. Using the current world map and the map on page 387, what modern nations are:

a. Catholic?
b. Anglican?
c. Lutheran?
d. Calvinist?
e. Eastern Orthodox?
f. Muslim?

2. What European nations are divided by religion?

3. How might two religions in a nation affect its development?

B. Map 16.2: Europe under Absolute Monarchy, 1715 (Page 392)

1. Which modern nations already exist in 1715?

2. Which modern nations have not yet emerged?

3. Why would it be different to govern the Holy Roman Empire and Italy?

V.   PHOTO ESSAY: Secularization of Western Society

Using photos on pages 380, 385, 386, 389, 395, and 399, look up and define secularization and humanism. The era 1450 – 1750 witnessed the increasing secularization of society and faith in human reason. How do the photos represent these qualities?

VI.   DOCUMENT ANALYSIS: *Controversies About Women* (Page 396)
A. Document Analysis

1. Who wrote each? (Attribution includes biographical references)

2. What were the authors' points of view?

3. How reliable are the documents? Why?

4. What were the intents or purposes behind the documents?

5. Who were the intended audiences?

6. What are the documents' tones?

B. Comparison

1. How do the two documents agree? Disagree?

2. What might account for these differences?

3. What biases do you detect?

4. How do they affect your understanding or the reliabilities of the authors?

5. What would account for changes in perspectives?

VII. MULTIPLE-CHOICE QUESTIONS

1. The major transformation of Western European society began with the
   A. invention of the printing press.
   B. Renaissance.
   C. Protestant and Catholic Reformations.
   D. Enlightenment.
   E. Glorious Revolution.

2. The Renaissance in Western Europe
   A. profoundly challenged absolutist traditions in government.
   B. was primarily religious in outlook.
   C. began in England and France but spread throughout Europe.
   D. challenged medieval values and intellectual constructs.
   E. was the last European intellectual movement to influence world cultures.

3. The Renaissance was largely influenced and financed by
   A. the Roman Catholic Church.
   B. Medieval institutions.
   C. popular culture and the lifestyles of the masses.
   D. scientists and the Scientific Revolution.
   E. the urban environment and commercial economy.

4. Renaissance humanism would have been most comfortable with the values and ideas of which world belief system?
   A. Christianity
   B. Buddhism
   C. Hellenism
   D. Confucianism
   E. Hinduism

5. The Protestant Reformation in Germany was equally a religious and political revolution because it challenged all of these authorities EXCEPT the:
   A. Papal position as the head of the Christian Church.
   B. noble and aristocratic class structure within society.
   C. influence of the Emperor as head of the Holy Roman Empire.
   D. church's ownership of land in Germany.
   E. influence of Roman and Italy over Germany.

6. The fragmentation of Christianity during the Reformation into Catholics and Protestants most closely resembles the
   A. Sunni-Shia divisions within Islam over political leadership of the Muslim community.
   B. Buddha's founding of Buddhism out of Hindu traditions.
   C. expulsion of the Christians from Judaism around 70 C.E.
   D. transformation of religions from polytheism to monotheism.
   E. absorption of Muslim ideas by Hinduism following contacts between the two religions.

7. In Western Europe following the religious wars in the 16th and 17th centuries,
   A. the popes reestablished their dominant religious and political positions.
   B. Christian unity was restored but the Pope was no longer head of the church.
   C. full religious freedoms were granted to practice and to choose one's faith.
   D. the different Christian sects accepted a limited toleration of other groups.
   E. Europe abandoned religions totally because of its divisiveness in society.

8. Changes during the Reformation influenced all of these developments EXCEPT:
   A. the political balance of power shifted.
   B. abolishment of classes and social hierarchies.
   C. the rise of the modern European family and marriage.
   D. increased literacy.
   E. the increasing secularization of West European society.

9. The cause of the massive inflation in 16th century Europe was the
   A. Renaissance monarchs' increased demand for art.
   B. Reformation challenged faith in the economy.
   C. large imports of gold and silver from overseas colonies.
   D. religious wars, which destroyed the economic structures.
   E. trade between Europe and the Muslim world.

10. The growing commercialization of Western Europe's economy and the Price Revolution most negatively impacted the
    A. rulers and bureaucracy.
    B. aristocracy and the ruling elite.
    C. churches and religious establishments.
    D. merchants.
    E. peasants, serfs, and the working poor.

11. The chief challenge in West Europe during the 17th and 18th centuries C.E. to the predominance and the traditional role of religion and theology as the primary influence on formal intellectual life was
    A. the ruler and his or her ideas about the arts and learning.
    B. the merchant and the profit motive.
    C. Military necessity.
    D. the scientist and scientific experimentation.
    E. the increasing paganism and atheism of the common people.

12. The 17th century Scientific Revolution in West Europe built heavily on
    A. the work of Muslim scientists.
    B. Hindu mathematics.
    C. Chinese mystical Daoism.
    D. Greek rational philosophies and classical scientists such as Aristotle.
    E. Christian theology.

13. In early modern Europe, in order to secure their predominant political positions within their states, West European rulers had to
    A. limit the rights of nobles and privileges of their institutions.
    B. replace the Christian clergy.
    C. restrict the power and influence of the military.
    D. limit the rights of their ethnic and religious minorities.
    E. discourage economic profits and entrepreneurial incentives.

14. West European monarchs employed all of these methods or groups to win "absolute" control of their states EXCEPT:
    A. increasing royal revenues through new taxes and supporting mercantilism.
    B. allowing representative assemblies to make and to pass laws.
    C. limiting the rights of medieval parliaments and diets.
    D. creating a professional army.
    E. recruiting trained bureaucrats from the middle (urban) classes.

15. Mercantilism differs from capitalism because mercantilism
    A. discourages colonies and overseas adventures.
    B. encourages skilled workers to demand better pay and benefits.
    C. does not encourage state or government intervention in the economy.
    D. allows imports and exports without tariffs and barriers.
    E. promotes the wealth of a national economy at the expense of free trade.

16. A nation-state differs from an empire or many medieval states because it
    A. grants rulers absolute rights to govern.
    B. rules a state with one dominant people, government, language, and culture.
    C. limits the power of monarchs and rulers.
    D. has many large and different ethnic groups under a common government.
    E. is democratic and representative of the people's wishes.

17. The major difference between the Enlightenment and Scientific Revolution was that Enlightenment philosophies
    A. encouraged religion and the piety of the people.
    B. had the support of rulers.
    C. applied scientific methods to benefit society at large.
    D. did not challenge traditional ideas, constructs, or ruling institutions.
    E. looked to the common people for support or encouragement.

VIII.   ESSAY QUESTIONS

    A. Compare and contrast the Enlightenment and Scientific Revolution with one of these: (1) 12th century Islamic achievements; (2) Italian Renaissance; (3) 5th century BCE Greek intellectual accomplishments; and (4) 11th century Song Chinese achievements.

    B. How did European government change from Charlemagne through the 18th century C.E.?

    C. Compare and contrast European absolutism with governmental policies under one of these states: (1) Tsarist Russia; (2) Ottoman Empire; (3) Mughal India; (4) Safavid Persia; or (5) Ming China.

    D. Compare and contrast the Reformation with religious schisms in Islam or Buddhism.

    E. Compare and contrast absolutism in France or Spain with Dutch and English representative government.

    F. Compare and contrast the Protestant belief system with any other world belief system.

    G. Compare and contrast mercantilism and capitalism.

    H. Compare and contrast the nation-state with any post-classical state.

155

CHAPTER 18
The Rise of Russia
Page 402 – 417

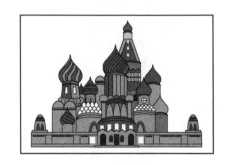

I.   SUMMARY

A. Russia's Expansionist Politics under the Tsar

Between1450 and 1650, Russia began its process of territorial expansion while working to strengthen the tsarist state in what proved to be the first phase of the empire's early modern development. This process was externally challenged by Russian neighbors especially Poland, Sweden, and the Ottoman Empire. Internally, the nobles were often the largest impediment to centralization and state power.

B.   Russia's First Westernization, 1690 – 1790

By the late 17th century, Russia was poised for dramatic, if selective, internal change. Peter the Great led the first westernization effort in history, changing Russia permanently and providing a model for later Westernization attempts elsewhere. Peter and his successors used westernization to bolster Russia's expansionist empire, without intending to become a truly Western society.

C. Themes in Early Modern Russian History

Russian society differed greatly from that of the West. It focused on serfdom and a deep-rooted peasant culture. The gap between Russia's traditional economic and social structure and its westernization efforts at the top set up some durable tensions in the nation's history, visible even today. Although Russian serfdom was particularly severe, a similar social system developed in other east European areas.

II.   CHAPTER REVIEW

A. Into what areas did Russia expand and how was this accomplished?

B. How did the Mongol rule affect Russia?

C. What role did the "West" play in early modern Russia?

D. What is "westernization" and what did it mean for Russia?

E. How did Peter the Great and Catherine the Great modernize Russia?

F. What forces resisted modernization and westernization in Russia? Why?

G. What was the connection between expansion and modernization?

H. What themes have dominated Russian history and how have they affected Russian development?

I. What is a multinational state and how does it differ from a nation-state?

III. VOCABULARY

A. Third Rome

B. Boyars

C. Cossacks

D. Time of Troubles

E. Old Believers

F. St. Petersburg vs. Moscow

G. Westernization vs. Modernization

H. Westernizer

I. Partition of Poland

J. Serf

K. Multinational states

IV. MAP EXERCISE

A. Map 18.1: Russian Expansion under the Early Tsars, 1462-1598 (Page 405)

B. Map 18.2: Russia under Peter the Great (Page 407)

1. What city-state formed the core of the Russian empire?

2. Where did Russia expand first? Later?

3. How would you describe Siberia?

4. What lands has Russia acquired since 1598?

C. Map 18.3: Russian Holdings by 1800 (Page 412)

1. Using maps at the back of the book, how have geography, climate and distance directed and limited Russian expansion?

2. How might geography, climate, and distance affect the governance of Russia?

3. Using the map on page 322, what states probably opposed Russian expansion?

V.   DOCUMENT ANALYSIS: The Nature of Westernization (Page 411)

A. Document Analysis

1. Who wrote the document? (Attribution includes biographical references)

2. What is the author's point of view?

3. How reliable is the document? Why?

4. What is the intent or purpose behind the document?

5. Who is the intended audience?

6. What is the document's tone?

B. Conclusions

1. To what degree is modernization really westernization? Are they the same?

2. Why would Russian tsars seek to modernize and westernize?

3. Why would Western thinkers admire Peter and Catherine?

4. Why would Russian peasants oppose Peter and Catherine?

VI.   PHOTO ESSAY: *The Two Worlds of Russia* (Pages 402, 406, 408, 409, and 415)

Although Russia westernized and modernized, the changes created a two-tiered society defined by two distinctive cultures. One segment favored by urban and aristocratic elites copied European culture and traditions and looked to the "West" for guidance. The other culture was based on the land of Russia and favored Russia's traditional heritage of serfs, the land, autocratic rule, and Orthodoxy.

Compare and contrast the two worlds of Russia – the Western cultures and the traditional Russian heritage – for daily lives, customs, education, work, and religion.

VII.   VISUALIZING THE PAST: *Oppressed Peasants* (Page 414)

Historical paintings are supposed to portray with a degree of accuracy, historical events. Accuracy is especially difficult if the subject is painted centuries after the events. And all paintings represent the artist's perception of the event and include his or her biases. Nevertheless, historical paintings can teach us about history.

1. Based on the painting describe 17th century peasant life.

2. Why is it unlikely that a 17th century Russian painter would have depicted peasants?

3. Why might a 20th century painting about 17th century peasants be inaccurate and biased?

4. If poverty levels are accurately rendered, what conclusions can you draw about 17th and 20th century peasant life?

5. About what items would the artist have had to guess?

VIII.   MULTIPLE-CHOICE QUESTIONS

1. In order to expand, Russia had to defeat all these neighboring states EXCEPT:
    A. Austria.
    B. Sweden.
    C. Poland-Lithuania.
    D. Ottoman Empire.
    E. Khanate of the Golden Horde.

2. Russia did not experience either the Renaissance or Reformation because
    A. Russia did not exist at the time of either movement.
    B. Russia was engaged in a 100 Years war with the Ottoman Empire.
    C. both revolutions were confined to Italy.
    D. Mongol rule cut Russia off and isolated her from western contacts.
    E. Russia had no intellectual elites able to understand either movement.

3. In order to acquire lands to the south and east (the Ukraine), the Russian tsars
    A. married into the ruling dynasties of neighboring states.
    B. recruited semi-nomadic peasants and adventurers and landlords to acquire and to farm lands.
    C. made an alliance with Poland.
    D. launched an Orthodox crusade against the Mongols and Muslims.
    E. became Roman Catholic and sought assistance from the Pope.

4. In Russia, prior to the 17th century, the group that was most receptive to western or European styles and ideas was
   A. landlords.
   B. Orthodox clergy.
   C. serfs.
   D. free peasants.
   E. tsars.

5. The only group to support the tsars' attempts to modernize Russia and increase the power of the central government was
   A. boyars.
   B. urban artisans and merchants.
   C. peasants.
   D. clergy.
   E. ethnic minorities.

6. Reforms in Russia during the 17th and 18th centuries
   A. were examples of the benefits of world trade.
   B. show cooperation by all classes for the benefit of the nation.
   C. failed to benefit Russia.
   D. led to a revolution against the ruling dynasty.
   E. were due to energetic rulers ordering changes against nearly universal social opposition.

7. Peter the Great's symbol of his reforms, westernization, and foreign policy was
   A. his visit to the West to learn first hand about institutions and technologies.
   B. toleration of religious minorities and laws granting freedom of worship.
   C. the shaving of the nobles' beards.
   D. building of St. Petersburg as the new capital and a port on the Baltic.
   E. his conversion to Islam.

8. All of Russia's reforms under Peter the Great were largely attempts to
   A. preserve Russian cultural identity from Western influences.
   B. protect the serfs from the harsh rule of the boyars.
   C. please his wife, who was Italian.
   D. undermine the power of the Russian Orthodox clergy.
   E. modernize the state and strengthen the army in order to conquer desired lands.

9. Most Russian reforms under Peter the Great and Catherine the Great
   A. were reversed following their deaths.
   B. were supported by the Orthodox Church.
   C. affected only the educated elites and landowners.
   D. benefited the serfs.
   E. discouraged trade and industry in favor of agriculture.

10. Modernization and westernization in Russia under Peter the Great and Catherine the Great did not include
    A. military reforms.
    B. liberalizing state policies and tolerating democratic ideas.
    C. educational reforms.
    D. improvements in the conditions of upper-class women.
    E. internal economic and industrial changes.

11. Although early modern Russia was paternalistic, evidence that reforms in Russia included women is proven by all of these changes EXCEPT the:
    A. right of women to sue in court and divorce their husbands.
    B. rule of four Russian tsarinas (empresses).
    C. right of women to appear in public.
    D. end to the tradition of husbands whipping their wives.
    E. decrees westernizing women's dress and manners, and permitting education.

12. In order to accomplish her domestic goals, Catherine the Great
    A. followed Enlightenment ideas and democratized her government.
    B. supported peasant demands for reform and free land.
    C. abolished serfdom and slavery.
    D. supported the French Revolution when it broke out.
    E. allied with the nobles and gave them absolute control over their peasants.

13. The majority of Russians in early modern Russia were
    A. educated.
    B. merchants and artisans living in Russian cities.
    C. non-Russian minorities.
    D. rural inhabitants, especially serfs.
    E. heavily-debted peasants forced into servile status.

14. As Russia expanded
    A. it acquired a larger Russian population.
    B. it became a largely Muslim state.
    C. serfdom spread.
    D. the free population expanded.
    E. nobles lost their influence to merchants and artisans.

15. In comparison to American slaves, Russian serfs
    A. had fewer rights.
    B. could neither be owned nor sold.
    C. were largely skilled laborers working in export industries.
    D. grew mostly cotton, sugar, and tobacco.
    E. produced only for a domestic, local economy.

16. Economically, early modern Russia was
    A. largely agricultural and dependent on western trade.
    B. largely industrialized.
    C. poor and backward with few items to export and unable to feed itself.
    D. uninterested in trade because she was economically self-sufficient.
    E. one of the leading partners in international trade.

17. The greatest source of social unrest in early modern Russia was
    A. noble opposition to westernization.
    B. the clergy and religious opposition to the non-Christian minorities.
    C. rapid growth of towns and factories.
    D. the lack of real reform especially rights for the serfs.
    E. caused by intellectuals and radicals opposed to the tsars' autocracy.

IX.   ESSAY QUESTIONS

A. Compare and contrast Russian serfdom with Latin American, African, and/or American slavery.

B. Compare and contrast Russian governmental policies and institutions with (1) any West European state (France, England, Spain or Netherlands), or (2) one of the successor states to the Mongols (Ming, Mughals, Safavids, or Ottomans).

C. How did Russia change from the time of Kiev through the rule of Catherine the Great?

D. Compare and contrast the role and influence of industry, trade, and commerce in Russia with Western Europe.

E. Compare and contrast the rise of the Russian Empire with any one Western European maritime empire (Spain, Portugal, England, or France).

F. Compare and contrast reform and change in Russia with changes that arose in Western Europe from the Renaissance through the Enlightenment.

CHAPTER 19
Early Latin America
Page 418 – 444

I.   SUMMARY

    A. Spaniards and Portuguese: From Reconquest to Conquest

The Spaniards and Portuguese came from societies long in contact with peoples of other faiths and cultures in which warfare and conquest were well-established activities. In the Caribbean, these traditions were modified by American realities as people with the backing of the state moved to conquer the mainlands.

    B. The Destruction and Transformation of Indian Societies

To varying degrees, all indigenous societies suffered from conquest. Demographic losses were extreme. The Spanish created institutions to control the native populations or make them work. These policies disrupted indigenous societies.

    C. Colonial Economies and Governments

Agriculture and mining were the basis of the Spanish colonial economies. Eventually, Spanish farms and ranches competed with Indian villages, but they also depended on Indians as laborers. Spain built a bureaucratic empire in which the church was an essential element and a major cultural factor.

    D. Brazil: The First Plantation Colony

In Brazil, the Portuguese created the first plantation colony of the Americas, growing sugar with the use of Indian and then African slaves. In the18th century, the discovery of gold opened up the interior of Brazil to settlement and the expansion of slavery. Brazil became the first major plantation zone, organized to produce a tropical crop, sugar, in great demand and short supply in Europe.

    E. Multiracial Societies

In three centuries, Spain and Portugal created large colonial empires in the Americas. To the American colonies, the Iberian nations transferred and imposed their language, laws, forms of government, religion, and institutions. Large numbers of immigrants came to the colonies. But Indian cultures persisted, and after Africans arrived as slaves, a multiethnic and multiracial society developed.

    F. The 18th Century Reforms

Increasing attacks on the Iberian empires by foreign rivals led to the Bourbon reforms in Spanish America and the reforms of Pombal in Portugal. These changes strengthened the two empires but also generated colonial unrest that eventually led to movements for independence.

II. CHAPTER REVIEW

A. How did Iberian society influence Spanish and Portuguese conquests?

B. What Iberian institutions were transplanted to the Americas?

C. How did the Caribbean serve as a model for the Spanish empire?

D. How did Spain acquire her American empire?

E. What effects did the Spanish contacts and conquests have on Indian societies?

F. What was the Great Exchange and how did it affect societies around the world?

G. How did Spain organize and manage its empire and colonial possessions?

H. How did the Portuguese experience in Brazil differ from the Spanish experience in Latin America?

I. What effects did the 18th century reform movements have on Latin America?

III. VOCABULARY

A. Encomiendas

B. Conquistador

C. Mita

D. Columbian Exchange

E. Haciendas

F. Casa de Contratacion

G. Treaty of Tordesillas

H. Council of the Indies

I. Viceroyalities, audencias, capitaincies

J. Miscegenation

K. Castas

L. Peninsulares, creoles

IV.   INTERPRETING GRAPHS

    A. Chart 19.4 Population Decline in New Spain (Page 429)

        1. What trends do you notice in the graph?
        2. When did the Indian decline bottom out and begin to rise?
        3. When did the population of "others" pass one million?
        4. How would this demographic transition affect New Spain?

    B. Chart 19.5: A Comparison of Human and Livestock Populations (Page 429)

        1. What trends do you notice in the graph?
        2. Why would decreases have gradually leveled off?
        3. What is the relationship between humans and livestock in central Mexico?
        4. How would the rise of ranching have affected central Mexico?

    C. Chart 19.6: Silver Production in the Americas (Page 432)

        1. What trends do you notice in the graph?
        2. What is the relationship between royal and total revenues?
        3. When does silver production begin to fall off?
        4. What might account for the decline of production?
        5. How would the export of silver in such quantities affect Europe's economy?

V.   PHOTO ESSAY: *Visualizing Society* (Pages 418, 423, 435, 436, and 440)

    A. How do the photos depict:
        1. Indians?

        2. Gender relations?

        3. Work?

        4. Social inequalities and class?

    B. What evidence do you find of the importance of each in society?

        1. Religion?

        2. The military?

VI. VISUALIZING THE PAST: Race or Culture – A Changing Society (Page 439)

   A. How do Mexico and Peru compare ethnically?

   B. What trends do you notice in the graphs?

   C. In which society would Indian influence have been strongest? Casta influence?

VII. DOCUMENT ANALYSIS: *A Vision from the Vanquished* (Page 425)

   A. Reliability and Validity
      1. Why is Guaman Poma reliable?

      2. What abuses does Poma condemn?

      3. How does he characterize Spanish ruling officials?

   B. Drawing Conclusions
      1. If the Spanish are as bad as Poma says, why did the Indians not revolt?

      2. How did the Spanish manage their empire?

      3. What evidence is there that the Church would oppose inhuman practices?

      4. How would the King of Spain have probably responded to Poma's letter?

VIII. MULTIPLE-CHOICE QUESTIONS

   1. An institution that had died out during Medieval Europe but survived in Iberia and that Spain and Portugal transplanted to the new world was
      A. feudalism.
      B. serfdom.
      C. slavery.
      D. a militarized aristocracy.
      E. capitalism.

   2. All of these Iberian traits influenced Spain and Portugal colonial patterns and society in the Americas EXCEPT:
      A. local political and religious autonomy.
      B. land grants to provincial nobles.
      C. the use of serfs.
      D. patriarchal family structures.
      E. an alliance between church and state.

3. In order to administer its Latin American possessions, Spain
    A. permitted nobles to administer lands without royal interference.
    B. retained local Indian rulers as clients provided they were loyal to Spain.
    C. transferred political authority to Catholic bishops and priests.
    D. intermarried with ruling Indian elites to create an administrative class.
    E. built capital cities staffed with trained bureaucrats and royal officials.

4. Prior to the 1520s, Spanish interest in the Caribbean was initially limited to
    A. exporting Indian slaves to Europe.
    B. harvesting sugar, cotton, and tobacco.
    C. obtaining land to resettle the overpopulation of Spain.
    D. the search for gold and spices.
    E. converting Indians to Catholicism.

5. To furnish labor for their estates in the Americas, Spain
    A. imported Spanish peasants.
    B. utilized Indian labor or imported African slaves.
    C. began to pay laborers wages.
    D. recruited European settlers.
    E. made land grants to immigrants, who worked the land and paid a percentage of their profit to Spain.

6. The Spanish assimilation of the American peoples and the replacement of Indian by Spanish cultures were facilitated by he
    A. demographic die off of Indian populations caused by European diseases.
    B. introduction of the Spanish language with its alphabet.
    C. use of superior weapons.
    D. utilization of European technologies.
    E. introduction of the institutions of government and law.

7. In regard to the atrocities and harsh treatment of the Indians by the conquistadors, the Spanish crown
    A. ignored complaints and supported the conquerors.
    B. appointed the Church protector of the Indians.
    C. often agreed with those who defended the Indians, but did not stop the conquests.
    D. created courts of inquiry and put the conquerors on trial for their crimes.
    E. stopped the conquests.

8. Exploitation of the Indians in the Americas
    A. was restricted to forced labor.
    B. included forced labor, taxes, low wages, and the appropriation of their lands.
    C. subsided in the mid-16th century when slavery was outlawed.
    D. drove the Indians to isolate themselves away from the Spaniards.
    E. was confined to the estates and plantation of the small ruling class.

9. The dislocation of native plants and animals by European crops and domesticated animals and the devastation of natives by European diseases is referred to as
   A. the Columbian Exchange.
   B. the Great Migration.
   C. an environmental disaster.
   D. ecological imperialism.
   E. the Great Die-off.

10. The Columbian Exchanges involved all of these EXCEPT the:
    A. transplanting of European crops and livestock to the Americas.
    B. voluntary or forced immigration of peoples to the Americas.
    C. spread of diseases to and from the Americas.
    D. migration of basic American crops and stimulants to Africa, Asia, and Europe.
    E. spread of American livestock to Africa and American Indians to the Pacific islands.

11. Prior to 1800, the most profitable economic activity for Spain in its colonies was
    A. the export of finished goods to Europe.
    B. mining and smelting of metals.
    C. ranching and herding.
    D. agriculture.
    E. manufacture and processing of cottons and cloth.

12. The export of silver from the Americas led to all of these outcomes EXCEPT:
    A. discouraging foreign rivals and pirates.
    B. paying for Spain's religious and dynastic wars.
    C. causing a sharp inflation in Western Europe.
    D. exchange of silver for Chinese luxuries Europeans desired.
    E. the increasing impoverishment and bankruptcy of Spain.

13. Within the Spanish American Empire, the Roman Catholic Church
    A. administered the state bureaucracy.
    B. administered the state judicial system.
    C. supported the state, influenced cultural life, and defended Indian rights.
    D. was the largest landholder.
    E. had no major role because the kings feared their influence amongst the Indians and the poor.

14. Unlike Spanish Latin America, in Portuguese Brazil
    A. Indians retained their rights and properties.
    B. gold was the most important mineral extracted prior to the 17th century.
    C. Caucasian Europeans flocked to settle the land.
    D. the Roman Catholic clergy administered the state.
    E. sugar and sugar refining provided the most important economic activity.

15. When Portuguese domination of the sugar refining market ended in Brazil,
    A. Holland seized control of Brazil.
    B. gold and gold strikes continually brought in new settlers and opened new lands.
    C. France bought Brazil from Portugal.
    D. Brazil began to grow wines for export.
    E. Brazil stagnated and much of the colony reverted back to Indian control.

16. The conquest and settlement of Latin America by Spain and Portugal
    A. led to the spread of native American cultures to Europe.
    B. encouraged the settlement of large numbers of Europeans in the Americas.
    C. led to the spread of Islam amongst the Indian populations.
    D. led to the rise of a multiracial, casted society with much miscegenation.
    E. had little effect on the culture of the Americas.

17. Under the doctrine of mercantilism, Spain and Portugal encouraged their Latin American colonies to
    A. buy manufactured goods only from the mother country.
    B. permit foreign merchants to trade within the empires.
    C. allow the free settlement of English colonists within the New World.
    D. practice free trade.
    E. become self-sufficient.

IX.   ESSAY QUESTIONS

    A. Compare and contrast Latin American and Russian systems of labor.

    B. Compare and contrast the Roman acquisition of its empire with the Spanish conquest of the Americas.

    C. How did Latin American demography and environment change from the classical age through the Spanish and Portuguese colonization?

    D. Compare and contrast Latin American colonial society with the institutions and practices of the Arab Empire.

    E. Compare and contrast Spanish colonial society with medieval European society.

CHAPTER 20
Africa and the Africans in
the Age of the Atlantic Slave Trade
Pages 446 – 471

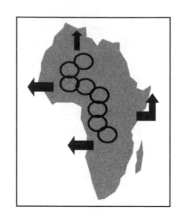

I. SUMMARY

A. The Atlantic Slave Trade

Early Portuguese contacts set the patterns for contact with the African coast. The slave trade expanded to meet the demand for labor in the new American colonies, and millions were exported in an organized commerce that involved African rulers and states and European slave traders.

B. African Societies, Slavery, and the Slave Trade

The slave trade influenced African forms of servitude as well as the social and political development of African states. Newly powerful states such as Ashante and Dahomey emerged in West Africa. In the Sudan and East Africa, slavery and the slave trade across the Sahara and in the Indian Ocean to Muslim lands also produced long-term effects.

C. White Settlers and Africans in Southern Africa

In Southern Africa, a Dutch colony eventually brought Europeans into conflict with the Africans, especially the southern Bantu-speaking peoples. One of these groups, the Zulu, created under Shaka a powerful chiefdom during the early 19th century in a process of expansion that affected the whole region.

D. The African Diaspora

The slave trade and the horrifying Middle Passage carried millions of Africans from their original homelands. In the Americas, especially in plantation colonies, they became a large segment of the population, and African cultures were adapted to new environments and conditions. Africans also resisted enslavement.

II. CHAPTER REVIEW

A. How did the arrival of Portugal (and other Europeans) affect West Africa?

B. Why did the slave trades arise and how did they affect Africa?

C. How many Africans were enslaved and where did they go?

D. What demographic patterns do historians see in the slave trade?

E. How was the slave trade organized and who controlled the trade?

F. How did African slavery differ from American slavery?

G. How did the slave trade influence African politics and the rise of states?

H. What developments occurred in East Africa?

I. What popular movements collided in South Africa and with what results?

J. How did African cultures, religions, and institutions change outside Africa?

III. VOCABULARY

A. Factories

B. Lançados

C. Royal African Companies

D. Indies piece

E. Triangular trade

F. Asante-hene

G. Benin

H. Voortrekkers

I. Great Trek

J. Mfecane

K. Chattel slavery

L. Salt-water slaves

M. Creole slaves

N. Diaspora

IV. MAP EXERCISES – Map 20.1: *Portuguese Expansion, African Kingdoms* (Page 450)

A. What African states existed when Portuguese explorers arrived in Africa?

B. To control Africa's coasts, what few territories would Portugal have had to acquire?

V. STATISTICAL EXERCISES

A. Table 20.1: Slave Exports from Africa, 1500 – 1900 (Page 452)

1. What different slave trades existed? (Think geographically about the origins of slaves and their destinations)

2. Which region exported the largest number of slaves?

3. When were the most slaves exported?

4. Between 1800 – 1900, why would the number of slaves crossing the Atlantic decline?

B. Table 20.2: Destinations of African Slaves (Page 452)

1. What regions received the most slaves? The least?

2. Why would the Caribbean and Brazil need such large numbers?

3. In British North America, what colonies would have received slaves?

4. Today, where would African influences and cultures be the greatest? Why?

VI. DOCUMENT ANALYSIS: *The Middle Passage* (Page 465)

A. Document Analysis

1. Who wrote the document? (Attribution includes biographical references)
2. What is the author's point of view?
3. How reliable is the document? Why?
4. What was the intent or purpose behind the document?
5. Who was the intended audience?
6. What is the document's tone?

B. Conclusions

1. How would an abolitionist use this document?

2. How did the Africans and Europeans perceive each other?

3. How would this have affected views of the slave trade and slavery?

VII.   PHOTO ESSAYS: *Symbols of Power* (Pages 451, 456, 457, 459, and 462)
      In order to rationalize the slave trade, Europeans and Muslims denigrated Africans and African civilization by calling the people savages and the cultures primitive.

      Do the photos support or refute this statement? Why?

VIII. MULTIPLE-CHOICE QUESTIONS

   1. The first European nation to visit and to exploit Africa was
       A. Spain.
       B. Portugal.
       C. France.
       D. England.
       E. Holland.

   2. In the beginning of the Early Modern Age, the relationship between Europeans in Africa and Africans was
       A. often one of relative equality in which no one power was dominant.
       B. one of mutual respect.
       C. an inferior status with Europeans predominating.
       D. dominated by superior European technology.
       E. contentious and led to constant warfare.

   3. Portuguese missionaries were most successful in their activities in
       A. Morocco.
       B. Senegambia.
       C. Benin.
       D. Ghana.
       E. the Zaire Region (Kongo).

   4. The European slave trade out of Africa arose and expanded when
       A. European began to supply Muslim slave markets in the Middle East.
       B. Europe conquered the coasts of West Africa.
       C. gold was discovered in Iberia necessitating greater numbers of laborers.
       D. sugar plantations were established on the Atlantic islands and in the Americas.
       E. Spain and Portugal launched their crusades against Muslim states in Africa.

   5. The large numbers and high volume of Africans in the slave trade was necessary because
       A. most Africans escaped from slavery before arriving in the Americas.
       B. Muslim fleets patrolled the Atlantic coast of Africa and freed the slaves.
       C. the mortality of slaves was high and their fertility rate was low.
       D. African slaves were also needed on estates in Europe after the Black Death.
       E. European slavers also supplied Muslim and Asian markets.

6. Most slaves transported out of Africa went
    A. to the Muslim states of the Red Sea.
    B. across the Sahara to North Africa.
    C. to African, Muslim, and Indian states along the Indian Ocean.
    D. across the Atlantic to the Americas.
    E. to Europe.

7. The largest number of African slaves sent to the Americas went to
    A. British and French islands of the Caribbean.
    B. Brazil.
    C. the slave states of the United States.
    D. Central America.
    E. the Spanish colonies along the Pacific coast.

8. Slavery in the United States differed from slavery and the slave trade to the rest of the Americas in all of the following ways EXCEPT:
    A. the slave trade to the United States was abolished after 1807.
    B. the United States supported its need for slaves with domestic breeding and internal trade.
    C. American plantations grew cotton and tobacco instead of sugar.
    D. the total slave population in the United States grew.
    E. the death rate of slaves due to brutality was higher in the United States.

9. The Trans-Atlantic slave trade differed from the Trans-Saharan slave trade to the Muslim world in that
    A. the Trans-Atlantic was less brutal than the Trans-Saharan slave trade.
    B. the Trans-Saharan slave trade included women for domestic work.
    C. the Atlantic route transported whole families to the Americas whereas the Trans-Saharan trade broke families up.
    D. the trade to the Muslim world ended before the Trans-Atlantic trade began.
    E. More people were transported across the Sahara than across the Atlantic.

10. The slave trade out of Africa was controlled by
    A. African trading guilds.
    B. key African forest kingdoms such as Benin, Oyo, Ashante, and Kongo.
    C. European slave traders and African rulers working jointly.
    D. Muslim traders.
    E. the Europeans, especially the Dutch and Portuguese.

11. The Trans-Atlantic slave trade had all of these effects EXCEPT:
    A. the European conquest of Africa.
    B. contributing to the growth of capitalism.
    C. the increased violence in Africa as slavers raided and warred for slaves.
    D. the settlement and development of vast areas of the Americas by Africans.
    E. the spread of African culture and institutions to the Americas.

12. The major difference between American and African forms of slavery was
    A. American slaves could own property.
    B. African slaves often acquired their freedom after years of work.
    C. slavery in Africa was largely unknown before Europeans arrived.
    D. the extreme brutality towards and high mortality rates of slaves in the Americas was higher.
    E. Americans used slaves as soldiers, administrators, and bureaucrats.

13. Which of these statements about slavery in Africa is a FACT?
    A. African societies did not practice chattel slavery.
    B. The Europeans introduced slavery as an important institution.
    C. Islam allowed slavery but not the enslavement of Muslims.
    D. Most African slaves could attain their freedom.
    E. The European slave trade tapped into a preexisting African institution.

14. With regard to the slave trade and slavery in Africa, contacts with the Europeans
    A. decreased warfare between African states as Africans united against European slavers.
    B. increased violence and the disruption of African societies as the search for slaves increased.
    C. led to the rise of a few, key African states that dominated the slave trade.
    D. led to open warfare between Christians and Muslims for the control of the slave trade.
    E. benefited most African states, which received high quality goods in exchange for slaves.

15. All of these popular movements affected Africa in the 19th century EXCEPT:
    A. Europeans immigrated and settled the coasts of South Africa.
    B. Boer farmers migrated from the Atlantic coast to the interior of South Africa.
    C. San and Khoikhoi migrated to Southwest Africa from Central Africa.
    D. the Nguni peoples united under the Zulus and expanded their empire.
    E. the Sultanate of Sokoto launched a series of jihads to spread Islam.

16. All American slave societies recognized social hierarchical distinctions based on
    A. religious affiliations.
    B. ownership of property.
    C. usefulness of skills performed.
    D. color of skin – the lighter the skin, the higher the status.
    E. countries from which the slaves originated.

IX.   ESSAY QUESTIONS

A. Compare and contrast African slavery, Latin American forced labor, Russian serfdom, and American slavery.

B. Compare and contrast the effects of the slave trade on Africa with the Black Death's effects in Europe.

C. Compare and contrast the effects of the slave trade on the development of African states with the effects of the Commercial Revolution on European states such as Holland, France, and England.

D. How did Islam change in Africa from its introduction in 600 C.E. to 1900 C.E.?

E. Compare and contrast the spread of Islam in Africa with the spread of Christianity in Europe.

X. SPECIAL DISCUSSION TOPIC

In 2001, a special United Nations conference on racism met in South Africa. Among its topics was one item of discussion, namely that Europe, Latin America, and the United States owe reparations to the African states and Africans transported during the slave trade.

A. Do these nations owe Africans and African states reparations? Why or why not?

B. What responsibilities do African states and rulers bear for the slave trade?

C. What responsibilities do Muslim states bear for their slave trades?

The slave trade in Africa predated the arrival of Europeans, and prior to the early 19th century, the world trade in and possession of slaves was legal and had been for millenia. Even after European and American nations began to end the slave trade and abolish slavery, many nations in Africa, Asia, and the Muslim world still permitted and today still practice slavery. Additionally, many cultures enserfed their peasants, casted whole populations into religious slavery, paid their workers slave wages, or assigned different ethnicities, such as the Irish, to plantations.

A. How do these facts change the above discussion?

CHAPTER 21
The Muslim Empires
Pages 472 – 497

I.   SUMMARY

    A. The Ottomans: From Frontier Warriors to Empire Builders

    From the devastation that the Mongol invasions brought to much of the Islamic heartlands, a new power arose in the 13th and 14th centuries. Founded by yet another Turkic people migrating from the central Asian steppes, the Ottoman dynasty gradually built an empire in the Eastern Mediterranean that rivaled the Abbasid imperium at its height. The Ottomans put an end to the Byzantine Empire and advanced into eastern and central Europe. The Ottomans built much of their empire on the ideas and institutions of earlier Muslim civilization. Internal weaknesses and the counteroffensives of their Muslim and European rivals reduced Ottoman power by the early 18th century. Increasingly the dynasty was forced to attempt administrative and social reforms to cope with the challenges from the expansive Western powers.

    B. The Shi'ite Challenge of the Safavids

    The Safavids founded a dynasty and conquered the region that makes up the present-day nation of Iran. From that point onward, Iran has been one of the strongest and most enduring centers of Shi'ism within the Islamic world. Under the Safavids, the Iranian region was restored as a center of political power and cultural activity at a level that it has rarely enjoyed since.

    C. The Mughals and the Apex of Muslim Civilization in India

    In the first decades of the 16th century, nomadic invaders established the most powerful of a succession of Muslim dynasties in South Asia and spread the power of the Mughal dynasty through most of the Indian subcontinent. Under their rule, a brilliant civilization blending Hindu-Islamic cultures arose. By the early 17th century, a familiar pattern of dynastic decline took hold. Wars of succession and internal revolts led to a recurrence of political fragmentation and sectarian strife that had dominated so much of south Asia's long history.

II.   CHAPTER REVIEW

    A. What is a gunpowder empire and how is technology critical to its success?

    B. What factors influenced the rise of the Ottomans, Safavids, and Mughals?

    C. How did the Ottomans, Mughals and Safavids govern their empires?

    D. What led to the decline of the Ottoman, Mughal, and Safavid empires?

E. In the Safavid Empire, what was the relationship between religion and state?

F. Describe the intellectual achievements of the Muslim gunpowder states.

G. Describe gender roles and society in the three Muslim gunpowder empires.

H. Describe the relationship between European and Muslim empires.

III. VOCABULARY

A. Gunpowder empire

B. Ottomans

C. Safavids

D. Mughals

E. Janissaries

F. Red heads (Red Turbans)

G. Shah

H. Vizier

I. Imams, Mullahs, ayatollahs

J. Sikhs

K. Marattas

L. Sati

M. Din-i-Ilahi

IV. MAP EXERCISES: *Muslim Gunpowder Empires*

A. Map 21.1: The Ottoman, Safavid, and Mughal Empires (Page 475)

B. Map 21.2: The Expansion of the Ottoman Empire (Page 476)

C. Map 21.3: *The Safavid Empire* (Page 483)

D. Map 21.4: *The Mughal Empire* (Page 490)

1. Which state governs the
   a. Largest empire?
   b. Most multicultural?
   c. Most populous?

2. How would the answers above make government difficult?

3. Which empire is nearest to Western Europe?

4. How would proximity to Europe affect an empire?

5. What modern states (consult a modern atlas) does each empire rule?
   a. Ottoman Empire
   b. Safavid Empire
   c. Mughal Empire

6. Which state would be most dependent on seapower? Why?

7. Which state would be the easiest and most difficult to defend? Why?

V.   PHOTO ESSAY: Accomplishments of the Muslim Gunpowder Empires

   A. Describe artistic accomplishments in (Pages 472, 478, and 487)

      1. Painting
      2. Architecture

   B. Describe military accomplishments in (Pages 477 and 480)

      1. Army
      2. Navy

VI.   VISUALIZING THE PAST: *The Basis of Imperial Power* (Page 491)

   A. What empire has the largest resource base? Why did you conclude this?

   B. What empire would be most threatened by internal difficulties? Why?

   C. How should this government rule its state most effectively?

   D. Which nations would be most threatened by European navies? Why?

   E. Which nation is most multinational? Why?

VII. DOCUMENT ANALYSIS: *An Islamic Traveler's Laments* (Page 481)

A. Document Analysis

1. Who wrote the document? (Attribution includes biographical references)

2. What is the author's point of view?

3. How reliable is the document? Why?

4. What was the intent or purpose behind the document?

5. Who was the intended audience?

6. What is the document's tone?

B. Conclusions

1. How might the Muslims' neglect of Western studies have hurt or hindered Muslims in the future?

2. What reasons does Abu Taleb give for his fellow Muslims' neglect of western studies?

VIII. MULTIPLE-CHOICE QUESTIONS

1. What event was most directly responsible for the rise of the gunpowder empires in Turkey, Iran, and India and similar states in Tsarist Russia and Ming China?
    A. The invention of gunpowder
    B. The collapse of the Mongol Empire and its khanates
    C. The arrival of West European merchants in the area
    D. The revival of trade across Eurasia
    E. Steppe nomads founded all five states

2. The Ottoman, Safavid, and Mughal empires possessed all of these shared characteristics EXCEPT:
    A. They originated in Turkish nomadic cultures of the steppe.
    B. They were Muslim led.
    C. They were based on conquest and the use of military technologies.
    D. They began with absolutist rulers and efficient bureaucracies.
    E. They ruled predominantly Muslim populations.

3. The chief source of rivalry between the Ottomans and Safavids was
   A. rivalry over control of trade in the Indian Ocean.
   B. disagreement over the treatment of Christians within their empires.
   C. religion – the Ottomans were Sunni and the Safavids were Shi'ites.
   D. dynastic – both dynasties arose within the same ruling family.
   E. their treatment of Hindu subjects.

4. The Ottoman advances into Central Europe ended
   A. with their defeat by Germans, Poles, and Italians at the siege of Vienna.
   B. when the Safavids invaded the Turkish empire.
   C. with the Christian naval victory at Lepanto.
   D. when Russia invaded the Turkish empire and reconquered Istanbul.
   E. after France and Spain attacked the Ottoman Empire.

5. The class which initially dominated the Ottoman, Safavid, and Mughal states and social hierarchy was
   A. descendant of slaves (Mameluks).
   B. a military aristocracy.
   C. the clergy.
   D. the merchant class.
   E. largely composed of intellectuals and scholars.

6. In order to supply its elites Janissaries and palace bureaucrats with soldiers, the Turks
   A. used feudal troops.
   B. relied on old Muslim nobles and aristocrats.
   C. forcibly conscripted young Christian boys, converted them to Islam, and trained them.
   D. imported trained foreigners and mercenaries.
   E. relied on Muslim clergy.

7. All of these developments weakened the absolute and efficient rule of the Ottoman government EXCEPT:
   A. powerful factions within the Janissaries and court bureaucrats.
   B. harem politics by rival wives and their sons, who were potential heirs.
   C. the hedonistic lifestyles of many sultans.
   D. corruption and graft.
   E. the development of a vizier or chief administrator who ran the bureaucracy.

8. Succession to the Ottoman throne when the previous sultan died was
   A. from father to eldest son.
   B. decided by the Muslim clerics and Quranic law.
   C. based on military successes and accomplishments.
   D. unclear, which caused great confusion including civil wars.
   E. determined by the sultan's eldest sister, whose eldest son inherited the throne.

9. Which of these statements about the decline of the Ottoman Empire is TRUE?
   A. Ottoman institutions were weak and failed to support the empire.
   B. foreign wars and defeats were responsible for the decline of the empire.
   C. internal corruption and harem life undermined Ottoman administration.
   D. the empire was too poor to maintain a strong government or army.
   E. domestic trade and agriculture were unaffected by the decline.

10. The Safavids arose to power in Persia primarily due to
    A. their support for the Shi'ite cause.
    B. an alliance with Portuguese merchants and soldiers.
    C. their conversion from Islam to Christianity.
    D. a monopoly on military technologies and guns.
    E. their control of trade along the Silk Road.

11. With regard to the west Europeans and their institutions and technologies, the Ottomans and Safavids
    A. borrowed freely and heavily any useful idea, tool, or institution.
    B. were clearly superior to the Europeans in all respects.
    C. heavily influenced West European political culture and military traditions.
    D. had no contacts because they had no trade with West Europeans.
    E. ignored and looked down upon all things European, which later hurt them.

12. During their reign, Safavid policies in Persia
    A. alienated the majority of the population.
    B. fostered a sense of Persian religious nationalism and social unity.
    C. fostered Turkish traditions and customs.
    D. favored the Arabic language and Arab trained bureaucracies.
    E. favored agriculture over trade and manufacturing.

13. Unlike the Ottomans and Safavids, the Mughals
    A. favored trade.
    B. were intolerant of religious differences.
    C. avoided the use of advanced military technologies.
    D. did not conquer lands for religious reasons.
    E. never developed a strong centralized state or government.

14. Akbar the Great used the following techniques to build a stable state in India EXCEPT:
    A. led a well-trained, well-led military.
    B. established an efficient bureaucracy and administration.
    C. supported the arts and intellectual developments.
    D. practiced religious toleration and reconciliation with the Hindus.
    E. promoted foreigners, especially Europeans, to positions of power in India.

15. Religiously, Akbar favored
    A. religious toleration and fostered his own invented faith.
    B. Sunni Islam.
    C. Shi'ite Islam.
    D. conversion to Hinduism.
    E. an atheism similar to the Confucian social philosophy.

16. Which of these statements about women in India during the Mughal Empire is TRUE?
    A. Child-bride marriages were ended.
    B. Seclusion (purdah) of upper class Hindu and Muslim women began.
    C. Widow remarriage was ended.
    D. The practice of sati (widow burning) ended.
    E. The birth of girl children was seen as an unlucky event.

17. All of these contributed to the decline of the Mughal empire EXCEPT:
    A. too many wars of conquest exhausted resources.
    B. good government and needed reforms were ignored.
    C. the arrival of the Europeans.
    D. local leaders largely ignored the government and kept the taxes they collected.
    E. the later Mughal religious policies favored Islam and alienated the Hindus and Sikhs.

IX. ESSAY QUESTIONS

A. Compare and contrast the rise and institutions of the Byzantine and Ottoman Empires.

B. Compare and contrast the interaction of any one of these empires (Ottoman, Safavid, or Mughal) with the West to Russia's interaction with the West.

C. Compare and contrast Portugal and Spain with any one of the "Gunpowder Empires" for imperial systems, governmental institutions, and military.

D. Compare and contrast empire building by gunpowder empires with any one classical or post-classical empire.

E. Compare and contrast religious policies of any one gunpowder state with Spanish religious policies.

F. How did India change from the Mauryan Dynasty to the Mughals?

G. How did gender relations in India change from the Aryans to the Mughals?

H. Compare the decline of any one of the gunpowder empires with the decline of any one classical or post-classical empire.

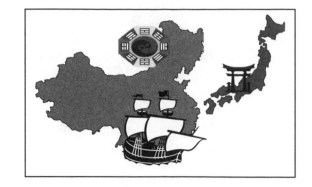

CHAPTER 22
Asian Transitions in an Age of Global Change
Pages 498 – 523

I.   SUMMARY

A. The Asian Trading World and the Coming of the Europeans

Several European seafaring nations were actively involved in South and Southeast Asia in the centuries after the arrival of Vasco da Gama. Most European enterprise was centered on trade and commerce, as the Europeans struggled to find profitable ways to obtain the products they wanted. Some Europeans went to Asia in search of Christian converts. Small numbers of Europeans also settled in the area.

B. Ming China: A Global Mission Refused

With the restoration of ethnic rule and the reunification of the country under the Ming Dynasty, Chinese civilization enjoyed an age of splendor. Renewed agrarian and commercial growth supported a population that was the largest in the world. The Ming's resources, technologies, numbers of skilled artisans and engineers, and military forces were vaster than any country in the world, and China's centralized bureaucracy remained the best organized and most efficient in the world. In its earlier decades, the Ming Dynasty also pursued a policy of overseas exploration, but turned inward and removed a formidable obstacle to the rise of the Europeans.

C. Fending Off the West: Japan's Reunification and The First Challenge

Fortunately for the Japanese, their ability to defend their islands was not tested in the early centuries of European expansion. In the decades before the arrival of the Europeans, the Japanese found leaders who had the skills and ruthlessness needed to restore the shogunate. By the early 1600s, with the potential threat from the Europeans looming ever larger in the Japanese imagination, the new Tokugawa shoguns gained sufficient control to let them gradually shut down contacts with outsiders and envelop the islands in a state of isolation.

II. CHAPTER REVIEW

A. How did the arrival of the Europeans affect the Asian trading network?

B. Describe the Asian sea-trading network.

C. How did the Europeans establish and maintain their trading empires in Asia?

D. Who challenged the Portuguese in Asia and with what results?

E. What was the relationship between trade and religion for Europeans in Asia?

F. How did the Ming Dynasty attempt to reform and govern its empire?

G. Describe the Ming social hierarchy.

H. What evidence is there that the early Ming rule was a revived Golden Age?

I. What were the motives for the Ming naval expeditions? Why were they ended?

J. What led to the decline of the Ming?

K. How did the Japanese deal with the European challenge?

III. VOCABULARY

A. Caravel

B. Asian sea trading network

C. Mercantilism

D. Ormuz, Goa, Malacca

E. Factories

F. Dutch trading empire

G. Philippine Islands

H. Jesuits in Asia

I. Friars

J. Ming Dynasty

K. Macao, Canton, Deshima

L. Tokugawa Shoguns

M. School of National Learning

IV. MAP EXERCISES

A. Map 22.1: Routes and Products in the Asian Trading Network, c. 1500 (Page 502)

1. Reading the Map

      a. Identify the three zones.

      b. What elements of geography define the zones? (see map at back of book)

      c. What are choke points?

      d. What are the major ports and where are they located?

      e. What religion controlled the Indian Ocean zone?

      f. What products are traded within the zones?

  2. Interpreting a Map

      a. To control the trade on the map, what would you need to do?

      b. Which zone would trade with both zones? Why?

B. Map 22.2: Ming China and the Zheng He Expeditions, 1405 – 1423 (Page 514)

Compare Maps 22.1 and 22.2. What conclusions do you reach? Why?

V.   PHOTO ESSAY: The Coming of the Europeans

A. How did the Asians perceive the European (Pages 498-499, and 520):

  1. Ships?

  2. Religions?

  3. Merchants and trade goods?

B. Describe Portuguese and European

  1. Naval technology (Page 503).

  2. Missionaries (Page 517).

C. Describe the worlds and perceptions of

  1. Ming Concubines (Pages 513).

  2. Scholar bureaucrats (Page 510).

  3. Japanese shogun (Page 519).

VI.   VISUALIZING THE PAST: *Intruders* (Page 506)

A. Europe in Asia

  1. Name the ports of each European nation.

        a. Portugal

        b. Spain

        c. The Netherlands

        d. England

2. Where did the Europeans locate their imperial capitals?

3. What regions did each power attempt to control?

        a. Portuguese

        b. Spanish

        c. Dutch

        d. English

B. Drawing Conclusions

1. Which European state had the strongest position in Asia? Why?

2. What nation had the least stake in Asia? Why would this be unimportant?

3. How did Europe redirect the flow of trade routes?

4. What areas seem least affected by the European presence? Why?

VII.   DOCUMENT ANALYSIS: *Chinese Examination System* (Page 509)

A. Document Analysis

1. Who wrote the document? (Attribution includes biographical references)

2. What is the author's point of view?

3. How reliable is the document? Why?

4. What was the intent or purpose behind the document?

5. Who was the intended audience?

6. What is the document's tone?

B. Conclusions

1. From the exam questions, what can we learn about Chinese society?

2. Where do the Chinese look for models to orient their social behavior?

3. What types of skills and knowledge do the Chinese value?

4. What are the advantages and disadvantages to the exam system?

VIII. MULTIPLE-CHOICE QUESTIONS

1. When the Portuguese arrived in India in 1498, they
   A. found they had little to offer in trade but could get rich by using force.
   B. quickly integrated themselves into the Asian trade system.
   C. exchanged their European goods for Asian luxury items.
   D. were unwelcome.
   E. established cordial relations with the Muslim merchants.

2. The periphery of the Indian Ocean trading network around 1500 C.E., specifically Africa, Southeast Asia, and Japan furnished what items to the network?
   A. slaves
   B. cotton textiles
   C. carpets and tapestries
   D. porcelain and silks
   E. mainly raw materials

3. The highest prices in the Asian network were paid for
   A. cotton textiles.
   B. spices.
   C. bulk items such as foodstuffs.
   D. silk and porcelains.
   E. gold and silver.

4. Long distance travel and trade in the Asian trade zone was based on
   A. foodstuffs transported to feed the population of India.
   B. Muslim pilgrimages to and from Mecca.
   C. tribute from client states to the Chinese Empire.
   D. products with the highest profit margins, which were easily transported.
   E. transport of slaves.

5. The largest portion of Asian trade by volume in the Early Modern Era was the trade in
   A. silk from China to the Middle East.
   B. cottons from India to the Middle East.
   C. bulk items, usually foodstuffs, exchanged within each of the main zones.
   D. spices from the East Indies.
   E. slaves from Africa.

6. The Portuguese were able to control trade in Asian waters because
   A. they had endless supplies of gold and silver to buy goods.
   B. states in the area granted Portuguese merchants a trade monopoly.
   C. they had superior weapons and controlled trade through force.
   D. the Chinese had withdrawn from trade in Asia.
   E. the Portuguese captains allied with the Mughals, who controlled the area.

7. Rather than try to control trade in the Indian Ocean as had Portugal, the Dutch
   A. attempted to monopolize the spice trade from the East Indies.
   B. cooperated with the Muslim and Hindu merchants.
   C. signed trading agreements with local rulers.
   D. abided by the traditional trading practices of the region.
   E. concentrated on trade in India.

8. The Dutch and Portuguese empires in Asia relied on all of these EXCEPT:
   A. fortified towns and bases.
   B. factories.
   C. migration of thousands of Europeans to settle in Asia.
   D. warships on patrol.
   E. monopoly control of a limited number of products.

9. Europeans learned that the greatest trading profits in Asia could be made by
   A. allying with the Hindus and warring on the Muslim states.
   B. transporting other peoples' goods and providing services as middlemen.
   C. seizing lands and creating land-based empires.
   D. peaceful cooperation with and integration into existing Asian trade networks.
   E. "turning" pirate and raiding other nations' merchant ships.

10. In Asia, European naval technologies and trade practices had little effect against
    A. Ceylon and Java.
    B. Asian states with strong militaries and determined rulers.
    C. the Philippine Islands.
    D. the coasts and peoples of East Asia.
    E. the islands of the East Indies.

11. Europeans learned that the most successful missionary work in Asia occurred by
    A. having missionaries use local languages and become acclimated to cultures.
    B. forcibly converting the Muslims and Hindus to Christianity.
    C. converting the poorest and lowest social classes first.
    D. converting the elites first; the other classes would follow.
    E. converting areas, that had never previously been converted by Muslims.

12. Following the defeat and expulsion of the Mongols from China,
    A. a legalist regime was established.
    B. the Ming Dynasty arose.
    C. peasants were granted equality with the scholar-gentry and noble classes.
    D. China converted to Buddhism.
    E. the civil service exam system of the Mongols was ended.

13. The first Ming emperors of China attempted to end all of these abuses EXCEPT:
    A. abolishing the position of chief minister, who had too much power.
    B. dishonesty, disloyalty, and laziness.
    C. court factions and conspiracies.
    D. the influence of the Emperor's wives and their relatives.
    E. the influence of the scholar-gentry.

14. During the Ming Dynasty, the true power of China resided with
    A. prosperous peasants.
    B. merchants in port cities who administer foreign trade missions.
    C. the eunuch bureaucrats in the capital city.
    D. rural landlord families with relatives in the imperial bureaucracy.
    E. aristocrats and nobles.

15. The Ming abandoned the naval expeditions for all these reasons EXCEPT:
    A. the Portuguese defeated the Chinese navies on the last voyage.
    B. the money spent on the voyages had little return.
    C. Northern steppe nomads were a greater threat than pirates and sea peoples.
    D. court rivals of Zheng He opposed the voyages.
    E. the last emperors were unenthusiastic about the voyages.

16. When the Europeans reached Japan, the Japanese
    A. were united and strong under an absolute emperor.
    B. were engaged in a cycle of civil wars.
    C. rapidly converted to Christianity.
    D. refused to admit foreigners to their nation.
    E. population was devastated by diseases.

17. The Japanese dealt with the long-term European challenge by
    A. allying with the Portuguese against the other Europeans.
    B. permitting the Jesuits to convert the Japanese to Christianity.
    C. permitting the Europeans to establish a trading monopoly in Japan.
    D. self-imposed isolation and forbidding most European contacts.
    E. adapting European customs and technology.

IX.   ESSAY QUESTIONS

A. Compare and contrast Japanese and Chinese reactions to the European arrival.

B. Compare and contrast Portuguese and Chinese maritime expeditions in Asia.

C. Compare and contrast the Indian Ocean trading network before and after the arrival of the Europeans. (Change over time)

D. Compare and contrast the spread of Christianity in Asia with the spread of Hinduism or Islam throughout Asia.

E. Compare and contrast the Indian Ocean trading network with the Iberian empires in the Americas.

PART IV REVIEW

I.   PART OVERVIEW

    A. What does the unit's title "The world shrinks" mean?

    B. What developments signaled the end of the Post-Classical Era?

    C. What characteristics, trends, and themes typified the Early Modern Period?

    D. What new states arose and became important actors during this period?

    E. How did Western Europe come to dominate the Early Modern Period?

    F. How did the world economy change?

    G. How would you describe labor systems during this period?

    H. What global exchanges occurred and how did they affect the globe?

    I. How did state structures change in this period?

II. VOCABULARY

    A. Columbian Exchanges

    B. Gunpowder Empires

    C. Colonial(-ism)

    D. Early Modern

III. MAP EXERCISE: *Changing World Boundaries, 1453 to 1700 C.E.* (p. 353)

    A. What are the main changes on the map from 1453 to 1700?

    B. What areas have had:
       1. The most changes?

       2. The fewest changes?

    C. Where did the Europeans spread and settle?

    D. Why do you think European colonial empires spread in some areas but not others?

IV. TIMELINE CHRONOLOGY: 1450 – 1750 (pp. 350–351)

A. Beginnings
1. If we begin at 1453, what event(s) seem(s) to signal this era?

2. Why would that be a major transition from post-classical to this age?

3. What other major events between 1300 and 1500 seem to involve radical departures from the past?

B. Trends
1. Which people seem to dominate the timeline?

2. What one trend or theme seems to predominate during this era?

C. The End
1. If we end at 1750, what breaks with tradition could be seen as a catalyst for changes? Why?

2. Why might it be difficult to end this period? Is the end date arbitrary? Why?

V. PHOTO ESSAY: *Da Vinci's Man*

This famous drawing typifies the creative spirit of the Italian Renaissance. Typically associated with the work is a famous statement, "Man is the Measure of All Things." What does this statement mean and what might it mean for the Early Modern Era?

VI. MULTIPLE-CHOICE QUESTIONS

1. During the Early Modern period in world history, which region, culture, ideology, or civilization came to dominate the world?
A. Muslim
B. Chinese
C. American
D. European
E. Communism

2. The most predominant form of state structure during this period was
A. land-based or maritime empires utilizing military technologies.
B. the small trade-based capitalist state such as the Netherlands (Holland).
C. democratic states.
D. decentralized government.
E. theocratic states.

3. All of these were gunpowder empires EXCEPT:
   A. Safavid Persia.
   B. Ottoman Turkey.
   C. Mughal India.
   D. Ming China.
   E. Tokugawa Japan.

4. The date and event which commonly begin this period are
   A. 1405 and the Chinese Indian Ocean naval expeditions.
   B. 1453 and the Ottoman conquest of Constantinople.
   C. 1492 and Columbus' discoveries.
   D. 1498 when Vasco da Gama reached India.
   E. 1517 when Martin Luther began his reformation.

5. A major feature of the early modern globalization of international trade was the
   A. dominance of trade by the Muslims.
   B. intentional isolation of countries from participating in international trade.
   C. unequal economic and commercial relationships and the dependence of many other states on European states.
   D. decline of the luxury trade.
   E. decrease of unfree labor such as slavery and serfdom.

6. The major development between 1450 and 1750 was the rise of
   A. the first truly global world trade network.
   B. empires ruling transcontinental land masses.
   C. mass migrations of peoples.
   D. capitalism as the dominant economic ideology.
   E. almost instantaneous global communication network.

7. Fundamental to the European acquisition of colonies between 1450 and 1750 was
   A. the superiority of European military technologies against the Turks, Persians, and Mughal Indians.
   B. the lack of immunity amongst Americans, Africans, and Asians to European diseases.
   C. European naval and maritime technologies.
   D. lack of opposition.
   E. European overpopulation, which allowed large armies and provided willing settlers.

8. The culture or lifestyle that had influenced world history since the Neolithic revolution but ceased to play any role after this era was
   A. Islamic civilization.
   B. Chinese civilization.
   C. agricultural societies.
   D. religion.
   E. pastoral nomadic cultures.

9. All world labor systems during the Early Modern period can be characterized as
   A. increasingly slave-oriented.
   B. increasingly serf, sharecropper or tenant farmer associated.
   C. increasingly capitalist with wages paid for work.
   D. largely unfree.
   E. machine-based and electrically powered.

10. The Columbian exchanges involved all of these global movements EXCEPT:
    A. European diseases devastated the Americas.
    B. American foodstuffs and crops spread around the world.
    C. Africans were forcibly transported to the Americas.
    D. European transplanted their crops, animals, and economic systems to the Americas.
    E. Indian populations were resettled to the Pacific islands and African lands.

VII. ESSAY QUESTIONS

A. Compare and contrast the Post-Classical and Early Modern periods for changes which ended the previous period and led to the rise of a new era.

B. How did the international situation change from the Post-Classical to the Early Modern period (change over time)?

C. How did the international role of Europe change from the Post-Classical to the Early Modern period (change over time)?

D. Compare and contrast the role of Islam in the Post-Classical Era with the dominance of Europe in the Early Modern period.

PART IV GEOGRAPHY: THE EARLY MODERN WORLD, 1450 - 1750

The oceans and seas were at the center of the Early Modern world. When the Europeans found land expansion limited, they took to the open water. The Atlantic Ocean and its neighboring seas and coasts joined the world system for the first time. On the continents, land-based empires utilizing military technologies and favoring trade established powerful empires. Consequently straits and islands became important as conduits for movement between empires and civilizations. Along these routes, great trading entrepôt trading cities arose. Primitive cities also established great importance as centers for government.

I. LOCATE
A. PHYSICAL GEOGRAPHY
1. Philippine Islands
2. Cuba
3. Hispaniola
4. Cape of Good Hope
5. Bab el Mandeb
6. Strait of Hormuz
7. Straits of Dover
8. English Channel
9. Cape Horn
10. Mozambique Channel
11. Bight of Benin

B. CITIES
1. London
2. Paris
3. Delhi
4. Amsterdam
5. Beijing
6. Moscow
7. St. Petersburg
8. Vienna
9. Isfahan
10. Malacca
11. Calicut
12. Guangzhou
13. Istanbul
14. Sofala
15. Mombasa
16. Goa
17. Lisbon
18. Cadiz
19. Kyoto

II. IDENTIFY AND LOCATE
A. HISTORIC STATES
1. Russian Empire
2. Ottoman Empire
3. Safavid Empire
4. Mughal Empire
5. Ming, Qing China
6. England
7. Spain
8. Portugal
9. France
10. Netherlands
11. Mali, Songhai
12. Congo, Angola
13. Monomotapa
14. Shogunate Japan

B. EUROPEAN COLONIAL EMPIRES
1. Dutch
2. English
3. French
4. Spanish
5. Portuguese

MULTIPLE-CHOICE ANSWERS

CHAPTER 16
1. D
2. A
3. C
4. E
5. D
6. A
7. D
8. B
9. C
10. E
11. A
12. D
13. B
14. B
15. D
16. A
17. E

CHAPTER 17
1. B
2. D
3. E
4. C
5. B
6. A
7. D
8. B
9. C
10. E
11. D
12. D
13. A
14. B
15. E
16. B
17. C

CHAPTER 18
1. A
2. D

3. B
4. E
5. B
6. E
7. D
8. E
9. C
10. B
11. A
12. E
13. E
14. C
15. E
16. A
17. D

CHAPTER 19
1. C
2. A
3. E
4. D
5. B
6. A
7. C
8. B
9. D
10. E
11. B
12. A
13. C
14. E
15. B
16. D
17. A

CHAPTER 20
1. B
2. A
3. E
4. D
5. C
6. D

7. B
8. E
9. B
10. C
11. A
12. D
13. E
14. B
15. B
16. C
17. D

CHAPTER 21

1. B
2. E
3. C
4. A
5. B
6. C
7. E
8. D
9. C
10. A
11. E
12. B
13. D
14. E
15. E
16. C

CHAPTER 22

1. A
2. E
3. B
4. D
5. C
6. C
7. A
8. C
9. D
10. B
11. E
12. B
13. E

14. D
15. A
16. B
17. D

PART 4 REVIEW

1. D
2. A
3. D
4. B
5. C
6. A
7. C
8. E
9. D
10. E

DOCUMENT-BASED QUESTION:
AMERICAN AND MUSLIM SLAVERIES

DIRECTIONS

The following question is based on the accompanying documents. (The documents have been edited for the purpose of this exercise). The question is designed to test your ability to work with and understand historical documents. Write an essay that:

- Has relevant thesis and supports that thesis with evidence from the documents.

- Uses all or all but one of the documents.

- Analyzes the documents by grouping them in as many appropriate ways as possible and does not simply summarize the documents individually.

- Takes into account both the sources of the documents and the authors' points of view.

ESSAY PROMPT

Determine how the two slavery systems – one in the Americas and the other in the Muslim states – were similar and different. What reasons would account for the differences in the two systems?

Based on the following documents, discuss the two slave trades. What types of additional documentation would help explain the differences in the two systems?

HISTORICAL BACKGROUND

Although American slavery and the Atlantic slave trade to the Americas are more widely studied, slavery is as old as the world's first civilizations. Contemporaneous to the era of the Atlantic slave trade were two other slave movements: one across the Sahara Desert and another along the East African coasts of the Indian Ocean. Both routes terminated in slave markets in the Muslim world.

DOCUMENT 1

CHART: EMANCIPATION AND ABOLITION OF SLAVERY			
THE AMERICAS		THE MUSLIM WORLD	
STATES	OFFICIAL END OF SLAVERY	STATES	OFFICIAL END OF SLAVERY
UNITED STATES	1865	YEMEN	1962
MEXICO	1829	SAUDI ARABIA	1962
CUBA	1886	IRAN	1929
HAITI	1794	MAURETANIA	1980
VENEZUELA	1854	TUNISIA	1846@
PERU	1854	SUDAN	1900@
BRAZIL	1888	KUWAIT	1947
CHILE	1823	TURKEY	1857
ECUADOR	1851	ALGERIA	1830-1850@
PUERTO RICO	1873	EGYPT	1882@
BR. WEST INDIES	1838@	SOMALIA	1903@
FR. WEST INDIES	1848@	ZANZIBAR	1873@
COLOMBIA	1851	TANGANIKA	1922@
CENTRAL AMERICA	1824	FR. WEST AFRICA	1903@
BOLIVIA	1831	AFGHANISTAN	1923
URUGUAY	1842	IRAQ	1924
CANADA	1832@	JORDAN	1929
VIRIGN ISLANDS	1848@	OMAN	1970

@ = Slavery ended as the result of European colonial occupation or action

DOCUMENT 2

Ahmed Baba, Muslim cleric from Timbuktu, Mali, his legal treatise, c. 1600 C.E.

"The origin of [Muslim] slavery is unbelief, and the black [slaves] are like Christians, except they are majus, pagans. The Muslims among them, like the people of Kano, Katsina, Bornu, Gobir, and all of Songhai, are Muslims, who are not to be owned. Yet some of them transgress on the others unjustly by invasion as do the Arabs, Bedouins, who transgress on free Muslims and sell them unjustly, and thus it is not lawful to own any of them. If anybody is known to have come from these [Muslim] countries, he should be set free directly, and his freedom acknowledged."

DOCUMENT 3

A letter from an African slave in Virginia to the Bishop of London, 1723 C.E.

"Here it is to be noted that one brother is the slave of another and one sister to another, which is quite out of the way. And as for me, myself, I am my brother's slave but my name is secret. We are commanded to keep holy the Sabbath day but we do hardly know when it comes for our taskmasters are as hard with us as the Egyptians were with the Children of Israel, God be merciful unto us. Here follows our severity and sorrowful service; we are hard used on every account. In the first place we are in ignorance of our salvation and in the next place we are kept out of the Church and matrimony is denied us and to be plain they do look no more upon us then we were dogs. We desire that our children be put to school and learned to read through the Bible, which is always at present with our prayers to God for its success before your honor these from your humble servants in the Lord. My writing is very bad, I hope your honor will take the will for the deed. I am but a poor slave that wrote it and has no other time but Sunday and hardly that at sometimes. My Lord archbishop of London, these with care, we dare not subscribe any man's name to this for fear of our masters for if they knew, we have sent home to your honor we should go near to swing upon the gallows tree."

DOCUMENT 4

THE USES OF SLAVES IN CUBA, 1825

USAGE OF SLAVES	# OF SLAVES	PERCENTAGE
SUGAR PLANTATIONS	50,000	19.45
COFFEE PLANTATIONS	50,000	19.45
SMALL FARMS, CATTLE RANCHES	31,065	12.08
TOBACCO FARMS	7,927	3.08
DIVERSIFIED RURAL OCCUPATIONS	45,000	17.51
TOTAL RURAL OCCUPATIONS	183,992	71.6
VARIOUS URBAN OCCUPATIONS	73,000	28.4
TOTAL	256,992	100.00

According to data gathered by Alexander von Humboldt, German geographer and scientist, 1811, and Ramon de la Sangra, Cuban botanist/demographer, 1830

DOCUMENT 5

Letter from the Turkish Grand Vizier Mustafa Reshid Pasha to the Governor of Tripoli (Libya), 1849 C.E.

"The Sultan has received, with sorrow, the shocking and evil news that a caravan which set out from Bornu in June with a great number of black slaves, bound for Fezzan, ran out of water on the way, so that 1,600 blacks perished. It is a well-known fact, which there is no need to state, and which was indeed sent in writing to your province in the time of your predecessor as governor, that while our Holy Law permits slavery, it requires that slaves be treated with fatherly care; those who act in a contrary or cruel manner will be condemned by God. Those people whose practice it is bring such slaves from inside Africa and make commerce with them, if they wish to bring thousands of God's creatures from such far places and bring them through such vast deserts, then it is their human duty to procure the necessary food and drink for the journey, and ensure that these unfortunates suffer as little as possible on the way. When these people in no way accept this duty, and cause the death of so many human beings in misery and suffering, they are behaving in a way that is not compatible with humanity. The Sultan can neither condone nor forgive such cruel conduct, and such inhumane behavior is categorically forbidden. If slaves perish on the way, the people engaged in the trade will be subjected to various severe punishments."

DOCUMENT 6

David Gomes Jardim, Brazilian doctor, from his report on Plantation Diseases and their Causes to the Medical Faculty in Rio de Janiero, Brazil, 1847 C.E.

"We have constantly observed that work is assigned without concern for the strengths of the individuals; that the weak and the strong share the work alike. From this lack of consideration can come only one result, that which daily occurs: the weakest slaves are the first to die, and when they do they are completely emaciated. When I asked a planter why the death rate among his slaves was so exaggerated, and pointed out that this obviously did him great harm, he quickly replied that, on the contrary, it brought him no injury at all, since when he purchased a slave it was with the purpose of using him for only a single year to grow sugar or coffee, after which very few could survive; but that nevertheless he made them work in such a way that he not only recovered the capital employed in the purchase, but also made a considerable profit."

DOCUMENT 7

Alfred von Kremer, Austrian scholar-diplomat, ex-ambassador to Egypt and the United States, from his published book, 1863

"The color prejudice that is maintained in so crude a form by the free sons of America, not only against genuine Africans but even against their descendants in the fourth and fifth degrees, is not known in the Orient (Middle East). Here a person is not considered inferior because he is a darker complexion. This can easily be explained from the nature of slavery in the Orient, where the slave is not separated by an insurmountable barrier from the family of his master, where the slave does not belong to a caste that is despised and barely considered human, but where in contrast, between master and slave, there is the most intimate and manifold relationship. In the Orient there can hardly be a Muslim family that is without slave blood."

DOCUMENT 8

J. F. Keane, English visitor to Arabia, notes from his travel journals, 1881 C.E.

"The Negro is to be found here in his proper place, an easily-managed, useful worker. The Negroes are the porters, water-carriers, and performers of most of the manual and domestic labor in Mecca. Happy, well-fed, well-clothed, they are slaves, proud of their masters, in a country where a slave is honored only after his master. Slavery has an elevating influence over thousands of human beings, and but for it hundreds of thousands of souls must pass their existence in this world as wild savages, little better than animals; it, at least, makes men of them, useful men, too, sometimes even superior men. Could the Arab slave trade be carried on with safety, it might be executed more humanely; and it would, philanthropically speaking, do good to many of the human race. While every settled town under Turkish or native rule in all wide Arabia has a slave market to be stocked, our greatest efforts [to ban the slave trade] can but increase the demand and raise the markets. That there are evils in Arab slavery, I do not pretend to deny, though not affecting the Negro, once a slave. The exacting slave-driver is a character wholly unknown in the [Middle] East, and the slave is protected from caprice of any abuse of any cruel master in that he is transferable and of money value. The man who would abuse or injure his slave would maim and willfully deteriorate the value of his horse."

DOCUMENT 9

Hans Sloan, from his Voyage to the Islands, 1706 describing conditions on the island of Barbados, 1706 C.E.

"The punishments for crimes of slaves are usually for rebellions [and include] burning them, by nailing them down on the ground with crooked sticks on every limb, and then applying the fire by degrees from the feet and hands, burning them gradually up to the head, whereby their pains are extravagant. For crimes of a lesser nature gelding (castration) or cropping off half of the foot with an axe are common. These punishments are suffered by them with great constancy. For running away they put iron rings of great weight on their ankles. For negligence they are usually whipped by the overseers with hard-wood switches, till they be all bloody. After they are whipped till they are raw, some put on their skins pepper and salt to make them smart. These punishments are sometimes merited by the slaves, who are a very perverse generation of people, and though they appear harsh, yet are scarce equal to their crimes, and inferior to what punishments other European nations inflict on their slaves in the East Indies."

FOOTNOTES

1. Patrick Manning, *Slavery and African Life: Occidental, Oriental, and African Slave Trades*. (Cambridge, England: Cambridge University Press, 1990), 154.

    Encyclopedia Americana: Grolier International Edition, vol. 25, *Skin to Sumac*. (Danbury, Connecticut: 2000), 24.

    Bernard Lewis, *Race and Slavery in the Middle East: A Historical Inquiry*. (Oxford: Oxford University Press, 1990), 79-84 in passim.

    Robert William Fogel and Stanley L. Engerman, *Time on the Cross: The Economics of American Slavery* (New York: W. W. Norton & Company, 1989), 33-34.

    Susanne Everett, *History of Slavery* (Edison, New York: Chartwell Books, Inc., 1999), 249.

2. Robin Blackburn, *The Making of New World Slavery: From the Baroque to the Modern, 1492-1800*. (London: Verso, 1997), 81.

3. Blackburn 473.

4. Herbert S. Klein, *Slavery in the Americas: A Comparative Study of Cuba and Virginia*. (Chicago: The University of Chicago Press, 1967), 151-152.

5. Lewis 161.

6. Ronald Segal, *The Black Diaspora* (London: Faber and Faber, 1995), 76.

7. Lewis 99-100.

8. Lewis 83.

9. Blackburn 345.

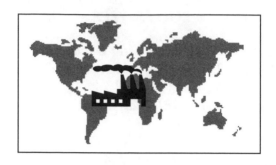

PART V
Industrialization and
Western Global Hegemony
1750 – 1914
Pages 524 – 531

SUMMARY

Between 1750 and 1914, world history was dominated by European imperialism. These were the decades in which Western civilization experienced the Industrial Revolution, which transformed the bases of production through new technology and new sources of power. European dominance in the world economy became overwhelming. In contrast to the Early Modern Period, when Western power on land was limited, no area could escape the possibility of extensive European or United States penetration. International commercial contacts increased steadily; they were enhanced by major technological innovations. By the 1850s, the leading issues began to revolve around either resistance or imitation to western influences.

Chronology: From Industrial Revolution to the Beginnings of a Western Breakdown

The beginning of this period focuses on no particular event. More important is the fact that during the 1750s, the forces that produced Europe's Industrial Revolution began to take shape: rapid population growth, expansion of manufacturing, and a surge of new inventions. Signs of the impact of western industrialization on the wider world followed quickly. European powers, the United States, and later, Japan opened markets, economically penetrated countries, fought wars, and seized colonies. This period drew to a close with the outbreak of World War I in 1914.

The Industrial Revolution

The period begins around 1750 when the forces shaping the Industrial Revolution emerged: population growth, expansion of manufacturing, a surge of inventions. The era closed with the beginning of World War I in 1914 because the conflict fundamentally weakened the Western world. The Industrial Revolution began first in Britain, and spread to Western Europe and the United States. Its essence was technological change, especially the application of coal-powered engines to replace humans and animals as the key energy sources. New production equipment followed to speed up processes. The British lead in the revolution came from its favorable internal resources and from the stimulus for innovation pressured by population growth. Enlightenment thinking provided ideological basis for change, and the previous accomplishments made in Western societies provided the essential foundations.

Population Movements

Western industrialization and imperialism led to huge shifts in the population structures of various parts of the world. Both basic dynamics and migration patterns were involved. In the West, birthrates began to decline, but high birthrates continued elsewhere in the world. Industrialization drew workers to the factories, while Europeans in nations slow to industrialize and Asians from India and China immigrated in the millions to the Americas and places offering employment.

Diversity in the Age of Western Dominance

The principal complexity in describing the period lies in detailing the diverse reactions to the growth of Western military and industrial might. One change was the incorporation of the United States, Canada, Australia, and New Zealand into an expanded Western civilization. Russia and Japan underwent dramatic internal changes. China and the Ottoman Empire, along with the Americas, retained their independence but were increasingly subject to Western influences. Most of the world experienced outright colonization as great inequalities in world politics, economics, and exchanges spread.

Major Themes Transformed

The relationship between humans and nature shifted dramatically in this era. New transportation methods, higher population, medicine, all a part of the Industrial Revolution, evened the odds for human survival but at a cost to soil conditions and water sources. Legal equality increased and slavery was abolished in most places.

Globalization

By the end of the nineteenth century, interconnections among all parts of the world intensified to an unprecedented level. The telegraph, steamship, railroad and, by the end of the period, radios, and telephones provided the means. Western industrialism and imperialism created an impressive network of global contacts.

CHAPTER 23
The Emergence of Industrial Society in the West, 1750-1914
Pages 534 – 561

I.   SUMMARY

A. The Age of Revolution

Even before industrialization, new ideas and social pressures caused a series of political revolutions, beginning with the American Revolution in 1776. The French Revolution of 1789 and the Napoleonic Period had an impact throughout Europe and beyond and encouraged new movements of liberalism and nationalism. Lesser revolutions followed in 1820 and 1830.

B. The Consolidation of the Industrial Order, 1850 – 1914

Industrial society developed more fully after 1850 and contained new family and leisure patterns. Political consolidation brought national unifications in Italy and Germany and new constitutions. Governments developed new functions, and the rise of socialism (Marxism and revisionism) changed the political spectrum.

C. Cultural Transformations

Western culture changed dramatically during the 19th century. Growing emphasis on consumers introduced new values and leisure forms. Science increased its hold but generated a new, complex view of nature, and new artistic movements demonstrated innovation and spontaneity.

D. Western Settler Societies

Western industrial growth and nationalist rivalry brought an explosion of imperialist expansion in the late 19th century. Along with this expansion, several societies, including the growing United States, extended many Western values and institutions to new areas. This expansion of the West to a number of vast settler societies was one of the crucial developments of the 19th century.

E. Diplomatic Tensions and World War I

Diplomatic and military tensions within Europe began to increase, particularly from the 1890s onward. Rival alliance systems built up their military arsenals. A series of crises, particularly in the Balkans, accelerated the tension.

II. CHAPTER REVIEW

A. What themes dominated the history of Western civilization between 1750 – 1914?

B. What ideas and pressures led to the Era of Atlantic Revolutions 1789 – 1830?

C. What two revolutions began the era; how did they transform Western society?

D. What ideas did the American and French revolutions unleash?

E. How did conservatives attempt to restore the balance of power?

F. What political ideologies challenged European conservatives?

G. What were the origins of the Industrial Revolution?

H. How did the Industrial Revolution affect traditional European lifestyles?

I. Why did the 1848 revolutions breakout and what did they achieve?

J. What role did nationalism play in European politics after 1848?

K. How did the social roles of European governments change after 1870?

L. What ideologies challenged the traditional social system after 1870?

M. How did Western culture change in the 19th century?

N. What advances occurred in the sciences and arts?

O. What factors led to the rise of the United States?

P. What role did the United States play in world history?

Q. What enclaves of Western culture arose outside of Europe?

R. What developments led to the outbreak of World War I?

III. VOCABULARY

A. Industrialization

B. Population Revolution

C. Proto-industrialization

D. American Revolution (1776)

E. French Revolution (1789)

F. Nationalism

G. Congress of Vienna

H. Liberals

I. Radicals

J. Conservatives

K. Greek Revolution

L. The Reform Bill of 1832

M. Factory System

N. Luddite

O. Revolutions of 1848

P. Chartist Movement

Q. Demographic Transition

R. Social Question

S. Socialism

T. Socialist Revisionism

U. Feminist Movement

V. Mass leisure culture

W. Romanticism

X. Triple Alliance, Triple Entente

Y. Balkan Nationalism

IV.   MAP EXERCISES

A. Map 23.1: *Napoleon's Empire* (Page 540)

1. The Grand Empire of Napoleon
   a. What areas did Napoleon acquire?

   b. What states allied with Napoleon?

   c. What states seem to be enemies of Napoleon?

2. Upsetting the Balance of Power
   a. How did Napoleon upset the balance of power?

   b. Based on Napoleon's campaigns, what can you predict about his plans?

B. Map 23.2: *Industrialization in Europe, c. 1850* (Page 543)
   1. Reading the Map
      a. Identify the industrial areas of England.

      b. What areas are emerging industrial areas?

      c. What nation(s) has (have) the densest concentration of railroads?

   2. Drawing Conclusions
      a. What nations would likely experience an industrial revolution?

      b. Why do you come to this conclusion?

C. Map 23.3: *The Unification of Italy* (Pages 547)

D. Map 23.4: *The Unification of Germany* (Page 547)
   1. What two states united Italy and Germany respectively?

   2. What other states did the two core nations acquire?

V.   PHOTO ESSAY: *Cultural Transformations* (Pages 534, 542, 549, 551, and 553)

What 19th century ideas and cultural values do the pictures represent regarding:
A. Dress?

B. Past times?

C. Politics?

D. Attitudes?

E. Social Class?

VI. DOCUMENT ANALYSIS: *Women in the Industrial Revolution* (Pages 545)
Write a document-based question based on these excerpts. The prompt is:

How did the status and traditional roles of women change during the Industrial
Revolution? What reasons would account for these changes?

Based on the following documents, discuss the status of women after the Industrial
Revolution. What types of additional documentation would help explain conditions that
bolstered or undermined women's position in society?

VII. MULTIPLE-CHOICE QUESTIONS

1. The chief intellectual cause of the French and American Revolutions was the
    A. Renaissance.
    B. Scientific Revolution.
    C. 1688 Glorious Revolution in England.
    D. Enlightenment.
    E. economic ideas of mercantilism.

2. The class most responsible for the intellectual ferment and forces of change in Europe
    between 1750 and 1914 was the
    A. middle class or bourgeoisie.
    B. aristocracy.
    C. peasants and serfs.
    D. urban workers or proletariat.
    E. clergy.

3. All of these were forces for change in Western Europe during the period 1750 – 1914
    EXCEPT:
    A. the ideas of the Enlightenment.
    B. the increasing wealth and success of the business classes.
    C. religious innovation.
    D. the population pressures caused by a demographic shift.
    E. industrialization and mechanization.

4. Which statement is a FACT about the world-wide influence of the American
    Revolution and early American government?
    A. The Americans abolished slavery and helped enforce the ban on slave trade.
    B. The American government modeled its constitution after France.
    C. Americans adopted a mercantilist approach to economics and established tariffs
        against European nations.
    D. Americans received little support from European nations in their struggle for
        independence.
    E. The American Revolution and early government impacted the later French,
        Haitian, and Latin American revolutionaries and their ideas.

5. All of these led to the outbreak of the French Revolution in 1789 EXCEPT:
   A. the inability of the French government to reform itself.
   B. an invasion of France by Prussia and Austria.
   C. a massive debt and need for tax reform.
   D. a desire to limit the powers and rights of the king, nobles, and clergy.
   E. bad harvests and rural (peasant) unrest.

6. The ideas of the French Revolution spread most widely throughout Europe as a result of
   A. the printing press, which popularized radical ideas.
   B. French radicals and the Reign of Terror.
   C. the advances of the French revolutionary and Napoleonic armies.
   D. the Catholic Church's support for reforms.
   E. the Allies victories against Napoleon and the Congress of Vienna in 1815.

7. The political ideology most favored by the victorious allied powers at the Congress of Vienna was:
   A. nationalism.
   B. radicalism.
   C. liberalism.
   D. conservatism.
   E. revolution.

8. The older European loyalty to established religions and God was often replaced after the French Revolution by
   A. devotion to the Pope.
   B. support of the king and national rulers.
   C. allegiance to local leaders.
   D. allegiance to strong military leaders.
   E. nationalism and loyalty to the nation-state.

9. All of these are ideas favored by 19th century European liberals EXCEPT:
   A. state regulation of tariffs and trade.
   B. limited government interference in individual life.
   C. the right of elected representation and the vote by propertied individuals.
   D. freedoms of religion, press, and assembly.
   E. restricted government intervention in the economy or commercial activities.

10. The most significant change caused by the Industrial Revolution was the
    A. movement of populations from rural to urban settings.
    B. mechanization of production and application of power to manufacturing.
    C. growth of a middle class.
    D. rise of a radical political movement.
    E. expansion of trade and commerce.

11. Which of these statements is a FACT about Europe's Industrial Revolution?
    A. Production of textiles was concentrated in living quarters and homes.
    B. Water and water wheels provided most power.
    C. Most transportation of resources and finished products was by sea.
    D. The Industrial Revolution led to an agricultural revolution.
    E. A major feature was the high pace of technological change and inventions.

12. All of these were disruptions caused by the Industrial Revolution EXCEPT:
    A. growth of large cities as populations moved from the country to the city.
    B. health conditions worsened in the cities.
    C. crime rates rose.
    D. increased birthrates and the rise of the middle class.
    E. traditional patterns of family and marriage changed.

13. Which revolution(s) was (were) directly influenced by the European Industrial Revolution during the Modern Period?
    A. the American Revolution
    B. the French Revolution
    C. the European Revolutions of 1848 – 1849
    D. the Greek nationalist revolution of 1820
    E. the Napoleonic Revolution

14. All of these demands were advocated by the 1848 revolutionaries EXCEPT:
    A. social reform.
    B. an end to serfdom and manorialism.
    C. nationalist independence and/or unification.
    D. liberal constitutions with political rights and protections.
    E. an end to colonialism and overseas acquisitions.

15. The new European power, which benefited from industrialization and nationalism, and which came to rival Great Britain in the 19th century, was
    A. the United States.
    B. Italy.
    C. Russia.
    D. France.
    E. the German Empire.

16. The social questions, demands for reform, and the need for monies to support the construction of railroads during the 19th century led to
    A. the expansion of and increasing intervention by governments in society.
    B. increasing radicalization of a majority of workers and peasants.
    C. numerous violent, socialist revolutions.
    D. the decrease in support for socialism, Marxist, or revisionist.
    E. the bankruptcy of many governments.

17. All of these conditions led to the outbreak of World War I EXCEPT:
    A. rival systems of alliance.
    B. international courts of justice and organizations such as the Red Cross.
    C. increased militarization of societies.
    D. the rivalry for and expansion of colonial empires.
    E. national rivalries between the states of the Balkans.

VIII. ESSAY QUESTIONS

    A. Compare and contrast the Neolithic Agricultural Revolution and the Industrial Revolution.

    B. Compare and contrast the demographic shifts caused by the Neolithic and Industrial Revolutions.

    C. How did European society change from 1500 to 1900?

    D. How did the balance of power change in Europe from 1500 to 1900?

    E.   Compare and contrast the governmental structures of the nation-state and monarchies.

    F. Compare and contrast the European Reformations and French Revolution.

    G. How did the role of religion change in Europe from 1500 to 1900?

    H. How did mankind's impact on the environment change from the Agricultural Revolution through the 19th century?

    I. How did women's roles in society change between 1000 and 1900?

    J. Compare and contrast lifestyles during the Agricultural Revolution and the Industrial Revolution.

    K. How did the roles of cities in Europe change from 1000 to 1900?

    L. Compare and contrast the roles of leisure, consumption, and material culture in 19th century Europe with any one other historical society.

CHAPTER 24
Industrialization and Imperialism:
The Making of the European Global Order
Pages 562 – 587

I.   SUMMARY

A. The Shift to Land Empires in Asia

From the mid-18th century onward, the European powers began to build true empires in Asia similar to those they had established in the Americas beginning in the 16th century. Using divide and conquer tactics, the Dutch in Java and the British in India, carved up Asia, Africa, and Oceania. Initially, Europeans were willing to adapt their lifestyles on the climates and cultures of the peoples they had gone out to rule. While the Dutch were hesitant to promote major changes in Javanese society, the British in India pushed for social reforms.

B. Industrial Rivalries and the Partition of the World, 1870 – 1914

The spread of the Industrial Revolution from Great Britain to continental Europe and North America greatly increased the advantages Western powers already enjoyed in manufacturing capacity and the ability to wage war. These advantages culminated in the domination and partition of the globe by Western powers by the late 19th century.

C. Patterns of Dominance: Continuity and Change

Widespread conquests were the dramatic manifestation of the great disparity in power that industrialization had created between the Europeans including North Americans and other peoples of the globe. The Westerners' sense of their own uniqueness and superiority, heightened by their unparalleled scientific and technological achievements, led to major changes in their economic, social, and cultural relations with the colonized. Europeans living in the colonies increasingly distanced themselves from the peoples that they governed. Europe and North America became more dominant in the world market system, with much of the rest of the globe supplying them with low-priced raw materials in return for the more highly priced, mass-produced consumer goods of the West.

II.   CHAPTER REVIEW

A. How did modern 19th century imperialism differ from 16th century colonialism?

B. How did the Europeans typically acquire colonial possessions?

C. How did the British rule India?

D. Describe the early colonial society in Java and India.

E. Why did Europe attempt social reforms in their colonies? With what results?

F. How did Western style education effect colonial peoples?

G. How did economic competition influence imperialism?

H. How did the Europeans organize and govern their empires?

I. Describe the social relationships between colonizer and the colonized.

J. How did Europeans change the economies of their colonies?

K. How did colonies with large European populations differ from other colonies?

III. VOCABULARY

A. Partition

B. British Raj

C. Presidencies

D. Princely states

E. Tropical dependencies

F. Settlement colonies

G. Gunboat diplomacy

H. White dominions

I. Contested settler colonies

J. Great Trek

K. Boer Republics

L. Boer War

IV. MAP EXERCISES

A. Map 24.1: *European Colonial Territories, Before and After 1800* (Page 566)
   1. The World in 1763

a. What was the largest European empire?

b. Which European nations had overseas empires?

2. The World in 1830
   a. Which European nation had the largest empire?

   b. Which European nations had largely lost their empires?

   c. What events between 1763 and 1830 would account for their changes?

B. Map 24.2: *The Stages of Dutch Expansion in Java* (Page 567)
C. Map 24.3: *The Growth of the British Empire in India* (Page 568)

1. Early Expansions prior to 1800
   a. What lands did the British and Dutch control?

   b. How would you describe the pattern of acquisition and control?

2. Expansion after 1800
   a. What patterns did British and Dutch pursue in acquiring colonies?

   b. What would be the benefit of having allies and dependent states?

D. Map 24.4: *The Partition of Africa* (Page 575)
1. Map around 1870
   a. Which European nations control what areas?

   b. Describe the pattern of settlement.

   c. What might account for this pattern of control?

2. Map around 1914
   a. Which two states have the largest African empires?

   b. What other states have African empires?

   c. Why might Germany be considered a "spoiler" in Africa?

V.   VISUALIZING THE PAST: *Capitalism and Colonialism* (Page 577)

A. Analysis
   1.   In what countries did Great Britain invest most heavily?
   2.   What did Great Britain:
   a. Export?

b. Import?

3.   Add up percentages. What percentages
a. did Britain invest in its colonies, Europe and American nations?

b. of total British imports were from its colonies, Europe, and America?

c. of total British exports went to colonies, Europe, and American nations?

4.   Upon whom were the British dependent for
a. trade in raw materials?
b. high technological manufactured goods?

B.   Conclusions
   1. Which was more important for Great Britain – trade with colonies or trade with the United States, the rest of Europe, and Germany?

   2. How valuable were the colonies to Great Britain?

VI.   DOCUMENT ANALYSIS: *Contrary Images* (Pages 581)

A. Document Analysis
   1. Who wrote each? (Attribution includes biographical references)

   2. What were the authors' points of view?

   3. How reliable are the documents? Why?

   4. What were the intents or purposes behind the documents?

   5. Who were the intended audiences?

   6. What are the documents' tones?

B. Comparison
   1. How do the two documents agree? Disagree?

   2. What might account for these differences?

   3. What biases do you detect?

   4. How do they affect your understanding or the reliabilities of the authors?

   5. What would account for differences in perspectives?

VII. PHOTO ESSAY: *Technology and Imperialism* (Pages 562, 567, 569, 574, 579, 580, and 585)

19th centuries European imperialism was imminently successful. But prior to 1800, European nations had made little progress against most Africans and Asians. This was largely due to the technological and military equalities between Europe and its rivals. The Industrial Revolution changed this.

What technologies and skills gave Europe a tactical and strategic edge over its rivals? How did this lead to empire building? How might medicine, agriculture, and ranching be "technological" weapons of imperialism?

VIII. MULTIPLE-CHOICE QUESTIONS

1. By 1830, the largest European colonial empire was
   A. Germany.
   B. Portugal.
   C. Spain.
   D. France.
   E. Great Britain.

2. Prior to the Industrial Revolution, most colonial acquisitions by European states
   A. were confined to South America.
   B. tended to be improvised and influenced by local officials and local actions.
   C. ceased.
   D. fulfilled military needs and imperial security.
   E. were limited to ports and forts in Africa to facilitate the slave trade.

3. British had first acquired its empire in India during the 18th century
   A. through purchase from local rulers.
   B. by intermarriage with local rulers.
   C. following successful wars against France for possessions in South Asia.
   D. from Portugal.
   E. from Spain.

4. Traditionally, British colonial practice in India during the 19th century was to
   A. leave defeated princes on the throne and control them through advisors.
   B. discourage warfare between local princes.
   C. encourage European intermarriage with local Hindu and Muslim ruling elites.
   D. support joint European control of trade and commerce.
   E. support the ruling Hindu and Muslim princes in exchange for trade privileges.

5. The most important British colonial possession in the 19th and 20th centuries was
   A. Canada.
   B. Australia.
   C. New Zealand.
   D. India.
   E. South Africa.

6. All of these institutions and technologies were transmitted by the British to India through their colonial rule EXCEPT:
   A. telegraph and railroad.
   B. an alphabet and an advanced literate culture.
   C. western style education.
   D. social reforms including an end to sati.
   E. application of science to farming and environment.

7. European-style language schools and education had the greatest impact on which colonial peoples?
   A. Peasants
   B. Merchants
   C. The children of the elite groups
   D. Indians
   E. East Asians

8. French educational policies of its colonial peoples were designed to
   A. create minor colonial officials and clerical staff.
   B. create a business staff.
   C. build a militarily trained group of colonial soldiers to support the empire.
   D. integrate French and native colonial ruling elites into one group.
   E. assimilate French-speaking Asians, Africans, and Pacific Islanders as citizens to offset Germany's higher birthrate.

9. The European educated colonial peoples tended to
   A. cling to their European rulers but became the leaders of future independence movements.
   B. side with traditional ruling elites in the colonies against the colonizers.
   C. immigrate to the mother countries, which owned the colonies.
   D. favor the peasants and poor people of their colonies.
   E. become merchants and businessmen.

10. Following the first Industrial Revolution, all of these nations challenged British traditional leadership in industry EXCEPT:
    A. the United States.
    B. Germany.
    C. Canada.
    D. France.
    E. Belgium.

11. Generally, European leaders saw colonies as
    A. wastes of money and resources.
    B. sources for raw minerals and potential markets.
    C. sources for cheap labor and slaves.
    D. places to settle their excess populations.
    E. military bases.

12. Active colonial policies seemed most popular with European
    A. ruling elites.
    B. religious leaders.
    C. the intelligentsia.
    D. peasants.
    E. lower middle and working classes.

13. The most likely reason for the success of European colonial acquisitions during the 19th century would be
    A. superior European military and transportation technologies.
    B. the enthusiasm by European Christian clergy to convert "the heathens".
    C. the epidemic amongst most native populations that preceded European arrival.
    D. lack of resistance to the Europeans.
    E. the successes in European agricultural technologies.

14. By 1914, all of these nations remained independent of European control EXCEPT:
    A. Ethiopia.
    B. Persia.
    C. Japan.
    D. India.
    E. Siam.

15. Most European, American, and Japanese colonial possessions could BEST be classified as
    A. settlement colonies.
    B. tropical dependencies.
    C. self-governing dominions.
    D. contested settler colonies.
    E. protectorates.

16. With regard to social policies towards their colonial peoples, European governing officials
    A. encouraged integration.
    B. promoted racial equality.
    C. practiced marrying local women.
    D. legally mandated racial and ethnic segregation.
    E. had no official policies.

17. Economically, European colonial powers encouraged their colonies to
    A. modernize.
    B. practice balanced agriculture and produce foodstuffs.
    C. become industrialized.
    D. be self-sufficient.
    E. remain dependent on the mother country.

IX. ESSAY QUESTIONS

    A. Compare and contrast the British colonial rule and acquisition of colonies with the Spanish model in the 16th and 17th century.

    B. Compare and contrast maritime and land-based empires.

    C. Compare and contrast European colonial society with the imperial society of any classical empire.

    D. Compare and contrast the impact of Western education on the Africans and Asians with the education of Western women (in overcoming inequalities).

    E. How did colonial societies change during the rule of Europeans?

    F. Compare and contrast frontier societies in the United States, Canada, and South Africa.

    G. Compare and contrast the treatment of colonial peoples by the Europeans with the treatment of the Dravidians by the Aryans, or the Arab treatment of non-Muslims peoples or dhimmis.

CHAPTER 25
The Consolidation of
Latin America, 1830 – 1920
Pages 594 – 619

I.   SUMMARY

A. From Colonies to Nations

Internal developments and the international situation of the French Revolution and Napoleonic wars set independence movements in motion. In Haiti, the ideas of the French Revolution led to a revolt of the slaves and the independence of the country. Hidalgo in Mexico, Bolivar in northern South America, and San Martin in the southern part of the continent led successful revolutions. In Brazil, an independent monarchy was created.

B. New Nations Confront Old and New Problems

The new nations confronted different problems: social inequalities, political representation, the role of the church, and regionalism. These problems led to political fragmentation. Local strongmen, representing various interests and their own ambitions, rose to prominence and dominated nations for decades.

C. Latin American Economies and World Markets, 1820 – 1870

In the mid-19th century, Latin American economies stagnated in the aftermath of the wars of independence. Dependence on exports of primary products created neo-colonial ties. Toward mid-century, a new prosperity began as some nations found new markets for their exports. The revenues earned allowed liberal governments to advocate a variety of social and political changes. By the end of the century Mexico, Brazil, and Argentina illustrate the general patterns from political instability or economic stagnation to the emergence of stable liberal regimes.

D. Societies in Search of Themselves

There was a tension in cultural life between European influences and the desire to express an American reality, or between elite and Indian or local culture. Social change came very slowly for Indians, blacks, and women, but by the end of the century economic resurgence was beginning to have social effects.

E. The Great Boom, 1880 – 1920

Between 1880 and 1920, Latin America and certain areas of Asia and Africa, experienced a tremendous spurt of economic growth, stimulated by the increasing demand in industrializing Europe and the United States for raw materials, foodstuffs, and specialized tropical crops. By the end of the 19th century, the United States was beginning to intervene directly in Latin American affairs.

II.   CHAPTER REVIEW

A. What causes led to the revolutions for independence?

B. How did Latin American nations achieve their independence?

C. How was Haiti's war for independence different from others in the area?

D. What factors led to political instability in Latin America?

E. How did the heritage of the past hinder the newly independent nations?

F. What was the role of the military and church in Latin American politics?

G. What economic problems did Latin American nations encounter?

H. How did the world trade system and foreign intervention affect Latin America?

I.   Compare and contrast the development of Brazil, Argentina, and Mexico.

J. What social tensions and inequalities existed in Latin America?

K. What paths did the developing cultures of Latin America take?

L. How did world economic concerns transform Latin America from 1880 – 1920?

M. What was the role of the United States in Latin America?

III.   VOCABULARY

A. Creoles (Criollos)

B. Toussaint L'Overture

C. Porteños

D. Caudillos

E. Centralists, Federalists

F. Monroe Doctrine

G. Positivism

H. Treaty of Guadalupe-Hidalgo (1848)

I. Mexican-American War

J. La Reforma

K. Fazendas

L. Underdeveloped

M. Modernization theory

N. Dependency theory

O. Spanish-American War

IV. PHOTO ESSAY: *New Nations, Old Problems* (Pages 588, 592, 600, 603, 604, 606, 607)

Although Latin American nations were newly independent, this freedom did not solve older problems associated with colonialism. How is each problem depicted in the above photos?

A. Race:

1. Western heritage?

2. Indian heritage?

3. African heritage?

B. Military and violence?

C. Economics?

D. Social stratification?

V. DOCUMENT ANALYSIS: *Hispanic Heritage* (Pages 596-597)

A. Document Analyses
   1. Who wrote each? (Attribution includes biographical references)

2. What were the authors' points of view?

3. How reliable are the documents? Why?

4. What were the intents or purposes behind the documents?

5. Who were the intended audiences?

6. What are the documents' tones?

B. Comparisons
   1. How do the two documents agree? Disagree?

   2. What might account for these differences?

   3. What biases do you detect?

   4. How do they affect your understanding or the reliabilities of the authors?

C. Conclusions
   1. What criticisms of Spanish rule did Bolivar mention?

   2. What problems did he foresee for an independent Latin America?

   3. What did Sarmiento admire and dislike about Latin American culture?

   4. What ideas and forces do both men support and oppose?

   5. How might these two traditions affect Latin American history?

VI.   MULTIPLE-CHOICE QUESTIONS

1. Which group led the independence movements in most of Latin America?
   A. Spanish and Portuguese officials born in the Iberian peninsula
   B. American-born whites or creoles
   C. Indians
   D. Mestizos or people of mixed Indian and European descent
   E. Mulattos or people of mixed African and European descent

2. All of these events helped cause Latin American independence EXCEPT:
   A. the Congress of Vienna.
   B. the American Revolution.
   C. the French Revolution.
   D. the slave revolt in Haiti.
   E. Napoleon's invasion of Spain and Portugal.

3. Haiti's independence differed from other Latin American movements in that
    A. it began as a slave revolt against slave owners and led to independence.
    B. the British landed troops to assist with the movement for independence.
    C. the United States supported the Haitians in their revolution with supplies.
    D. France and Napoleon welcomed and recognized Haiti's independence.
    E. Spain supported the movement for independence.

4. Leaders of Latin American independence revolts were generally
    A. monarchists, who wanted monarchs to govern their states.
    B. radicals, who supported the ideas of the French Jacobins.
    C. moderates, who wanted some democratic institutions but feared the masses.
    D. liberals, who wanted universal male suffrage.
    E. conservative republicans, who favored the church and rich landowners.

5. Brazil's independence differed from the rest of Latin America in that it was
    A. the result of a successful slave rebellion.
    B. not supported by the locally born European population.
    C. much earlier than the other Latin American revolutions.
    D. declared and led by the Portuguese regent in Brazil, who became emperor.
    E. extremely violent with conflicting armies led by different factions.

6. Throughout Latin America, the Indian population
    A. generally supported the new republican governments.
    B. remained largely outside the national political life.
    C. revolted against Europeans and later the newly independent governments.
    D. acquired rights in some countries but not all.
    E. was indifferent to whoever ruled.

7. The new maps and divisions of Latin American countries after 1820 reflected
    A. old Indian languages and cultures.
    B. racial and linguistic divisions.
    C. no relationship to older colonial boundaries.
    D. geographic barriers, the great distances, and isolated regions.
    E. years of warfare between the newly independent states.

8. In many 19th century Latin American nations, governments were in the hands of
    A. independent leaders or army commanders, who ruled regions by force.
    B. the Roman Catholic Church and its bishops.
    C. European born aristocratic elites, who survived the wars of independence.
    D. monarchists.
    E. leaders sympathetic to the Indians and working poor.

9. What statement about 19th century Latin American politics is a FACT?
    A. Centralists supported local autonomy and states' rights.
    B. Liberals wanted a centralized government with absolute control.
    C. Federalists wanted tax and commercial policies set by local governments.
    D. Conservatives supported equal rights and the franchise for all citizens.
    E. Most Latin Americans were monarchists and wanted royal dynasties.

10. The Monroe Doctrine
    A. was supported by Europeans eager to acquire lands in Latin America.
    B. supported a return of Latin America to Spanish and Portuguese control.
    C. encouraged European intervention in Latin America.
    D. was initially resented by Latin Americans, who felt the U.S. was a bully.
    E. was proclaimed by the U.S. and supported by British navies.

11. The country that had the greatest commercial and financial investments and interests in Latin America in the 19th century was
    A. France.
    B. Spain.
    C. Great Britain.
    D. Portugal.
    E. the United States.

12. The early-19th century economies of Latin America can be described as largely
    A. autarkic and self-sufficient.
    B. dominated by slave labor.
    C. unconnected and unaffected by the larger world economy.
    D. industrialized with a large population of factory workers.
    E. dependent on the export of primary products such as coffee and minerals.

13. The economic resurgence in Latin America at the end of the 19th century
    A. led to the rise of a powerful middle class.
    B. encouraged liberal reforms modeled after American or European examples.
    C. decreased the influence of large landowners.
    D. led to a rise in the living standards for the poor, ex-slaves, and Indians.
    E. discouraged foreign investments and European immigration to the area.

14. The Roman Catholic Church in Latin America
    A. usually opposed liberal reforms.
    B. supported the Indians and their concerns.
    C. was a leader of the liberal movements and their reforms.
    D. was generally neutral in disputes and acted as a moderator.
    E. had little influence with any groups and was marginalized in society.

15. Brazil was different than most Latin American nations in the 19th century for all of these reasons EXCEPT:
    A. it was a monarchy until 1889.
    B. Africans, mestizos, and mulattos outnumbered people of European descent.
    C. Brazil remained a centralist state with few local autonomous institutions.
    D. slavery was permitted until abolished in 1888.
    E. Brazil received millions of European immigrants after 1850.

16. After independence Latin America nations
    A. emancipated women and granted them rights denied during colonial times.
    B. ended legal systems of discrimination but strong social barriers persisted.
    C. gave Indians the right to reclaim their lost lands.
    D. prohibited educational opportunities for women and Indians.
    E. saw increased conflict between the old landed elite and the commercial middle classes.

17. All of these led to increased U.S. interest in Central America and the Caribbean EXCEPT:
    A. the American acquisition of Puerto Rico following the Spanish-American War.
    B. the desire for Latin American imports especially coffee, sugar, and oil.
    C. investments in Mexico, Central America, and Caribbean economies.
    D. the desire to build a canal between the Pacific and Atlantic Oceans.
    E. the suppression of the slave trade and slavery in the region.

VII. ESSAY QUESTIONS

    A. Compare and contrast Latin American independence movements with the French or American Revolutions.

    B. How did Latin American society, economics, and politics change from colonial times to the 1920s?

    C. Compare and contrast the Industrial Revolution in Europe with economic and social changes in Latin America.

    D. Compare and contrast Latin American economic dependence on the West with European colonialism in Africa.

    E. Compare and contrast Brazil with Argentina or Mexico between 1820 and 1920.

    F. Compare and contrast the British and American roles in Latin America.

CHAPTER 26
Civilizations in Crisis –
The Ottoman Empire, the Islamic
Heartlands, and Qing China
Pages 620 – 645

I. SUMMARY

A. From Empire to Nation: Ottoman Retreat and the Birth of Turkey

By the 18th century, the days of the Ottoman Empire seemed numbered. Weakened by internal strife, the Ottomans were unable to prevent their European rivals from whittling away territories on all sides. Ottoman rulers and reformers, however, devised strategies and initiated changes that slowed the decline of the European powers. Rather than disappear, leaders committed to westernization and modernization took over the Ottoman regime from within.

B. Western Intrusions and the Crisis in the Arab Islamic Heartlands

The crisis of confidence brought on by successive reverses and the ever-increasing strength of the Muslims' old European rivals elicited a wide variety of responses in the Islamic world. Islamic thinkers debated the best way to reverse the decline and drive back the Europeans. Some, such as the Mahdi of the Sudan, argued for a return to the Islamic past and instigated jihads against the advancing Europeans. Others such as Muhammad Ali of Egypt favored a large-scale adoption of western ways; others tried to combine both approaches.

C. The Last Dynasty: The Rise and Fall of the Qing Dynasty

Although China was strong enough to get away with its policies of isolation and attitudes of disdain in the early centuries of European expansion, by the late 18th century these policies were outmoded and dangerous. Not only had Europeans grown stronger, but China was also crumbling from within. More than a century of strong rule gave way to rampant official corruption, severe economic dislocations, and social unrest. The Western powers took advantage of these weaknesses to force open China's markets, humiliate its military defenders, and reduce its leaders to puppets. China's intellectuals were locked in debates over how to check the power of the Europeans and restore China's collapsing political and social order.

II. CHAPTER REVIEW

A. What domestic and foreign forces threatened Qing China and Muslim states?

B. How did Muslim and Chinese leaders respond to westernization?

C. How successful were Muslim and Chinese leaders in reforming their states?

D. Would westernization fail in Muslim states? Why or why not?

E. How successfully did Muslims and Chinese resist Western penetration?

F. Were Europeans responsible for Chinese and Muslim internal problems or did they just take advantage of the situation?

G. What internal forces arose to challenge Qing and Ottoman leadership?

H. Why were Muslim culture and states able to survive when the Qing could not?

III. VOCABULARY

A. Tanzimat reforms

B. Ottoman Society for Union and Progress (Young Turks); Mustafa Kemal

C. Muhammad Ali; Khedives

D. Suez Canal

E. Mahdist Revolt; The Mahdi

F. Manchu (Qing Dynasty)

G. Banner Armies

H. Compradors

I. Opium War

J. Taiping Rebellion

K. Boxer Rebellion

L. Self-strengthening movement

M. Empress Cixi

N. Foreign concessions; extraterritoriality; treaty ports

IV. MAP EXERCISES

A. Map 26.1: *Ottoman Empire, Late 18th Century* (Page 619)
1. What three continents does the empire straddle?

2. What modern states were once ruled by the Ottomans (refer to a modern atlas)?

3. Drawing Conclusions
   a. What different ethnic groups does the empire rule?

   b. How might different ethnic groups weaken Ottoman rule?

   c. What European states would be the greatest threat to the empire?

B. Map 26.2: *China during the Qing Dynasty* (Page 629)
   1. What is a treaty port?

   2. What powers had treaty ports in China?

   3. What ports did each European power "rule"?

   4. Which states likely had territorial designs on China? Support your answer.

V. DOCUMENT ANALYSIS: *Building a New China* (Page 636)

A. Document Analysis
   1. Who wrote the document? (Attribution includes biographical references)

   2. What is the author's point of view?

   3. How reliable is the document? Why?

   4. What were the intents or purposes behind the document?

   5. Who was the intended audience?

   6. What is the document's tone?

B. Drawing Conclusions
   1. What western institutions and values does Liang esteem?

   2. What should China borrow from the West?

   3. How might Western ideas and values impact China?

VI. PHOTO ESSAY: *Civilizations in Crisis – Old Meets New*

A. Comparisons: Before and After Modernization
   1. In Photograph 26.1 on page 622, how did the Europeans view the Ottomans?

2. In Photograph 26.2 on page 623, how had the Young Turks changed?

VII. MULTIPLE-CHOICE QUESTIONS

1. The decline of the Ottoman Empire in the 18th and 19th century can be traced to all of these reasons EXCEPT:
   A. sultans who were weak or inept rulers.
   B. frequent defeat of the Ottoman Empire and annexations of its land.
   C. religious divisions within Islam.
   D. decline in the productivity of peasants and artisans.
   E. Christian and non-Turkish populations, who resented Turkish rule.

2. Which of these statements is a fact about Turkish foreign relations between 1850 and 1914?
   A. Turkey fought frequent wars with Russia and lost.
   B. Turkey suppressed the Greek and Serbian revolts for independence.
   C. European powers supported the partition of the Ottoman Empire.
   D. Arabs resented Turkish rule because the Ottomans were Christians.
   E. The Turkish leaders resented Western ideas and institutions.

3. The group that opposed most internal Ottoman reforms was the
   A. university-educated students.
   B. Christians.
   C. merchants.
   D. peasants.
   E. ruling religious, political, and social elites.

4. The Tanzimat reforms in the Ottoman Empire
   A. were defeated by the Janissaries and provincial officials.
   B. benefited the merchants and artisans.
   C. granted women legal rights and protections.
   D. improved the empire's ability to fend off foreign aggressors.
   E. were opposed by non-Muslim religious groups.

5. Reforms under the late Ottoman sultans and Young Turk leaders
   A. attempted to modernize Turkey without westernizing.
   B. sought Muslim solutions to internal problems.
   C. emphasized westernization and copied western models openly.
   D. were universally opposed by most members of Turkish society.
   E. had no effect.

6. Muhammad Ali's attempts to reform Egypt in the 19th century failed because
   A. the powerful landlord class opposed them.
   B. the peasants revolted.
   C. the Europeans invaded Egypt and seized control.
   D. he spent too much time attempting to conquer lands and failed to implement real reforms.
   E. the Egypt clergy opposed westernization.

7. The strategic importance of Egypt was changed by
   A. Napoleon's invasion in 1798.
   B. the khedive's conquest of the Middle East and defeat of the Ottoman Empire.
   C. building the Suez Canal.
   D. the conversion of a majority of Egyptians to Christianity.
   E. building Alexandria and Cairo.

8. The Muslim Sudanese revolted under the Mahdi for all of these reasons EXCEPT:
   A. opposition to the British-led effort to end the slave trade.
   B. the conquest of the Sudan by the British.
   C. opposition to British influence in the area.
   D. a desire to purge Islam of western influences.
   E. opposition to Egyptian rule in the area.

9. Although they were nomadic tribesmen from beyond the Great Wall, the Manchus, when they conquered China
   A. freely settled amongst the Chinese people.
   B. reformed the Ming bureaucracy and removed local elites.
   C. emancipated women and peasants.
   D. retained the Ming emperors as nominal leaders.
   E. retained the Confucian gentry-scholars and much of the political system.

10. Socially, the Manchu (Qing) rulers
    A. encouraged innovative organizations such as unions.
    B. reinforced much of the Confucian value system including the family.
    C. began to slowly emancipate women.
    D. discouraged Manchu elites from adopting Chinese ways.
    E. refused to reinstate the Confucian testing system.

11. The sector of the Chinese economy and society over which the Qing rulers exercised the least control was the
    A. peasants.
    B. Confucian scholars.
    C. traditional landed elite.
    D. merchants and commercial interests.
    E. non-Chinese living within the empire.

12. All of these incidents were signs of the decline of the Qing Dynasty in China EXCEPT the:
    A. breakdown of honesty on the Chinese bureaucratic exams.
    B. diversion of taxes and revenues to enrich bureaucrats and their families.
    C. rise of banditry.
    D. rise of a wealthy group of merchants.
    E. neglect of public works and utilities.

13. The British reversed their imbalance of trade in the 18th century with China by
    A. selling opium to the Chinese.
    B. selling the Chinese British manufactured goods.
    C. negotiating treaties with the Chinese government.
    D. bartering their goods for Chinese luxury items.
    E. ending trade with China.

14. When the Chinese decided to end the illegal drug trade destroying their country
    A. few Chinese supported the government's decision.
    B. the Chinese successfully stopped the importation of the drug.
    C. the British attacked China to protect their opium trade.
    D. Chinese drug dealers openly established independent states and raised armies to protect their network.
    E. many European nations defended the Chinese decision and supported them.

15. The most immediate result of the Opium Wars was
    A. the partition of China between European nations.
    B. the collapse of the Qing Dynasty and its replacement.
    C. the beginning of a powerful reform movement to strengthen China.
    D. the cessation of Korea to Japan.
    E. China was forced to open its ports to European trade and grant Europeans extraterritoriality.

16. All of these ideas were supported by the Taiping rebels EXCEPT:
    A. outlawing Christian missionaries.
    B. social reform.
    C. land redistribution.
    D. liberation of women.
    E. a simplified script and universal literacy.

17. In the last decades of the 19th century, the Chinese inability to reform or modernize was largely due to
    A. foreign pressures not to modernize at all.
    B. constant rebellions and peasant revolts.
    C. the lack of a prosperous merchant class.
    D. elites and the Dowager Empress, who would do nothing to limit their authority.
    E. the lack of an educated elite willing to lead or propose reforms.

VIII. ESSAY QUESTIONS

A. Compare and contrast Turkish and Chinese responses to westernization.

B. Compare and contrast the reactions to Western influence, culture, and trade of one from each group: Turkey, Egypt, or China; and Brazil, Argentina, or Mexico.

C. Compare and contrast reforms, industrialization, and westernization of Russia and any one of these countries: Egypt, Turkey, or China.

D. Compare and contrast the colonization of Africa with the Western penetration of Muslim nations or China.

E. Compare and contrast the decline of China and Turkey with the decline and fall of any previous classical or post-classical civilization.

F. Compare and contrast the resistance to European influence and penetration in Turkey, the Sudan, or China with African or Indian resistance.

G. How did the government, society, and economics change (or remain the same) over the course of the Ottoman Empire?

CHAPTER 27
Russia And Japan –
Industrialization Outside the West
Pages 640 – 661

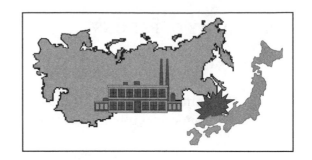

I.   SUMMARY

A. Russia's Reforms and Industrial Advances

After half a century of conservatism, in which the official national ideology was represented by the phrase "autocracy (tsar's absolute authority), orthodoxy (conservatism and Orthodox Christianity) and nationality (Great Russian nationalism and a Pan Slavist foreign policy) and the humiliating loss in the Crimean War, Russia moved into an active reform period in 1861. Social and political changes beginning with the emancipation of the serfs set the basis for industrialization by the 1890s. But social strain persisted as Russian leaders tried to defend the tsarist autocracy.

B. Protest and Revolution in Russia

A rising tide of unrest and assassinations accompanied Russia's period of transformation. The autocratic government refused to make any changes, which would have threatened the rule of the tsars and aristocrats. By the 1880s nationalist agitation gave way to outright revolution. Russia remained a profoundly unstable society in which any national catastrophe could endanger the entire system.

C. Japan: Transformation without Revolution

Like Russia, Japan faced new pressure from the West during the 1850s, although this pressure took the form of a demand for more open trade rather than outright military conflict. Japan's response was more direct than Russia's and more immediately successful. Despite Japan's long history of isolation, its society was better adapted than Russia's to the challenge of industrial change. Market forms were more extensive, reaching into peasant agriculture, and literacy levels were higher. Nevertheless, Japan had to rework many of its institutions during the final decades of the 19th century, and the process produced significant strain.

II.   CHAPTER REVIEW

A. Describe Russian society between 1815 – 1860.

B. What constituted the "peasant problem" in Russia?

C. Why did the Russians emancipate their serfs and with what results?

D. What reforms did Alexander II attempt and with what results?

E. How did Russia industrialize?

F. What radical groups arose in Russia and what did they advocate?

G. What caused the 1905 Russian Revolution and what results did it achieve?

H. What effects did Russian nationalism have on Eastern Europe?

I. Describe Japanese society during the late Tokugawa Shogunate.

J. How was Japan opened to foreign influences and with what results?

K. Why was Japan better able to modernize than China?

L. How did Japan change politically after the Meiji Restoration?

M. Describe the industrialization of Japan.

N. What social and cultural effects and conflicts did modernization cause in Japan?

O. How did Japan create an empire between 1895 and 1910?

III. VOCABULARY

A. Russo-Japanese War

B. Holy Alliance

C. Decembrist Uprising

D. Crimean War

E. Emancipation of the Serfs

F. Zemstvo

G. Trans-Siberian Railroad

H. Intelligentsia

I. Anarchists

J. Lenin and the Bolsheviks

K. 1905 Russian Revolution

L. Duma

M. Kulaks

N. Dutch Studies

O. 1853 and Matthew Perry

P. Meiji Restoration

Q. Diet

R. Zaibatsu

S. Sino-Japanese War

T. Yellow Peril

IV.   VISUALIZING THE PAST: *Two Faces of Western Influence* (Page 657)

    A. What values do the two images convey?
      1. Of Commodore Perry?

      2. Of Parliament?

    B. Why would the artists want to depict each scene in the way that they did?

V.   PHOTO ESSAY: *Russia in Turmoil* (Pages 643, 646, and 648)

    A. What aspects and problems about Russian society do these photos reflect?

    B. If these photos are typical of 19th century Russian history, what could you predict about future Russian history? (Consider the Document on page 647)

VI.   MAP EXERCISES

    A. Map 27.1: *Russian Expansion 1815 – 1914* (Page 644)
      1. What modern states did the Russians rule in 1914 but not 1999?

   a. In Europe
   b. In the Caucasus area
   c. In Central Asia

  2. Geo-Politics and Geo-Economics
   a. How far is it from St. Petersburg to Vladivostok in East Asia?

   b. How would the size and distances in Russia make government difficult?

   c. What relationship is there between Russian ports and access to seas?

   d. Why would ports on the Barents Sea and Arctic Ocean not be practical?

B. Map 27.2: *Japanese Colonial Expansion* (Page 659)
  1. Geography and Japan
   a. What lands block Japanese expansion?

   b. If Japan were to expand abroad, what would she need?

   c. Why would Japan covet Korea?

  2. Geography and War
   a. If Japan expanded into Korea, what countries would contest the move?

   b. What two wars did Japan fight?

   c. What geographic problems plagued Russia but helped Japan?

VII. DOCUMENT ANALYSIS: *Russia's Industrialization* (Page 647)

A. Document Analysis
  1. Who wrote the document? (Attribution includes biographical references)

  2. What is the author's point of view?

  3. How reliable is the document? Why?

  4. What were the intents or purposes behind the document?

  5. Who was the intended audience?

  6. What is the document's tone?

B. Drawing Conclusions
  1. Describe working conditions in the Russian factory.

2. Why would Russian workers be drawn to Bolshevism and radical ideas?

3. Why would a conservative Russian government support this critical report?

VIII. MULTIPLE-CHOICE QUESTIONS

1. 19th century ruling elites in Russia embraced which philosophy and ideas?
   A. Autocratic government, Orthodox religion, and extreme nationalism
   B. Liberalism, including the emancipation of serfs and British style democracy
   C. Socialism with land reform for the peasants and protections for workers
   D. Bolshevism or a worker led revolution and abolition of private property
   E. Constitutional monarchy with an elected parliament and limitations on the ruler's powers

2. In Russia, the supporters of westernization and radical ideas were often
   A. nobles.
   B. the Russian Orthodox clergy.
   C. peasants.
   D. intellectuals and university-educated students.
   E. ethnic minorities especially the Jews, Catholics, and Muslims.

3. In the 19th century and into the early 20th century, Russia
   A. developed a large middle class of businessmen and entrepreneurs.
   B. industrialized and urbanized at a rapid pace.
   C. remained a largely peasant society with an agrarian economy.
   D. kept pace with much of West European developments.
   E. developed no industries and relied largely on imports of manufactured goods.

4. Russia's 19th century underdevelopment was most dramatically revealed by
   A. the French Revolution's impact on Russia.
   B. Napoleon's invasion of Russia, which nearly succeeded.
   C. the 1825 Decembrist Revolution.
   D. the Crimean War.
   E. the Russo-Japanese War.

5. Despite the emancipation of the serfs in Russia,
   A. serfdom persisted in many parts of Russia.
   B. Russian aristocrats opposed the emancipation.
   C. few new numbers of workers joined the factories or industrial workforce.
   D. slavery persisted in Russia.
   E. Russia was careful to preserve imperial and aristocratic power and influence.

6. Industrially and socially, Russia was most transformed by
   A. the emancipation of the serfs, which furnished millions of workers.
   B. the construction of railroads, which opened markets, jobs, and movement.
   C. compulsory education for women and the peasants.
   D. the state's support of free enterprise, free trade, and entrepreneurship.
   E. the government's land reform policy giving the peasants land and money.

7. Russia was initially assisted in its modernization and industrialization by
   A. the creation of an armaments industry to build up its armed forces.
   B. giving aristocracy, church, and imperial lands to landless peasants.
   C. huge influxes of foreign investments and capital, especially from France.
   D. frequent wars against weaker neighbors.
   E. a massive immigration of highly trained technicians to Russia.

8. All of these influences led to the 1905 Revolutions EXCEPT:
   A. businessmen and professionals pressuring the government for political rights.
   B. students agitating amongst the peasants.
   C. anarchist assassinations and agitations amongst peasants and workers.
   D. Count Witte's social and economic policies.
   E. the spread of Marxism and socialism amongst workers and intellectuals.

9. Prior to the arrival of the American fleet and Commodore Perry, Japan
   A. was dominated by a Buddhist and Shinto religious hierarchy.
   B. had not developed a literate and educated population.
   C. was in self-imposed isolation.
   D. lacked a centralized, effective government.
   E. knew little of western developments or western ideas.

10. Westernization and modernization in Japan was most opposed by the
    A. Japanese intellectuals.
    B. shogun's bureaucrats.
    C. samurai class.
    D. merchants and commercial class.
    E. landed aristocrats.

11. Which of these statements is a FACT about the policies of the Meiji restoration?
    A. Political power was centralized and the Emperor's authority was restored.
    B. Feudalism was retained although it was limited.
    C. The samurai retained some of its rights and privileges.
    D. The samurai and educated Confucian elite staffed the state bureaucracy.
    E. The Diet obtained rights and powers similar to British parliament.

12. Japan avoided the fates of Qing China and the Ottoman Empire by
    A. closing its country to foreign influences.
    B. accepting the United States as a protector to balance European influences.
    C. defeating American, British, and other European expeditions to Japan.
    D. reforming, modernization, westernization, and industrialization.
    E. relying on its samurai, bushido, and Shinto traditions.

13. Industrialization in Japan
    A. had begun before the arrival of the Americans and opening of Japan.
    B. relied heavily on foreign investments in Japanese factories.
    C. relied heavily on government-supported and financed plans.
    D. was begun and led by Japanese combines called zaibatsu.
    E. relied little on imports of raw materials.

14. All of these social and cultural changes were the results of the Japanese Industrial Revolution EXCEPT:
    A. the secularization of Japanese society.
    B. massive population growth due to better nutrition and medical provisions.
    C. a universal educational system.
    D. the explosive growth of towns as rural populations migrated to cities.
    E. an increased emphasis on technological and scientific education.

15. Japanese imperialism
    A. was unpopular amongst the Japanese masses.
    B. sought natural resources for industry and gave ex-samurai jobs in the military.
    C. was restricted to Korea.
    D. avoided conflicts with China and Russia.
    E. was discouraged by the Japanese emperors and his bureaucracy.

16. As a way to smooth over strains within Japanese society caused by the Industrial Revolution, the government
    A. granted extensive rights and benefits to workers, women, and peasants.
    B. established a social welfare and retirement system.
    C. tolerated unions and radical groups if they worked with the government.
    D. gave the Japanese Parliament (Diet) powers over ministers and government.
    E. supported Japanese nationalism and foreign expansion.

17. The nation which threatened Japanese colonial aspirations most in the late 19th and early 20th century was
    A. Great Britain.
    B. Russia.
    C. China.
    D. Korea.
    E. The United States.

IX.   ESSAY QUESTIONS

A. Compare and contrast Japanese and Russian paths to modernization.

B. Compare and contrast Japanese and Chinese responses to the western threat.

C. How did Japan change socially, politically, and economically from 1500 – 1900?

D. Compare and contrast Russia's reaction to westernization or modernization with the reaction of any one of these: Brazil, Mexico, Argentina, Egypt, Ottoman Empire, or China.

E. How did Russia change socially, politically, and economically from 1400 – 1900?

F. Compare and contrast Russian society and its changes with any one West European nation.

G. Compare and contrast the emancipation of the Russian serfs, American slaves, and end to slavery in the Americas.

H. Compare and contrast the Industrial Revolution in Russia with the British Industrial Revolution.

I. Compare and contrast Russian imperialism with the expansion of Great Britain in the 19th century.

J. Compare and contrast the demographic shift in Japan with similar changes in one of these: China, Russia, Western Europe, or any Latin American nation.

PART V REVIEW

I.   PART OVERVIEW

     A.   What themes dominated this period of history?

     B.   What influences did Western civilization have on non-European areas?

     C.   How did non-Western civilizations respond to Western contacts and influences?

     D.   What was the connection between industrialization and Western imperialism?

     E.   What demographic transitions and population movements occurred?

     F.   How did industrialization and population changes affect the environment?

     G.   How did industrialization lead to greater social and economic inequality?

     H.   What scientific, intellectual, and artistic movements influenced this period?

II.   VOCABULARY

     A.   Imperialism

     B.   Hegemony

     C.   Industrialization

     D.   Demographic Transition

III.   TIMELINE CHRONOLOGY: BETWEEN 1700 – 1900
     Using the timeline, identify these major events.

     A.   Major inventions and technologies

     B.   Major wars

     C.   Major rebellions and revolutions

     D.   Major independence movements

     E.   Colonial annexations

     F.   Which countries tend to dominate this period?

IV.	GEOGRAPHY

   A. Industrial Development in Key Regional Centers, c. 1900
      1. Identify
         a. Centers of industrialization worldwide.

         b. The most-industrialized continents.

      2. Foreign Investment
         a. What nation is the world's largest investor abroad?

         b. Which nation is the largest investor in:
            (1) North America?
            (2) South America?
            (3) Africa?
            (4) Asia?

         c. Who is the second largest investor in the world?

   B. Main Colonial Holdings, c. 1914
      1. What was the world's largest empire? Second largest?

      2. Which continents are:
         a. Largely European-dominated?

         b. Freest from European control?

   C. Comparison of Maps

   Even if Great Britain did not "own" Argentina, Brazil, and Russia, for example, if the British invest money and own capital in these nations, how independent is the country in question?

V.	MULTIPLE-CHOICE QUESTIONS

   1. The period 1750 – 1914 is characterized by the
      A. rise of civilizations.
      B. rise of classical religions.
      C. rise of transregional civilizations.
      D. first global connections.
      E. predominance of European imperialism.

2. European and many North American areas were transformed during the period 1750 – 1914 by
   A. colonialism.
   B. the Industrial Revolution and technology.
   C. world war.
   D. global trade.
   E. the great religions.

3. During this period, the region, which had resisted European penetration from 1450 – 1750, that was mostly carved up into colonies was
   A. Africa.
   B. South America.
   C. North America.
   D. East Asia.
   E. Southwest Asia.

4. International commercial connections between 1750 and 1914 were enhanced by
   A. the rise of the first global trade network.
   B. the first mass immigration between continents.
   C. the invention of the telephone and television.
   D. major technological innovations.
   E. the spread of a common system of international diplomatic laws.

5. The period 1750 – 1914 began with
   A. the outbreak of World War I, the first global war.
   B. the beginning of the Industrial Revolution.
   C. the American Revolution.
   D. a Demographic shift.
   E. no particular event.

6. The period 1750 – 1914 ended when
   A. the European colonial empires collapsed.
   B. the Panama Canal opened.
   C. World War I broke out.
   D. the Industrial Revolution moved from Europe and North America to Africa, Latin America, and Asia.
   E. the Russian Revolution.

7. The demographic transition from 1750 – 1914 was due to all of these causes EXCEPT:
   A. declining birthrates in industrial nations.
   B. the spread of new food plants around the world.
   C. decreased death rates due to public health measures.
   D. Europe's percentage of the total world population declined.
   E. high birthrates in Afric, Latin America, and Asia.

8. During the 19th century, mass immigration was generally
   A. from less developed countries to industrialized nations.
   B. surpassed by numbers from the slave trade.
   C. from Mexico and Central America to the United States.
   D. from China and India to coastal areas.
   E. religious in nature.

9. One new development during the period 1750 – 1914 was the
   A. first mass migrations between continents.
   B. first global trading network.
   C. rise of diplomatic relationships.
   D. decrease of economic inequalities between regions.
   E. rise of international non-governmental agencies such as postal exchanges, the Red Cross, and the Olympics.

10. For most non-European nations during the period 1750 – 1914, the major influence on their development was
    A. mass population shifts.
    B. industrialization.
    C. the relationship to the West and its political, economic, and social values.
    D. the continuing degradation of the environment.
    E. the expansion of the slave trade to include non-Africans.

VI.   ESSAY QUESTIONS

   A. Compare and contrast the responses to westernization in any two: Russia, the Ottoman Empire, China, Japan, or Iran.

   B. Compare and contrast the political, economic, and social changes in Russia around 1905 with Japan in the late 19th century.

   C. Compare and contrast the first Industrial Revolution in Western Europe with the second Industrial Revolution (which spread to Russia, Japan, the United States, etc.).

   D. Compare and contrast any two types of labor systems common in the period: serfdom, slavery, caste system, or paid workers.

   E. Compare and contrast the European 19th century world system with the Muslim civilization of the 11th century C.E.

PART V GEOGRAPHY: THE MAP OF THE FIRST GLOBAL CIVILIZATION

Between 1750 and 1914, the world's geography was defined by technology and colonialism. Technologies of transportation and communication, trade, venture capital, and migration created the world's first global civilization and fueled the competition for and acquisition of empires. Centers of industry such as the vast Canadian-American complex around the Great Lakes and the Ruhr of Germany became critical. To facilitate trade and military power, canals were dug between seas and oceans.

I. LOCATE (Page 525)
    A. PHYSICAL GEOGRAPHY

    1. Panama Canal
    2. Suez Canal
    3. Saint Lawrence Seaway
    4. Great Lakes
    5. Lake Victoria

    6. Nile River
    7. Niger River
    8. Congo River
    9. Korean Peninsula

    B. REGIONS
    (Page 525)

    1. The Ruhr
    2. The Balkans
    3. Indonesia

    4. The Sudan
    5. Central Asia
    6. Siberia

II. IDENTIFY AND LOCATE
    A. HISTORIC STATES

    1. United States
    2. Japan
    3. Germany
    4. Canada
    5. Brazil
    6. Mexico
    7. Haiti

    8. Argentina
    9. Ottoman Empire
    10. Egypt
    11. South Africa
    12. China
    13. India

    B. CITIES

    1. Hong Kong
    2. Shanghai
    3. New York City
    4. Chicago
    5. Berlin
    6. London

    7. Paris
    8. Manchester
    9. Birmingham
    10. Tokyo
    11. Bombay

    C. COLONIAL EMPIRES

    1. British
    2. French
    3. German
    4. Italian
    5. Portuguese
    6. Dutch

    7. Japanese
    8. American
    9. Russian
    10. Belgian

MULTIPLE-CHOICE ANSWERS

CHAPTER 23

1. D
2. A
3. C
4. E
5. B
6. C
7. D
8. E
9. A
10. B
11. E
12. D
13. C
14. E
15. E
16. A
17. B

CHAPTER 25

1. B
2. A
3. A
4. C
5. D
6. B
7. D
8. A
9. C
10. E
11. C
12. E
13. B
14. A
15. C
16. B
17. E

CHAPTER 24

1. E
2. B
3. C
4. A
5. D
6. B
7. C
8. E
9. A
10. C
11. B
12. E
13. A
14. D
15. B
16. D
17. E

CHAPTER 26

1. C
2. A
3. E
4. D
5. C
6. D
7. C
8. B
9. E
10. B
11. D
12. D
13. A
14. C
15. E
16. A
17. D

CHAPTER 27

1. A
2. D
3. C
4. D
5. E
6. B
7. B
8. D
9. C
10. E
11. A
12. D
13. C
14. A
15. B
16. E
17. B

PART V

1. E
2. B
3. A
4. D
5. E
6. C
7. B
8. A
9. E
10. C

DOCUMENT-BASED QUESTION:
DECOLONIZATION IN THE 20th CENTURY

DIRECTIONS

The following question is based on the accompanying documents. (The documents have been edited for the purpose of this exercise). The question is designed to test your ability to work with and understand historical documents. Write an essay that:

- Has relevant thesis and supports that thesis with evidence from the documents.

- Uses all or all but one of the documents.

- Analyzes the documents by grouping them in as many appropriate ways as possible and does not simply summarize the documents individually.

- Takes into account both the sources of the documents and the authors' points of view.

ESSAY PROMPT

Determine the methods colonies and colonial peoples used to achieve their independence and end colonial rule in the 20th century.

Based on the following documents, discuss decolonization and the movement for independence by colonial peoples. What types of additional documentation would help explain the different paths taken and methods used by independence movements?

HISTORICAL BACKGROUND

In 1921, Ireland became the first colony to achieve independence from Great Britain. Egypt and the Philippines both achieved autonomy in the mid-1930s, but it was not until 1947 that decolonization really began. Between 1947 and 1948, Great Britain granted independence to Sri Lanka, Burma, Pakistan, and India. By 1970, most empires had granted their former colonies independence. Only Portugal resisted. In 1991, the breakup of the last remaining colonial empire – the Soviet Union – occurred. By the dawn of the 21st century, there were few remaining colonial possessions left.

DOCUMENT 1

CHRONOLOGY OF THE FILIPINO INDEPENDENCE MOVEMENT

1899	United States annexes Philippines
1899-1902	Guerrilla war between US-Philippines

1900	Colonial administration established
1900	Filipino Party established to work with US toward independence
1901	Filipinos join colonial administration
1902	Colonial schools, courts created
1903	Filipino coinage created; US buys church lands for poor farmers
1907	Independence party formed; free elections to colonial legislature

1913	Law allows Filipino goods into the US without duties
1916	Filipino national bank established; elective Senate created

1924	Filipino politicians split over independence question

1931	US President says Philippines need economic independence
1933	US Congress passes 1st Independence Act
1934	Filipino legislature declines to accept 1st Independence Act
1934	US Congress passes 2nd Independence Act
1934	Filipino legislature agrees to independence in twelve years
1935	Philippines Commonwealth established with Filipino president; US retains control of defense, foreign policy, national finance
1938	Fear of Pacific war leads Filipinos to reject earlier independence

1941	Japanese invade islands, establish collaborationist government
1944-1945	US liberates Philippines
1946	US grants independence including payments for war damage and trade bill to allow Filipino goods into US without tariffs

DOCUMENT 2

Aung San, Burmese nationalist and military leader, from his pamphlet, *Burma Challenge*, 1940

"Personally though I felt that international propaganda and assistance of our cause was necessary, the main work, I thought must be done in Burma which must be the mobilization of the masses for the national struggle. I had a rough plan of my own – a country-wide mass resistance movement against British imperialism on a progressive scale . . . co-extensive with international and national developments in the form of a series of local and partial strikes of industrial and rural workers leading to a general and rent strike finally, also all forms of militant propaganda such as mass demonstrations, and peoples marches leading finally to mass civil disobedience, also economic campaign against British imperialism in the form of boycott of British goods leading to mass non-payment of taxes, to be supported by developing guerrilla action against military and civil and police outposts, lines of communications, etc. leading finally to complete paralysis of the British administration in Burma when we should be able along with the developing world situation (World War II) to make the final and ultimate bid to capture power. And I counted then upon the coming over of the troops belonging to the British government to our side – particularly the non-British sections. In this plan I also visualized the possibility of the Japanese invasion of Burma."

DOCUMENT 3

Dmytro Pavlychko, Ukrainian poet and key figure in the reform movement, also a member of the Ukrainian People's Assembly, from a 1990 interview.

"I am for total independence and opposed to any sort of compromise concerning the so-called Union treaty. But I think we must move towards this independence through the slow, peaceful progress of parliamentary struggles. It has to be a gradual affair – an immediate secession from the Soviet Union is, first of all impossible . Moreover, it would provoke a harsh, chauvinistic reaction, and blood would flow. There are many Russified Ukrainians; there are many who will view such a step negatively. The matter must be carried out with considerable tact and diplomacy. We must quietly leave the Soviet Union and close the door gently, so that Gorbachev does not awaken. But if the entire Ukrainian people were convinced of the merits of such an ideal and were to announce in union that we desire complete independence, then there is not a force that could stop such a movement. There can be no compromises at least until Ukraine has its own constitution. After independence, when matters become clearer, Ukraine can form agreements with Russia according to its needs, for example political, economic, cultural, and national."

DOCUMENT 4

Premier Gamal Abdel Nasser, Egyptian leader who nationalized the Suez Canal, his July 1956 speech to the Egyptian people

"Is history to repeat itself again with treachery and deceit? Will economic independence or economic domination and control be the cause of the destruction of our political independence and freedom? Whenever we turn backwards, we aim at the eradication of the past evils which brought about our domination, and the vestiges of the past which took place despite ourselves and which were caused by imperialism through treachery and deceit. Today, the Suez Canal where 120,000 of our sons lost their lives in digging it by corvee, and for the foundation of which we paid eight million pounds, has become a state within the state. It has humiliated ministers and cabinets. Britain has forcibly grabbed our rights, our 44 percent of its shares. Britain still collects the profits of these shares from the time of its inauguration until now. The income of the Suez Canal Company in 1955 reached 35 million pounds, or 100 million dollars. Of this sum we, who have lost 120,000 persons, who have died digging the canal, take only one million pounds or 3 million dollars. This is the Suez Canal Company, which was dug for the sake of Egypt and its benefit! We shall not repeat the past. We shall eradicate it by restoring our rights in the Suez Canal. This money is ours. This canal is the property of Egypt because it is an Egyptian Joint Stock Company."

DOCUMENT 5

Syrian Nationalist leader, Fakhri al-Barudi, his 1941 speech before the Syrian Chamber

"I do not believe that the nationalists have agreed to assume the responsibilities of the new national government because Free (anti-Nazi) France proclaimed the independence of Syria. They have seen how many times in the past independence was granted but soon withdrawn; and in the events of 1936, 1937, and 1938, we have a conclusive proof of French insincerity and faithlessness. They have assumed official responsibilities only when it was made clear to them that, this time, the offer of independence was guaranteed and insisted upon by Great Britain. [Even if their sole purpose was to keep the Germans out of Syria and win the war, and because the Arabs are of a greater importance than are the French], the Allied guarantee of our independence is, and has been, our only weapon against the [League of Nation's 1919] colonial mandate."

DOCUMENT 6

Amilcar Cabral, Secretary-General and president of the War Council of the African Party for the Independence of Guinea (Bissau) and Cape Verde (from Portugal), from a lecture in the United States, 1970; he was assassinated in 1973.

"The armed liberation struggle requires the mobilization and organization of a significant majority of the population, the political and moral unity of the various social classes, the efficient use of modern arms and of other means of war, the progressive liquidation of the remnants of tribal mentality, the rejection of social and religious rules and taboos, which inhibit development of the struggle – gerontocracies, nepotism, social inferiority of women, rites and practices incompatible with the rational and national character of the struggle. Consider these features inherent in an armed liberation struggle – the practice of democracy, of criticism and self-criticism, the increasing responsibility of populations for the direction of their lives, literary work, creation of schools and health services, training of cadres from peasant and worker backgrounds. The conquest of national independence and in the perspective of developing the economic and social progress of the people must be at least the following: development of a popular culture and all positive indigenous cultural values; development of a national culture; constant promotion of the political and moral awareness of the people and patriotism."

DOCUMENT 7

Reverend Nbadaningi Sithole, president of the Zimbabwean African National Union, guerrilla leader, and Anglican minister, comments from his book, *African Nationalism*, 1958.

"Broadly speaking, there are two methods that African nationalism employed, and still employs in trying to realize its aspiration: nonviolence, and violence. Men tend to employ methods that yield dividends. They discard those methods, which do not show results. Where constitutional arrangements were satisfactory, African nationalist participated in the various legislative bodies. When parliamentary participation was found not to yield the expected results, African nationalists usually organized mass rallies throughout the county. At the mass rallies nationalists took every opportunity to detail eloquently the oppression of white rule. And African nationalists used everything at their disposal to gain the sympathy of the European public. Where nonviolence failed, nationalists resorted to violence. It was only resorted to as a desperate measure. If there was no constitutional channel to address wrongs, this meant defying the law. Often this resulted in riots. Boycotts and strikes which began on a nonviolent basis ended in violence when they broke out into looting, stoning of vehicles, and other acts of destruction. When the powers-that-were refused to come to terms with popular demands, armed revolt was inevitable."

FOOTNOTES

1. William L. Langer, comp. and ed., *An Encyclopedia of World History: Ancient, Medieval, and Modern Chronologically Arranged* (Boston: Houghton Mifflin Company, 1972), 937 – 938, 1118 – 1119, and 1352 – 1353 in passim.

    Theodore Friend, *Between Two Empires: The Ordeal of the Philippines, 1929 – 1946* (New Haven, Connecticut: Yale University Press, 1965), 272 – 275.

2. Aung San Suu Kyi, *Aung San of Burma: A Biographical Portrait by his Daughter*, 2nd ed. (Edinburgh, Scotland: Kiscadale Publications, 1991), 87-88.

3. Roman Solchanyk, ed. *Ukraine: From Chernobyl to Sovereignty: A Collection of Interviews*, with a forward by Norman Stone (New York: St. Martin's Press, 1992), 120 – 121.

4. L. S. Stavrianos, *A Global History: From Prehistory to the Present*, 4th ed. (Englewood Cliffs, New Jersey, 1988), 711.

5. Howard M. Sachar, *Europe leaves the Middle East: 1936-1954*, with an introduction by William L. Langer (New York: Alfred A. Knopf, 1972), 286.

6. J. Ayo Langley, *Ideologies of Liberation in Black Africa 1856 – 1970: Documents on Modern African Political Thought* (London: Rex Collins, 1979), 719.

7. J. Ayo Langley 278 – 289 in passim.

PART VI

The 20th Century in World History

Pages 662 – 669

SUMMARY

The 20th century has provided a rare break in world history, comparable in scope to the 5th century or 15th century. The contemporary period in world history had just taken shape even at the end of the 1990s. Two impulses of the 20th century affect the periodization. One impulse emphasizes the continuities of the century. At the other extreme, many other observers reflect a modern culture that emphasizes rapid and fundamental change and the creation of very strong and influential global contacts. These historians see the 20th century as a third revolution comparable to the Neolithic and Industrial Revolutions. There are three phases. The first was between 1914 and 1945 including the two wars and the Great Depression, which led to a new international order. Between 1945 and 1991, decolonization and the Cold War dominated much of the world. The end of the Cold War either began a third phase, or, as some argue, perhaps a new period.

The Repositioning of the West

Western decline resulted in part from the two world wars. Western population decreased as a percentage of the world total and immigration to western countries increased rapidly. The West has also lost its technological monopoly including its military superiority, and has been challenged as the preeminent world trader and manufacturer. More decisive was decolonization in which European empires broke up and the rise of non-European super powers, namely the Soviet Union (Russia), the United States, China, and Japan.

International Contacts

The intensification of international contacts was a basic feature of the 20th century. Technology was critical: Innovations included faster communication, faster transport, and larger capacities for communication and the movement of goods. Levels of world trade increased and more corporations operated internationally. Diplomatic contacts were internationalized and influential international organizations arose. International cultural influences spread.

International Challenges in Politics and Culture

Change undermined long-standing traditions in all institutions and structures. Governments have changed, often adopting Western style institutions, and all governments have taken on new roles in societies and economies. Belief systems have been modified or challenged by systems that were more secular. Growing interest in science also challenged them. Another change was the displacement of long-standing beliefs in rigid social inequalities.

The 20th Century as a New Period in World History

The new period of the 20th century has at least two phrases. Between 1914 and 1945, two major wars and a great depression brought forward a new international order. Since 1945, there have been many adjustments – such as decolonization – to the working out of a new world order.

Globalization

As the 20th century began, globalization was clearly accelerating. The spread of industrialization, new developments in communication and transportation, and the cultural influence of the West created unprecedented linkages around the world.

CHAPTER 28
Descent into the Abyss:
World War I and the Crisis of
the European Global Order
Pages 670 – 699

I. SUMMARY

A. The Coming of the Great War

By 1914 diplomatic tensions had escalated fairly steadily among the major European powers. Colonial rivalries and arms races had led to the formation, beginning in the 1890s, of two increasingly hostile alliances. Each of the alliances were anchored on secret treaties that committed those who joined to come to each other's assistance in case of attack by an outside rival power. The participants in each alliance also made plans to coordinate both military preparations and operations should war break out in Europe.

B. A World at War

Part of the reason European leaders let their nations into war in 1914 was that most of them expected the conflict to be brief and decisive. They saw a war between the European powers as a way to break the logjam of tension and unresolved disputes built up by decades of confrontations between the two alliance systems. Many were also convinced that because the economics of the industrial powers, particularly Britain and Germany, were so interdependent, Europe could simply not remain at war for more that several months or at best a year.

C. Failed Peace

The widespread bitterness evoked by the unprecedented cost in lives and destruction of the war was redoubled by the utter failure of the peace conference convened by the victorious allies at Versailles. The Germans' willingness to negotiate an armistice owed much to their faith in Woodrow Wilson's frequent promises that he would seek a peace that was not aimed at punishing the defeated powers but focused on establishing a viable new world order in which such a war could never again occur.

D. World War I and the Nationalist Assault on the European Colonial Order

Four long years of intra-European slaughter severely disrupted the systems of colonial domination that had been expanded and refined in the century leading up to World War I. The conflict also gave great impetus to the forces of resistance that had begun to well up in the decades before the war. Although the actual process of decolonization would occur in most areas only after a second global conflict two decades later, World War I enhanced the standing of nationalist leaders, such as Gandhi, in major ways. The demands placed on colonized peoples during the war also contributed significantly to popular dissatisfaction with Western domination and widespread protest in a number of colonies during and after the conflict.

II. CHAPTER REVIEW

   A. What moves toward internationalism preceded World War I?

   B. What long term causes led to World War I?

   C. How was World War I fought that made it different from previous wars?

   D. How did World War I change Western governments and societies?

   E. Why would any conflict between European nations involve the world?

   F. How did World War I end?

III. VOCABULARY

   A. Internationalization

   B. World Court

   C. Submarine warfare

   D. Balfour Declaration

   E. League of Nations

   F. Archduke Ferdinand

   G. Western front

   H. Effendi

IV. MAP EXERCISES

   A. Map 28.1: *World War I* (Page 673)
      1. Alliances
          a. Identify nations belonging to the Entente powers.

    b. Identify nations belonging to the Central Powers.

  2. Geography and War
    a. What geographic advantages did the Central Powers possess?

    b. Why is Russia virtually isolated? How would this affect her?

    c. Why is the Ottoman Empire exposed to Allied attack?

    d. What problems relative to sea movement do Britain and Germany have?

V.   INTERPRETING CHARTS AND TABLES

A. Chart 28.1: *World War I Loses* (Page 681)
  1. Loses
    a. Which country had the most killed and wounded? The least?

    b. How might these loses affect Germany, Russia, Austria, and France?

    c. Why might the U.S. have a different perspective on the war?

  2. Drawing Conclusions
    a. Russia had greater loses than listed here. Why?

    b. How would number of wounded be a burden of a society at war?

    c. Most killed would have been young men. How would this affect a society?

VI.   MULTIPLE-CHOICE QUESTIONS

1. The immediate cause for the outbreak of World War I was
    A. nationalist tensions.
    B. a naval race between Germany and Great Britain.
    C. colonial disputes over Morocco.
    D. conflicting alliances.
    E. the Industrial Revolution.

2. The influence of technology on modern warfare is demonstrated by all of these developments in World War I EXCEPT:
    A. submarines.
    B. airplanes and aerial warfare.
    C. the destructive power of artillery and machine guns.
    D. mechanized warfare as demonstrated during the Blitzkrieg.
    E. poisonous gases and barbed wire.

3. Which of the following statements about the effects of World War I and the Great Depression on world governments is a FACT?
   A. Both made governments more responsive to the needs of the governed.
   B. Both made it easier for the military to dominate the government.
   C. Both supported the rise of totalitarian dictatorships.
   D. Both encouraged the growth of democracy and representative governments.
   E. Both led to the unprecedented growth of governments and their intervention in society.

4. It was inevitable the conflict in Europe would become a world war because
   A. Great Britain and France had existing alliances with Japan and the U.S.
   B. the European combatants had colonies and forces around the world.
   C. Germany attacked China and Japan.
   D. Germany had alliances with Brazil, Argentina, and Mexico.
   E. the U.S. was heavily invested in German industry and protected its ally.

5. The biggest battles outside of Europe during World War I occurred in
   A. African colonies of Europe.
   B. East Asia where Japan and China fought each other.
   C. the Middle East where the Turks fought Britain, Russia, and France.
   D. the Pacific where Germany and Japan fought for control of many islands.
   E. Latin America where Mexico invaded the United States.

6. The immediate result of World War I was the
   A. rise of the United States as a great power.
   B. beginning of European decolonization.
   C. rise of Japan to great power status.
   D. Great Depression.
   E. collapse of all European empires.

7. The principle of Woodrow Wilson that influenced future decolonization was
   A. immediate independence for all colonies.
   B. evacuation of all occupied territories.
   C. popular self-determination.
   D. reparations for war damage.
   E. the League of Nations.

8. The Indian Congress Party
   A. was composed primarily of peasants and Muslim holy men.
   B. from the outset took part in acts of violence against the British Raj.
   C. included only Hindus.
   D. was initially loyal to the British rulers and primarily concerned with interests of the Indian elite.
   E. was a radical faction devoted to the ousting of British rule by any means needed.

9. Which of the following statements concerning British administration of India in the last decades of the nineteenth century is most accurate?
   A. The British demilitarization of India caused substantial unemployment, particularly in Punjab.
   B. The enlightened British policy, begun in the 1880s, of fostering Indian industrialization through tariffs on imported British goods began to improve the Indian economy.
   C. British emphasis on the production of cash crops such as jute, cotton, and indigo led to shortages of food production in India.
   D. Indian economic dependency on Britain was beginning to end, as more of the steel for the production of railways was produced on the subcontinent.
   E. India never had a strict dependency on the British.

10. Who was the first Indian leader with a genuine mass following?
   A. J. Nehru
   B. M. K. Gandhi
   C. M. A. Jinnah
   D. B. G. Tilak
   E. C. J. Bodisramda

VII. ESSAY QUESTIONS

A. What caused World War I?

B. Compare and contrast the effects of World War I upon the domestic political and economic affairs of the involved nations.

C. Discuss the consequences of the agreements concluding World War I.

D. What forces led to European loss of colonial dominance?

E. What was the "Indian prototype" of decolonization movements?

F. How did the early Egyptian nationalist movement vary from that of India?

CHAPTER 29
The World by the 1920s: Challenges to European Domination
Pages 700 – 725

I.   SUMMARY

A. The Disarray of Western Europe

The interwar period, the 1920s and 1930s, was influenced by the political and economic changes brought by World War I and the crises that ended with World War II. Important social and cultural developments occurred. The emergence of revolutionary and authoritarian regimes was another unsettling factor. The rise of Japan and the United States intensified international competition.

B. Industrial Societies Outside Europe

World War I brought the United States to a world leadership position. But the nation opted for isolationist policies, although it did intervene in Latin America. The American economy boomed during the 1920s, producing consumer goods for domestic and foreign markets. The United States became the first mass-consumer society. Corporations were efficient and innovative, and introduced new product lines and production approaches. American culture, such as jazz and films, spread widely.

C. Revolution: The First Waves

Revolutions and anticolonial movements in Mexico, Russia and China posed a direct challenge to more established powers. Alternatives were advanced to Western political, economic, and social forms.

II. CHAPTER REVIEW

A. What changes occurred as a result of the Mexican Revolution?

B. Characterize the "Roaring 20s".

C. What factors led to the rise of the Fascists in Italy?

D. Why did the liberal experiment in Russia fail?

E. Why did Europe accept decolonization and what were its effects on Europe?

F. How did the post-war era represent a fundamental diplomatic shift for Europe?

G. What elements led to Nationalist seizure of power in China?

H. Why did the Nationalists fail to achieve permanent success in China?

I. What was the basis for Lenin and Stalin's domestic and economic policies? How did they differ?

III. MAP EXERCISES

A. Map 29.1: *Eastern Europe and the Soviet Union* (Pages 706)
   1. Post-War Boundaries
      a. What was the Treaty of Brest-Litovsk?
      b. Who lost the most territory?

B. Map 29.3: *China in the Era of Revolution and Civil War* (Page 721)
   1. In what region of China did the Communists eventually exert the most control?

   2. What nations belong to the European Union?

IV. MULTIPLE-CHOICE QUESTIONS

1. World War I and the immediate aftermath of the Versailles Treaty
   A. produced a decade in the 1920s of great economic instability.
   B. resolved many if not most of the issues affecting World War I.
   C. led to the political polarization of European parties between right and left.
   D. saw a realistic appraisal that wars could be avoided.
   E. had little demographic or social impact on Western society.

2. All of these conditions were characteristic of the 1920s in the West EXCEPT:
   A. industrial production boomed.
   B. mass consumption standards rose.
   C. technology increasingly impacted the economy and daily life.
   D. unemployment declined.
   E. women joined the work force in ever-larger numbers.

3. Which of the following statements concerning women's suffrage in the 1920s is most accurate?
   A. Despite their service in World War I, women remained without the vote everywhere but in the United States.
   B. Women had been briefly granted the vote during the war, but the female franchise was rapidly withdrawn when the conflict ended.
   C. Women's suffrage was granted after World War I in Britain, Germany, and the United States.
   D. Granting women's suffrage during the war converted many governments to feminist principles.
   E. Women had the vote throughout the pre-war period, but it was suspended indefinitely during the early years of mobilization.

4. Which of the following factors limited Japanese economic advance prior to World War II?
   A. continued dependence on relatively few export products
   B. low population growth
   C. the failure of the agricultural economy
   D. rapidly increasing wages in the work force
   E. none of the answers are correct

5. Francisco Madero
   A. was a member of the elite whose failed opposition to Díaz initiated the Mexican Revolution.
   B. was an Indian lawyer from Oaxaca who led the liberal revolution against Díaz.
   C. was removed from power by Porfirio Díaz.
   D. was able to initiate land reform and the expropriation of foreign property in Mexico.
   E. was the Hapsburg emperor of Mexico.

6. Which of the following reforms was NOT included in the Mexican Constitution of 1917?
   A. the state takeover of property belonging to the Catholic Church
   B. limited foreign ownership of key resources
   C. land reform
   D. guaranteed rights for workers
   E. all of the answers are correct

7. The Mexican muralist movement was indicative of
   A. the anti-Communist spirit of the Mexican Revolution.
   B. the policy of indigenism that was incorporated into the post-revolutionary reforms.
   C. the failure of the revolution to incorporate the Indians.
   D. the failure of Latin America to develop a significant indigenous cultural form.
   E. The muralist movement was Chilean, not Mexican.

8. How did Stalin's view of Communism differ from that of Lenin?
   A. Lenin was only interested in the Russian Revolution and did not visualize any further revolutionary process.
   B. Lenin was more interested in including a broad swath of the Russian population in the Communist movement.
   C. Stalin concentrated on a strongly nationalist version of Communism and concentrated on socialism in one country.
   D. Stalin was not a member of the Communist party.
   E. Their views did not differ.

9. Who succeeded Lenin as head of the Soviet state?
   A. Joseph Stalin
   B. Nikita Khrushchev
   C. Leonid Brezhnev
   D. Leon Trotsky
   E. Nicola Carsnekov

10. Sun Yat-sen was the
    A. first leader of the Communist discussion group at the University of Beijing.
    B. most powerful regional warlord of northern China.
    C. leader of the Revolutionary Alliance and first elected president of China.
    D. head of the Whampoa Military Academy.
    E. last of the Japanese shoguns.

11. What nation supplied most of the early support for the Chinese Nationalist movement?
    A. the United States
    B. the Soviet Union
    C. Japan
    D. Germany
    E. Australia

12. Who emerged as the head of the Nationalist party and the de facto ruler of China by the late 1920s?
    A. Sun Yat-sen
    B. Mao Zedong
    C. Chiang Kai-shek
    D. Li Dazhao
    E. Lui Haidong

V. Essay Questions

    A. What conditions led to the outbreak of the first Russian Revolution?

    B. How did Lenin change Marxism to fit the needs of Russian society and realities?

    C. How was the Bolshevik Party organized and what policies did it pursue?

    D. How did the Communists gain control in Russia between 1917 and 1921?

    E. What patterns did 20th century revolutions take?

    F. How did Stalin centralize control within Russia? With what results?

CHAPTER 30
The Great Depression and the Authoritarian Response
Pages 726 – 749

I.   SUMMARY

A.   The Global Great Depression

The economic depression that dominated the 1930s was international in scope. Economic shocks were particularly severe in Western Europe and the United States. The depression triggered important new governmental policies and also furthered extremist political forces in many countries. The Great Depression resulted from problems in the industrial economies of the West, combined with long-term structural weaknesses in other parts of the world. The result was a worldwide collapse that spared few economies.

B.   Economic and Political Changes in Latin America

During and after World War I, Latin American economies expanded and the population continued to increase, especially in the cities. The growth of middle class and working class populations challenged traditional oligarchies and resulted in new political parties, often populist and nationalist. These new parties and the traditional elites attacked liberalism and laissez-faire capitalism, which were clearly in crisis by the time of the Great Depression.

C.   The Militarization of Japan

The first decades of the 20th century brought important changes to east Asia as China was consumed with internal problems and Japan surged ahead economically and militarily. Japan's economic strength showed in its quick rebound from the Great Depression, but after some experiments with fuller democracy, its political system moved toward growing militarism.

D.   Stalinism in the Soviet Union

After an experimental phase in the 1920s, Stalinism dominated the Soviet system for nearly two decades. Stalin's system involved increased police repression, rapid industrialization, agricultural collectivization, and ultimately the Soviet Union's successful defense against the German invasion in World War II.

E. New Political and Economic Realities

Change undermined long-standing traditions in all institutions and structures. Governments changed, often adopting Western style institutions, and all governments took on new roles in societies and economies. Belief systems were modified or challenged by systems that were more secular. Growing interest in science also challenged them. Another change was the displacement of long-standing beliefs in rigid social inequalities.

II. CHAPTER REVIEW

G. What conditions led to the Great Depression?

H. How did western Europe and the U.S. respond to the Depression?

I. Discuss the factors that combined and resulted in breeding Fascism in Germany.

J. How did World War I affect Latin America?

K. Discuss the ascendancy of Japan's military during the 1930s, and their economic and industrial advancements.

L. Why and how did the Soviet Union become a great power and how did it create and administer its empire?

M. What economic and cultural policies did Communist regimes follow?

III. VOCABULARY

A. Soviet, Congress of Soviets

B. Bolshevik

C. Social Revolutionary Party

D. Russian, Bolshevik Revolutions

E. Nationalization

F. Red Army

G. New Economic Policy (NEP)

H. Kulaks

I. Union of Soviet Socialist Republics (USSR)

J. Supreme Soviet, Politburo

K. Joseph Stalin

L. Socialism in One Country

M. Collectivization

N. 5-Year Plans

O. Centralized (Command) Economy

P. Socialist Realism

IV. MAP EXERCISES

A. Map 30.1: *The Spread of Japan to the Outbreak of World War II* (Page 741)
  1. Manchukuo
    a. Trace the control of this Chinese region from 1910 to 1938.

    b. Why was this region desirable to the Japanese?

    c. How did World War I affect the geography of Russia?

V. VISUALIZING THE PAST: *Socialist Realism* (Page 746)

A. What values does the picture represent about:
  1. Women?

  2. Work?

  3. Technology?

B. How does the picture conform to the description of Socialist Realism discussed in the document?

VI. PHOTO ESSAY: *Soviet Realities* (Pages 726, 744, and 746) Despite all the propaganda that the Soviet regime put out, Soviet citizens had to live very real and often bleak lives. How do the pictures depict the realities of living in a Socialist state and what values do they represent? Lenin and Communism talked about building a worker's paradise. To what extent do these pictures represent and depart from this idea?

VII.   DOCUMENT ANALYSIS: *Socialist Realism* (Pages 745)

    A. Document Analysis
        1. Who wrote it? (Attribution includes biographical references)

        2. What was the author's point of view?

        3. How reliable is the document? Why?

        4. What was the intent or purpose behind the documents?

        5. Who was the intended audience?

        6. What is the document's tone?

    B. Analysis
        1. What purpose did culture and art serve in Soviet society?

        2. How did the Soviets view Western life?

        3. What was the proper role of the intellectual in Soviet society?

        4. How did the intellectual internalize socialism and socialist reality?

VIII.   MULTIPLE-CHOICE QUESTIONS

    1. The state called the Union of Soviet Socialist Republics (U.S.S.R.)
        A. allowed local autonomy to smaller governmental units.
        B. granted equality to the different nationalities.
        C. permitted a free market economy with no central control of economics.
        D. respected human rights.
        E. recognized the multinational character of the state but put the peoples under the
            control of the communists.

    2. In order to fund his rapid industrialization and provide labor for his factories, Stalin
        A. borrowed money from the Western allies.
        B. reestablished trade relations with Russia's old trading partners.
        C. collectivized Russian agriculture.
        D. gave land to the richer, more successful peasants in order to raise money.
        E. allowed freedom of enterprise and profit if a percentage of the earnings were paid
            to the state.

3. Stalin's economic policies are BEST categorized as a(n)
   A. free market.
   B. traditional economic system.
   C. laissez faire economy.
   D. centrally planned economy.
   E. mixed system.

4. Throughout Soviet history, the weakest sector of the Russian economy due to collectivization and lack of initiative was the
   A. industrial sector.
   B. foreign trade sector.
   C. agricultural sector.
   D. technological sector.
   E. defense industries sector.

5. Which of the following actions did governments take in 1929 with the onset of the depression?
   A. National tariffs were raised to keep out the goods of other countries.
   B. A new spirit of cooperation led to the formation of international trade agreements between nations.
   C. Most governments increased spending to provide an economic stimulus to their threatened economies.
   D. Governments successfully reduced unemployment through the creation of public service jobs.
   E. None of the answers are correct.

6. What event historically triggered the Great Depression?
   A. World War II
   B. World War I
   C. Collapse of the American stock market
   D. The attack on Pearl Harbor
   E. None of the answers are correct

7. What was the Scandinavian response to the Great Depression?
   A. Martial law
   B. Increased governmental spending
   C. An invasion of Holland
   D. Withdrawal from the League of Nations
   E. An immediate switch to the silver standard of currency

8. In 1935, Italy invaded what country?
   A. France
   B. The Sudan
   C. Algeria
   D. Ethiopia
   E. Madagascar

9. Franklin Roosevelt's program introducing several social insurance programs in the U.S. was called the
   A. Five year Plan.
   B. Fair Deal.
   C. New Deal.
   D. Fast Deal.
   E. Popular Front.

10. The Anschluss was the longed-for reunification of Germany and
    A. Poland.
    B. the Sudetenland.
    C. Russia.
    D. Austria.
    E. the Netherlands.

IX.   ESSAY QUESTIONS

   A. In what ways did Stalinism alter the original concepts of Soviet economy and government?

   B. In what ways did the cultural policies of the Stalin regime depart from traditional Russian practices? In what ways did it emphasize them?

   C. Compare and contrast Soviet industrialization and the West's Industrial Revolution.

   D. Compare and contrast the Soviet political system with its Western counterpart.

CHAPTER 31
A Second Global Conflict and the End of the European World Order
Pages 750-777

I.   SUMMARY

A. Old and New Causes of a Second World War

When the Kuomintang appeared to be successfully reunifying China, the Japanese military moved to secure their gains. Manchuria was proclaimed the independent state of Manchuko in 1931. Germany under Hitler pushed its aggressive response to the loss of World War I and the rise of the Soviet Union. Italy conquered Ethiopia, and both Germany and Italy aided the defeat of the Spanish republic.

B. Unchecked Aggression and the Coming of War in Europe and the Pacific

In 1937, the Japanese began a massive invasion of China. The Kuomintang retreated inland and continued resistance. The Germans invaded Poland in 1939 to begin the war in Europe.

C. The Conduct of a Second Global War

The reluctant Western democratic and Russian reaction to the aggressions of the Axis gave them initial success. Once the Nazis were checked in the Soviet Union, and the United States entered the war, the balance turned.

D. War's End and the Emergence of the Superpower Standoff

The victors in the war attempted to make a peace avoiding the mistakes made after World War I. The United Nations was established to allow for peaceful settlement of disputes. The great powers – the United States, the Soviet Union, Britain, France, China — controlled decisions in the Security Council. The defeated powers and newly independent colonial nations later gained membership. The United Nations took over the more specialized international agencies, such as the World Court of Justice, and played a key role in humanitarian endeavors.

E. Nationalism and Decolonization

World War II was fatal to the European colonial empires. European states populations were too devastated to consider fighting to keep Asia and Africa subjugated. Both the United States and the Soviet Union were hostile to continuation of European colonies. A reluctant Britain, in return for American support, in 1941 agreed to the Atlantic Charter, a pact recognizing the right of people to choose their own government.

II.   CHAPTER REVIEW

A. How did totalitarianism lead to World War II?

B. How was World War II fought and ended?

C. What is a total war and how does it affect the societies involved?

D. What agreements settled World War II and structured the post-war world?

III.   VISUALIZING THE PAST: *On National Leadership* (Page 770)

A. Leaders
    1. What do the dress and poses of each of the leaders tell you about the images they wished to project?

    2. How well did these leaders interact with their European counterparts?

IV.   DOCUMENT ANALYSIS: *Japan and the Loss in World War II* (Pages 763)

A. Document Analysis
    1. Who wrote it? (Attribution includes biographical references)

    2. What was the author's point of view?

    3. How reliable is the document? Why?

    4. What was the intent or purpose behind the document?

    5. Who was the intended audience?

    6. What is the document's tone?

B. Analysis
1. Why did the author accept defeat? Why did he ignore the military?

2. What attitudes and values of the author will help post-war reconstruction?

3. How did Japan and American ways of dealing with issues differ?

4. How do you think the author will view American suggestions and ways?

V.   MULTIPLE-CHOICE QUESTIONS

1. World War II officially began in what year?
   A. 1940
   B. 1941
   C. 1939
   D. 1935
   E. 1918

2. In 1931, the Japanese army marched into _____ and declared it an independent state.
   A. Korea
   B. Vietnam
   C. the Philippines
   D. Manchuria
   E. Laos

3. Adolph Hitler was the political and ideological leader of the
   A. Social Democratic Party.
   B. National Socialist Party.
   C. Christian Democratic Party.
   D. Conservative Union.
   E. None of the answers are correct.

4. Hitler came to power in Germany
   A. as a result of entirely legal and constitutional means.
   B. with the support of socialists.
   C. after a short, but violent, overthrow of the constitutional government.
   D. after a lengthy civil war between forces of conservatives and communists.
   E. as the result of a political assassination.

5. In order to avoid a two-front war, Hitler signed a nonaggression pact with this country in 1939.
   A. Russia
   B. Japan
   C. Italy
   D. France
   E. Great Britain

6. A 1944 allied landing in this country created a European front against the Germans.
   A. Belgium
   B. France
   C. Sicily
   D. Spain
   E. Egypt

7. This country chose a path of neutrality and cooperation with Japan in the Pacific theater of WWII.
   A. Australia
   B. The Philippines
   C. Indonesia
   D. Thailand
   E. New Zealand

8. This institution was created as a result of WWII.
   A. The League of Nations
   B. The United Nations
   C. The World Bank
   D. The International Monetary Fund
   E. The World Court

9. The Afrikaner National Party in South Africa established a rigid system of racial segregation called
   A. Boer prejudice.
   B. voortrekker.
   C. apartheid.
   D. swartzfrei.
   E. Jim Crow.

10. Which of the following nations achieved independence without violence?
    A. Indonesia
    B. Philippines
    C. Indochina
    D. India
    E. The United States

VI. ESSAY QUESTIONS

A. Discuss the common elements of colonization movements in south Asia, the Middle East, and Africa.

B. Discuss the proposition that both the outcomes of World War II were the result of problems created in the Treaty of Versailles.

C. Define "total war." How did the World Wars of the twentieth century demonstrate the application of "total war"?

D. In what ways did the settlement of World War II repudiate the Versailles treaties that ended World War I? In what ways did the settlement affirm the concepts included in the Versailles treaties?

CHAPTER 32
Western Society and Eastern Europe in the Decades of the Cold War
Pages 778-811

I.   SUMMARY

   A. After World War II: International Settings for the West

   Western European physical and economic structures were in ruins after the war. Millions of displaced peoples were refugees. Colonial societies took advantage of the weakness of their rulers.

   B. The Resurgence of Western Europe

   New leaders emerged who worked to avoid the mistakes of the past. After 1945, their nations moved forward on three fronts: extension of democratic political forms; modification of inter-European rivalries; and a commitment to economic growth.

   C. Political Stability and the Question Marks

   Contentious political issues were lacking in most of Europe during the post-1945 years as more conservative governments replaced reforming administrations. The conservatives supported existing programs; their less conservative successors had few dramatic programs to offer. The state's new social and economic role had been accepted. The calm was jolted by student protests in many countries during the late 1960s. The United States had a strong civil rights movement seeking equal treatment for African-Americans. Most of the agitation was contained by repression or reform by the 1970s, although new issues — feminism, environmentalism - became important. As economic growth slowed, conservative politicians emerged to boost private enterprise and reduce the impact of the welfare state. Despite the change, the principal lines of postwar government endured.

   D. Cold War Allies: The United States, Canada, Australia, and New Zealand

   Although the overseas western world had suffered less from the crises of the century, they developed similarly to western Europe. An important change occurred in foreign policy. The United States became an active world power. The dominions moved closer to the United States and made new contacts with other world areas.

E. Culture and Society in the West

Economic and political changes altered the pattern of previous industrial development. Many of the differences between Western societies, including the United States, disappeared. By the 1950s, the West became the first example of an advanced industrial society.

F. Eastern Europe After World War II: A Soviet Empire

Both eastern and western Europe experienced similar social changes after the war. Important differences were due to the regions distinctive traditions, the effects of the Cold War, Communist rule, and less-developed industrialization.

G. Soviet Culture: Promoting New Beliefs and Institutions

The Soviet government had a vigorous cultural agenda. It declared war on religion and aimed at creating Marxist secularism. The Orthodox Church remained, but it was under firm state control. Religious freedom for Jews was curtailed; Muslims fared better if they were loyal to the regime. Artistic and literary styles were kept within the party line. Modern Western ideas were regarded as decadent, but traditional classical music and ballet received state support. There was some interaction with Western styles; jazz and rock music bands emerged by the 1980s. Despite the imposed state limits, Russian literature remained diverse and creative; their freedom of expression depended upon the changing mood of the leadership. Even critical writers, like the exiled Aleksander Solzhenitsyn, maintained distinctive Russian values. Soviet culture placed great emphasis on science and social science. Although they were monitored by the state, significant developments occurred. In all, Soviet culture, with its state control, was neither traditional nor Western.

II.   CHAPTER QUESTIONS

A. How did the Cold War affect Western Europe?

B. What is the "welfare state"?

C. How did the social structure of the West change in the period after Word War II?

D. How did Soviet foreign policy change after 1945?

E. How was Soviet economy and society similar to that of the West?

F. Describe the cultural experience occurring in Western and Soviet-influenced societies during the late 20th century.

III.   VOCABULARY

A. Cold War

B. Eastern block

C. Harry Truman

D. Iron curtain

E. Marshall Plan

F. North Atlantic Treaty Organization

G. Warsaw Pact

H. Welfare state

I. Green Movement

J. Margaret Thatcher and Ronald Reagan

K. European Union

IV.   DOCUMENT ANALYSIS: *A New Wave of Soviet Reform* (Pages 808–809)

A. Document Analysis
   1. Who wrote the document? (Attribution includes biographical references)

   2. What was the author's points of view?

   3. How reliable are is the document? Why?

   4. What was the intent or purpose behind the document?

   5. Who was the intended audience?

   6. What is the document's tone?

B. Comparison
   1. What barriers must each woman overcome?

   2. Which women would have an easier time of changing society? Why?

3. How might Latin Americans of African descent see these issues?

V.   MAP EXERCISES – *Soviet and Eastern European Boundaries* (Page 781)
   1. Alliances
      a. What countries were allied with the U.S.? The Soviet Union?
      b. What nations were neutral?
      c. Why are Yugoslavia and China critical to both alliances?

   2. Geo-politics and military considerations
      a. How does geographic location help and hinder the
         (1) American-led alliance?
         (2) Soviet-led alliance?

VI. MULTIPLE-CHOICE QUESTIONS

   1. What crisis emerged in 1956 that demonstrated the diminished powers of European nations in world affairs?
      A. Portugal attempted to reassert its control over Goa.
      B. The Netherlands sought to establish colonial rule in South Africa.
      C. Britain and France attempted forcibly to halt Egypt's nationalization of the Suez Canal.
      D. France was driven from Libya.
      E. None of the answers are correct.

   2. What French leader negotiated Algeria's independence in 1962?
      A. King Charles V
      B. Marshal Petain
      C. General Boulanger
      D. Charles de Gaulle
      E. Emile Zapata

   3. What phrase did Winston Churchill coin to describe the division between free and repressed societies after World War II?
      A. the red menace
      B. the iron curtain
      C. the Berlin Wall
      D. the cold war
      E. the Marshall Plan

   4. Where was the focal point of the Cold War in Europe immediately after World War II?
      A. Hungary
      B. Czechoslovakia
      C. France
      D. Germany
      E. Italy

5. Which of the following was consistent with the political viewpoint of the Christian Democrats?
   A. totalitarian government
   B. democratic institutions and moderate social reform
   C. abolition of trade unions
   D. nationalization of all industries
   E. suppression of the Catholic Church

6. What work by Simone de Beauvoir signified the beginning of the new feminism in 1949?
   A. *Patriarchal Society*
   B. *The Feminine Mystique*
   C. *The Second Sex*
   D. *Fear of Flying*
   E. *The Solidarity of Women*

8. Which of the following nations did NOT remain independent of direct Soviet control by 1948?
   A. Greece
   B. Albania
   C. Yugoslavia
   D. Poland
   E. Turkey

9. The independent labor movement in Poland that challenged Soviet dominance was called
   A. Comintern.
   B. Solidarity.
   C. Izvestia.
   D. Pravda.
   E. Perestroika.

10. What Soviet leader emerged to take primary power in 1956?
    A. Joseph Stalin
    B. Mikhail Gorbachev
    C. Yuri Andropov
    D. Nikita Khrushchev
    E. Yuri Gagarin

VII. ESSAY QUESTIONS

A. Describe some of the societal and political changes of the 1970s.

B. In what ways did Stalinism alter the original concepts of Soviet economy and government?

C. In what ways did the cultural policies of the Stalin regime depart from traditional Russian practices? In what ways did it emphasize them?

D. How did the failures of the Soviet economy lead, in part, to the changes in Soviet policy after 1985?

CHAPTER 33
Latin America –
Revolution and Reaction
in the 21st Century
Pages 812-833

I.   SUMMARY

A. Latin America After World War II

The Mexican Revolution (1910 – 1920) was a violent reaction to authoritarian modernization. It produced a new sense of nationalism, reforms, and an institutionalized party that took over the presidency and remained in power through the mid-1990s.

B. Radical Options in the 1950s

Frustration with the failures of social, political, and economic reforms led to radical solutions that were often influenced by socialist or communist ideas. In Bolivia, Guatemala, and Cuba, revolutionaries tried to change the nature of government and society, and eliminate foreign economic controls, but such changes also had to accommodate the reality of the Cold War and the interests of the United States.

C. The Search for Reform and the Military Option

Programs based upon Catholic, Marxist, and capitalist doctrines were used to seek solutions for Latin American problems. Military governments based on nationalism and advocating economic development created a "bureaucratic authoritarianism," which served the Cold War interests of the United States. By the 1980s, a new wave of democratic regimes was emerging.

D. Societies in Search of Change

Social relations changed slowly in Latin America. Inequalities based on ethnicity continued in many places. Women had entered the labor force in great numbers but only began to gain the right to vote after 1929. Population growth, urbanization, and migration continued to challenge the region.

II. CHAPTER QUESTIONS

A. What caused the Cuban Revolution?

B. What motivated the post-revolutionary culture and politics in Mexico?

C. How did revolution change Mexican society? Cuban?

D. What unresolved challenges has Mexico faced during the last decade?

E. How did labor, middle class, and ideology influence society in the 20th century?

F. What pressures led to radical changes during the 1950s?

G. What ideologies were common in the 1960s and 1970s? What did they advocate?

H. How did the military affect Latin American politics in the 20th century?

I. Since the 1980s, what successes has democracy had?

J. What role has the United States played in the 20th century?

K. What social developments has Latin America experienced this century?

L. What demographic shifts and movements has the region experienced since 1980?

III. VOCABULARY

A. Third World

B. Indianize

C. Cristeros

D. Party of the Institutionalized Revolution (PRI)

E. North American Free Trade Agreement (NAFTA)

F. Import Substitution Industrialization

G. Peronism (Argentina)

H. Corporatism

I. United Fruit Company; Arbenz

J. Cuban Revolution

K. Liberation Theology

L. Salvador Allende and Chile, 1973

M. Banana Republics

N. Good Neighbor Policy

O. Alliance for Progress

P. Sandinistas (Nicaragua)

IV. PHOTO ESSAY: The Muralist Movement

Note: Find any mural by Diego Rivera. Anyone of his murals can teach the history of Mexico in a visual format. They are excellent Document Based Questions. See the following websites:

1. THE DIEGO RIVERA MURAL PROJECT
   http://www.riveramural.org

2. THE ARTCHIVES
   http://www.artchive.com/

3. CAROL GERTEN'S ART MUSEUM
   http://sunsite.auc.dk/cgfa/index.html

V. DOCUMENT ANALYSIS: *The People Speak* (Pages 822–823)

A. Document Analysis
   1. Who wrote each? (Attribution includes biographical references)

   2. What were the authors' points of view?

   3. How reliable are the documents? Why?

   4. What were the intents or purposes behind the documents?

5. Who were the intended audiences?

6. What are the documents' tones?

B. Comparison
1. What barriers must each woman overcome?

2. Which woman would have an easier time of changing society? Why?

3. How might Latin Americans of African descent see these issues?

VI. TIMELINE: *Latin America and the World* (Page 814)

What role have revolutions, wars, and the United States played in Latin American diplomatic history?

VII. READING GRAPHS: Chart 32.3 – *Participation in the Mexican P.R.I.* (Page 817)

A. Which social group dominated the PRI in:
1. 1936?

2. 1959?

3. 1988?

B. What does the occupation category "people in general" represent?

C. What does your above answer say about change in Mexican society?

D. How revolutionary do you think the PRI was in 1988?

VIII. MAP EXERCISES – *U.S. Intervention in Central America* (Page 826)

A. Reading the Map
1. What territories in Central America and the Caribbean does the U.S. own?

2. In what countries did the United States intervene?

B. How might communists in Cuba and Nicaragua threaten the U.S.?

C. What other American interventions are not listed on the map? (See timeline)

D. How might the Latin Americans perceive the United States? Why might the U.S. look upon the area as its empire?

IX.   MULTIPLE-CHOICE QUESTIONS

1. All of these were 20th century Latin American revolutionary movements or
    revolutions EXCEPT:
    A. Liberation Theology.
    B. Nicaraguan Revolution.
    C. Cuban Revolution.
    D. Mexican Revolution.
    E. Haitian Revolution.

2. Which of these statements about post-Revolutionary Mexico is a FACT?
    A. Mexican revolutionaries attempted to assimilate Indians into national society.
    B. The revolution disapproved of land redistributions to peasants.
    C. The Roman Catholic Church was unaffected by the Revolution.
    D. The U.S. accepted the revolution and its changes largely without comment.
    E. Mexico nationalized foreign economic holdings throughout the country.

3. All of these are traditional Latin American populist political practices or ideas
    EXCEPT:
    A. anti-imperialism especially anti-American and anti-European.
    B. acceptance of communism.
    C. nationalism.
    D. nationalization of foreign assets.
    E. anti-establishment (supported by urban workers and rural peasants).

4. In 20th century Latin America, the military was typically
    A. small and usually ineffective.
    B. liberal and reform-minded.
    C. anti-Catholic and in favor of a secular society.
    D. democratic but involved in politics.
    E. socially conservative, elitist, and authoritarian.

5. Argentina's Peron and Brazil's Vargas regime were
    A. pro-European or Western.
    B. favorable to foreign investments in national industries.
    C. often simultaneously fascist, nationalistic, socialist, and populist.
    D. supportive of the communists.
    E. anti-union and anti-worker.

6. The largest impediment to radical reforms and leftist regimes in Latin America during the 1950s and 1970s was
   A. a working class unwilling to support radicalism.
   B. reactionary local militaries backed by American money and support.
   C. a small, ineffective working class.
   D. reforms carried out by the elites to democratize the society.
   E. opposition by the Roman Catholic Church.

7. Throughout 20th century Latin America, the group most often excluded from influence or marginalized in society was the
   A. intellectuals, especially writers and artists.
   B. clergy, especially Roman Catholic priests and nuns.
   C. indigenous peoples and descendants of African slaves.
   D. peasants and rural landowners.
   E. workers and miners.

8. The Latin American country and rulers who most directly challenged American regional hegemony during the Cold War was
   A. Mexico's Cardenas.
   B. Chile's Allende.
   C. Argentina's Peron.
   D. Brazil's Vargas.
   E. Cuba's Castro.

9. All of these Latin American nations experienced military dictatorships and repression during the 20th century EXCEPT:
   A. Chile.
   B. Argentina.
   C. Peru.
   D. Mexico.
   E. Venezuela.

10. Which statement about Latin America since the 1980s is a FACT?
    A. Economic development came at the expense of enormous foreign debts.
    B. Democracy and democratic rule was threatened by military takeovers.
    C. Conservative groups and elite parties still dominate Latin America.
    D. The U.S. has abandoned its long time role of intervention in the region.
    E. Latin America has been able to exterminate the Drug Trade and cartels.

11. The American policy most favored by the majority of Latin Americans in the 20th century has been
    A. Kennedy's Alliance for Progress.
    B. Franklin Roosevelt's Good Neighbor Policy.
    C. Jimmy Carter's return of the Panama Canal to Panama.
    D. Jimmy Carter's human rights campaign.
    E. the periodic occupation of many nations by United States' troops.

12. All of these are demographic trends and problems in 20th century Latin America EXCEPT:
    A. rapid urbanization.
    B. migration of unskilled laborers, the poor and politically repressed to richer countries.
    C. millions of refugees due to wars and famines.
    D. excessively large population growth rates.
    E. staggering growth of metropolitan primate (capital) cities.

X.   ESSAY QUESTIONS

    A. Compare and contrast gender relations in 20th century Latin America with any one of these regions: Western, African, or Asian equivalents.

    B. How have trade and industry in Latin America changed from 1800 – 2000?

    C. Compare and contrast American relations with Latin America and Britain's relations with its 19th and 20th century colonial empire.

    D. Compare and contrast Latin American populism, fascism and corporatism to Italian Fascism or German Nazism.

    E. Compare and contrast demographic and environmental changes in Latin America with Western lands or Asia.

CHAPTER 34
Africa, the Middle East, and Asia in the Era of Independence
Pages 834-861

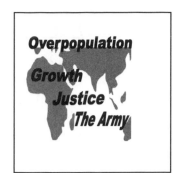

I. SUMMARY

A. The Challenges of Independence

In the early decades of independence, the existence of nation-states carved out of the colonial empires was challenged by internal rivalries, and in some cases, civil wars between different ethnic, religious, and social groups. Economic growth was hampered by unprecedented rates of population growth with rapid and often extreme urbanization, changes in the international market, and the continuing underdevelopment of most of the states. While some groups benefited, women continued to be disadvantaged in nearly all aspects of their lives.

B. Paths to Economic Growth and Social Justice

Leaders of newly independent African, Middle Eastern, and Asian nations had to deliver on their promises of social reform and economic prosperity. Different leaders adopted different approaches, and some tried one approach after another. Basic strategies included one party authoritarian rule with frequent coups and revolutions often by the military. Governments nationalized foreign assets and attempted land reforms in a combination of socialist and nationalist policies. And while the states attempted to develop what resources their states possessed, often it was development for some but not all of the people. Consequently, states fall into categories largely based on their development and stability. The first tier includes nations like India and Thailand, but very few African nations. Nations of this group have adequate resources, are relatively stable, and have made serious attempts to control population. The second tier of nations such as Nigeria, South Africa, Pakistan, and Iran has resources, but has been hampered by revolutions or internal conflicts. The third group of nations is too poor and too beset with troubles to remain viable.

II. CHAPTER REVIEW

A. What problems confronted the newly independent ex-colonial states?

B. How has ethnicity threatened many of the region's states?

C. What demographics-related problems threatened the region's states?

D. Why is the environment endangered in many of the region's states?

E. What achievements and disappointments have women faced in these states?

F. How have international economic conditions impacted development?

G. What political patterns have governments and politics followed in these states?

H. What role has the military played in post-colonial politics? With what results?

I. What different paths have Egypt, Iran, India, and South Africa taken?

III. VOCABULARY

A. "Artificial Nations"

B. Demographic transition

C. Parasitic cities

D. Religious revivalism

E. Primary products

F. Neo-Colonialism

G. Conditionalities

H. Green Revolution

I. Iranian Revolution

J. Globalization

K. Apartheid

L. Separatism, ethnic nationalism

IV. MAP EXERCISES:
A. Map 34.4: *The Middle East* (Page 852)
   1. The acronym PATIO meaning Persians, Arabs, Turks, Israelis, and Others best explains the Middle East. What culture and languages would each have?

2. Drawing Conclusions: Cause and Effect
   a. Iran and Iraq have large or predominant Shi'ite populations. How would this affect diplomatic relations with the rest of the region?

   b. Turkey abandoned the Arabic script and secularized the state in the 1920s. How might this affect Turkey's relations to the region?

   c. The Persian Gulf states are oil-rich. How might this affect their domestic and international policies?

   d. Egypt, Lebanon, Iraq, and Syria have large Christian populations, while Iraq, Turkey, and Lebanon have sizeable ethnic minorities. How might this affect domestic politics?

   e. Iran, Iraq, Syria, and Yemen are politically radical, Saudi Arabia is conservative, and Egypt, Jordan, Kuwait, Qatar, the United Arab Emirates, and Oman are moderate. How might this affect international alliances and domestic politics?

   f. Israel is largely Jewish and occupies Jerusalem, the third holiest city in Islam and the home of Christianity. The country is a regional power and allied to the US. How might this affect regional international relations?

V.   PHOTO ESSAY: *Challenges* (Pages 834, 839, 840, 841, 844, 850, 851, 853, and 859)

The newly independent nations have faced many problems. According to the photographs, what problems have plagued nations in the post-colonial era?

1. Political?

2. Economic?

3. Religious?

4. Social?

5. Environmental?

VI. DOCUMENT ANALYSIS: *Cultural Creativity* (Page 847)

A. Document Analysis
   1. Who wrote each? (Attribution includes biographical references)

   2. What were the authors' points of view?

3. How reliable are the documents? Why?

4. What were the intents or purposes behind the documents?

5. Who were the intended audiences?

6. What are the documents' tones?

B. Comparison
   1. How is the neo-colonial struggle evident in these literary selections?

   2. Are the problems Western in cause or do they predate Western arrival?

   3. How do the problems mirror situations in American society?

VII. STATISTICAL ANALYSIS:– *Populations* (Page 841)

A. What does the graph describe?

B. The graph uses two colors. What do they represent?

C. What trends characterize the change over time of the populations?

D. Which region(s) have had the greatest population growth?

VIII. MULTIPLE-CHOICE QUESTIONS

1. One dominant feature of post-colonial Asian and African nations was the
    A. Cold War rivalry between the U.S. and U.S.S.R.
    B. constant warfare between neighboring states over borders.
    C. class struggles and ethnic tensions that produced political instability.
    D. rise of socialist ideologies, which were blended with nationalist policies.
    E. persistence of European and Western economic controls.

2. The boundaries of many contemporary states, especially African nations,
    A. are representative of ethnic realities in the region or continent.
    B. generally conform to elements of physical geography such as rivers.
    C. have been rearranged since independence.
    D. are subject to frequent change.
    E. were set by colonial rivalries irrespective of ethnic or cultural realities.

3. In order to rule their colonies, Europeans frequently
   A. established a parliamentary system and allowed their subjects to vote.
   B. used one group to rule and played groups against each other.
   C. brought in foreign bureaucrats.
   D. failed to utilize traditional native elites.
   E. encouraged land reform and industrialization.

4. All of these modern African problems resulted from or were exacerbated by European colonial policies EXCEPT:
   A. intertribal warfare based on linguistic, cultural, and religious differences.
   B. wars of independence and secession by excluded ethnic groups.
   C. lack of loyalties to the nation-state.
   D. widespread reliance on the military and generals to rule nations.
   E. privileged economic and social elites ruling without mass support.

5. Most problems affecting the modern states in post-colonial Africa and Asia can be traced to
   A. overpopulation.
   B. industrialization.
   C. continuing neo-colonialism.
   D. linguistic, cultural, and religious differences.
   E. international warfare.

6. Inability to limit population growth in Africa and Asia is BEST attributed to
   A. lack of family planning and birth control programs.
   B. international demand for labor.
   C. cultural values and social traditions which block changes.
   D. European and Western successes in eliminating diseases, famine, and war.
   E. lack of educated elites and resources to implement programs.

7. The most destabilizing aspect of the 20th century demographic transition in Africa and Asia has been the
   A. rapid growth of the older segment of the population especially the elderly.
   B. international migration by productive populations to richer nations.
   C. decrease in poverty.
   D. increase of the productive portion of the population, especially those between 15 and 50.
   E. extreme urbanization with its accompanying urban problems with its drain on most national resources.

8. Which statement BEST describes women's situation in post-colonial Africa and Asia?
   A. While women have legal equality, they are rarely afforded equal opportunity for jobs, education, and in politics.
   B. Upper class educated women have established rights and exercise considerable power.
   C. Women's life spans in the developing world are longer than their male counterparts.
   D. Women are allowed to vote and encouraged to participate in the political process.
   E. As religious and cultural traditions erode, and secularism spreads, women are acquiring rights.

9. In the contemporary world economic system, ex-colonial Asian and African nations have
   A. developed industrialized, free market economies.
   B. built considerable infrastructures to support industry and commerce.
   C. attracted foreign developmental capital and industries from wealthier nations.
   D. remained largely sources for exportable raw minerals and cash crops.
   E. relied on tourism to develop.

10. A problem affecting development in ex-colonial states has been the
    A. lack of resources to trade.
    B. antiquated economic structures.
    C. lack of an entrepreneurial middle class.
    D. lack of funds to invest or to develop their nations.
    E. widespread corruption amongst officials and the ruling elites.

11. The style of government MOST favored in ex-colonial African and Asian states can be BEST described as a(n)
    A. one-party communist dictatorship.
    B. authoritarian military dictatorship.
    C. blend between socialism, democracy, and nationalism.
    D. traditional constitutional monarchies.
    E. largely democracies with elected executives and legislatures.

12. The army has become an important institution in many nations since 1950 for all of these reasons EXCEPT
    A. army units are usually disciplined and loyal to officers.
    B. it has a monopoly of force and power within society.
    C. soldiers and officers are often more educated and technically trained.
    D. the army is less susceptible to religious and ethnic rivalries.
    E. no other local or native institutions survived the colonial era.

13. The role of the Egyptian military and its leaders in their country's development since independence most closely parallels the
    A. military in Latin America during the 1960s, 1970s, and early 1980s.
    B. Red Army under the communists in the Russian Civil War.
    C. fascist armies of Franco and Mussolini in 1930s Spain and Italy.
    D. Indian National Congress Party of Nehru and Gandhi.
    E. depoliticized, neutral militaries in the US and Western Europe.

14. India differs from other ex-colonial 20th century nations such as Pakistan, Egypt, Burma and Nigeria in that
    A. its army constantly intervenes in national politics.
    B. it has avoided overpopulation.
    C. it preserved civilian and democratic rule of law and government since independence.
    D. it has failed to develop an important industrial and business sector.
    E. it avoided sectarian religious strife.

15. During the last decades of the 20th century, the event which has most determined Iranian development has been the
    A. autocratic reign Reza Pahlavi or the shah.
    B. Iranian religious revolution of the ayatollahs.
    C. alliance with the United States.
    D. war with Iraq.
    E. discovery and development of oil.

16. All of these developments are examples of late 20th century religious revivalism and sectarian nationalism EXCEPT the
    A. rise of fundamentalist movements across the Muslim and Hindu worlds.
    B. victory of extremely xenophobic nationalist parties in many nations.
    C. incidents of ethnic cleansing and genocide in many nations.
    D. founding of anti-colonial independence movements.
    E. rise of the religious radical right in the United States.

17. The apartheid program in South Africa could BEST be compared to
    A. the Nazi Holocaust against the Jews.
    B. the Israeli treatment of the Palestinians on the West Bank.
    C. segregation, "Jim Crow" and "separate but equal" laws in the United States.
    D. Gandhi's satyagraha campaign in India.
    E. immigration restrictions on foreign workers in Western Europe.

IX.   ESSAY QUESTIONS

A. Compare and contrast gender roles in Africa and Asia with one: Latin America, the Western world, or East Asia.

B. Compare and contrast post-colonial politics and economics of Africa with the newly independent Latin American states of the 1820s.

C. Compare and contrast 20th century economic development in Africa with either Latin America or East Asia.

D. How has Africa changed from 1000 to 2000 C.E.?

E. Compare and contrast 20th century roles of the military in African and Latin American societies.

F. Compare and contrast the demographic shift of 20th century Africa and Asia with the Neolithic Revolutions or the Industrial Revolution.

G. Compare and contrast African and Asian nationalisms with 19th century Western nationalism.

H. Compare and contrast the Iranian Revolution of the 1980s with any one of these revolutions: Russia, 1917; Mexico, 1910; Cuba, 1958, or China, 1911.

I. Compare and contrast social reforms and developments in post-colonial Africa and 1920s Soviet Russia.

J. Compare 20th century developments in any two of these nations: Iran, Egypt, India, South Africa, Argentina, Brazil, or Mexico.

K. Compare and contrast the legacies of colonialism in any two regions: Latin America, Africa, and Asia.

L. How has the Muslim world changed between 1000 and 2000 C.E.?

M. How has India changed from 1000 to 2000 C.E.?

CHAPTER 35
Rebirth and Revolution:
Nation-Building in East Asia and the Pacific Rim
Pages 862-891

I.   SUMMARY

A. East Asia in the Postwar Settlements

Adjustments at the end of World War II defined the Pacific Rim into the 1950s, as a zone of reasonably stable noncommunist states developed. Linked to the West, these states maintained a neo-Confucian emphasis on the importance of conservative politics and a strong state.

B. Japan, Incorporated

The keynotes of Japanese history from the 1950s onward were a fierce concentration on economic growth and distinctive political and cultural forms as the nation proved that industrial success did not depend on a strict Western pattern.

C. The Pacific Rim: New Japans?

Economic and some political developments in several other nations and city-states on Asia's Pacific coast mirrored elements in Japan's 20th-century history, although at a later date. The states of South Korea, Taiwan, Hong Kong and Singapore are called The Four Dragons. Political authoritarianism was characteristic, though usually with bows to parliamentary forms and with recurrent protests from dissidents. Government functions extended to careful economic planning and rapid expansion of the educational system, which emphasized technical training. Group loyalties promoted diligent labor and a willingness to work hard for low wages. Economic growth burgeoned, although problems appeared in the 1990s.

II.   CHAPTER REVIEW

A. Describe Japanese development between 1920 and 1940.

B. What factors led to the growth of militarism in Japan prior to World War II?

C. How did World War II affect the Pacific Rim?

D. How was Korea at the center of the Cold War?

E. Why did the Four Dragons emerge as leaders in the region?

F. What political, economic, and cultural styles developed in post-war Japan?

G. How did Japanese society differ from traditional Western societies?

H. To what extent did the Four Dragons economically, politically, and socially conform or depart from Japanese or Western counterparts?

I. What has been the American role in the Pacific Rim?

III.   VOCABULARY

A. Singapore

B. Douglas MacArthur

C. Liberal Democratic Party

D. Republic of Korea

E. Democratic People's Republic of Korea

F. Korean War

G. Taiwan

H. Hong Kong

I. Hyundai

J. Great Leap Forward

K. Cultural Revolution

L. Viet Minh

M. Viet Cong

IV. PHOTO ESSAY: *The Pacific and the World* (867, 868, 870, 871, 872, 879, and 882)

What is the military, economic or commercial, and cultural relationship between the Pacific Rim nations and the wider, especially Western world?

V. MAP EXERCISES: Map 35.1 – *China in the Civil War* (Page 876)
    A. 1934
        1. What groups controlled lands in China?

2. Who was the Nationalists' chief opposition?

3. Why might it be said that no one ruled China?

B. 1945
1. What was the Chinese power base like in 1935? 1945?

2. Why would Communists choose the route they took during the Long March?

VI. DOCUMENT ANALYSIS: *Women in Revolutionary Struggle* (Page 881)

A. Document Analysis
1. Who wrote each document? (Attribution includes biographical references)

2. What are the authors' points of view?

3. How reliable are the documents? Why?

4. What were the intents or purposes behind the documents?

5. Who were the intended audiences?

6. What are the documents' tones?

B. Analysis
1. What traditional roles did women have in Vietnam and China?

2. How do women plan to acquire equality with men?

3. How do these plans fit into the larger revolutionary struggle?

4. Comment: Women had to fight two revolutions – one against imperialists and another against men.

VII. MULTIPLE-CHOICE QUESTIONS

1. All of these nations are economic powerhouses of the Pacific Rim EXCEPT:
   A. Vietnam.
   B. Taiwan.
   C. Hong Kong.
   D. South Korea.
   E. Singapore.

2. One economic weakness of the Pacific Rim nations is a(n)
   A. vulnerability to economic conditions abroad especially trade fluctuations.
   B. large, uneducated force of workers.
   C. lack of ports or infrastructure to facilitate trade.
   D. inability to compete against Western industries.
   E. declining population.

3. During the 1930s in Japan the
   A. nation resisted the rising trend towards militarism and nationalism.
   B. nation worked closely with the League of Nations to avoid war.
   C. government granted Korea and Taiwan its independence.
   D. military ignored the elected political authorities and intervened in civilian government.
   E. government recognized the Communist states in Russia and China.

4. Between 1910 and 1945 Korea
   A. Allied with the United States to resist Japanese aggression.
   B. was invaded and occupied by China.
   C. remained neutral and isolated from outside influences.
   D. experienced an economic boom.
   E. was ruled by Japan, which suppressed indigenous institutions and culture.

5. The chief stimulus for the collapse of Western colonial rule and influence in the Pacific Rim was due to the
   A. communist victory in the Chinese civil war in 1945.
   B. British grant of independence to India in 1947.
   C. initial Japanese defeat of the Western colonial powers.
   D. American insistence during World War II that Europe grant its colonies independence.
   E. Russian invasion of Asian colonial territories in World War II.

6. Before 1950, the American role in Asia and the Pacific Rim is BEST described as
   A. largely colonial – the U.S. had obtained a large colonial empire.
   B. isolationist – the U.S. retreated to its prewar boundaries.
   C. interventionist – U.S. troops landed in China to support the Nationalists.
   D. militarily critical for Japan, the Philippines, and the Pacific islands with a temporarily waning influence on the Asian mainland.
   E. tolerant of colonialism and revival of the Japanese Empire.

7. Japan's postwar government is BEST characterized as a
   A. communist people's democracy.
   B. traditional monarchy with a hereditary emperor and little popular sovereignty.
   C. democracy dominated by a political and economic oligarchy.
   D. democratic republic with an unstable party system.
   E. militaristic state.

8. The chief tension within postwar Japan has been
   A. the lack of social mobility.
   B. a large non-Japanese ethnic minority deprived of any rights.
   C. limited rights for women and minorities.
   D. severe demographic dislocation due to rapid industrialization.
   E. a conflict between indigenous traditions or values, and Western influences.

9. Postwar Korean development has been largely determined by the
   A. occupation of the country by China and the Soviet Union.
   B. division of the peninsula between pro-Soviet and pro-capitalist states.
   C. long and autocratic rule by the Korean king.
   D. extreme hunger and poverty of the Korean peoples.
   E. devastation caused by World War II.

10. Following its defeat on mainland China, the Kuomintang or Nationalist Party led by Chiang Kai-shek
    A. collapsed.
    B. fled to Korea.
    C. fled to the island of Formosa and established a government.
    D. sought support from the U.S.S.R. for a prolonged fight against Mao's communists.
    E. joined with the Chinese Communist Party to form the People's Republic of China.

11. As a modern culture, the Japanese people most value
    A. stability.
    B. tradition.
    C. innovation.
    D. Western-style institutions.
    E. social equality.

12. The relationship between business and government in Japan, Korea, and Taiwan in the later half of the 20th century is BEST described as
    A. a communist style command economy.
    B. a socialist-capitalist mix of private property and public welfare.
    C. separated by American style constitutions.
    D. cooperative – the government encourages and protects businesses in an almost mercantilist manner.
    E. antagonistic towards each other.

13. In contemporary Japan and Taiwan,
    A. Christianity replaced the older Shinto and Confucian belief systems.
    B. both have military alliances with the United States.
    C. individualism and competitiveness are valued.
    D. populations are increasingly abandoning traditional ways and values.
    E. group consensus and collective decision making are most highly valued.

14. The second largely Christian country in the Pacific Rim (after the Philippines) is
    A. Taiwan.
    B. South Korea.
    C. Singapore.
    D. Japan.
    E. Hong Kong.

15. The Pacific Rim nation that has recently emerged as an economic giant and whose industries and products have challenged Japan, the United States, and Western Europe is
    A. North Korea.
    B. Taiwan.
    C. Hong Kong.
    D. South Korea.
    E. Singapore.

16. The chief concern and worry of contemporary Taiwan is
    A. its relationship to the communist regime in China, which claims to rule the island.
    B. its military alliance with the United States.
    C. its declining industrial base.
    D. widespread pollution caused by industry.
    E. the lack of democracy.

17. All of these problems are shared by the contemporary Pacific Rim nations EXCEPT:
    A. falling growth rates.
    B. a rise in unemployment.
    C. antagonisms between the United States and China, which threaten war.
    D. declining power of their national currencies.
    E. popular pressures for change in traditional political practices.

VIII. ESSAY QUESTIONS

    A. Compare and contrast the Chinese and Vietnamese communist revolutions with one of these: the Russian Revolution, Mexican Revolution, Cuban Revolution, or Iranian Revolution.

    B. How has China changed (politically, socially, economically, internationally, culturally or gender-wise) between 1000 C.E. and 2000 C.E.?

    C. Compare and contrast the role of women in the Chinese Revolution with the role of women in 20th century Western Europe or the United States.

    D. Compare and contrast industrial development in Communist China with similar developments in any one of these: (1) the European 19th century Industrial

Revolution, (2) Latin American economic developments in the 20th century; (3) developments in the USSR; or (4) 20th century developments in India.

E. Compare and contrast the Vietnamese struggle for independence with the campaign against apartheid in South Africa.

CHAPTER 36
Globalization and Resistance:
World History 1990-2003
Pages 892 – 925

I. SUMMARY

A. The End of the Cold War

By the 1980s, reforms began a process ending in the disintegration of the Soviet empire and the end of communism in eastern Europe. Conservative and untalented Soviet leaders were unable to solve growing problems. To counter the threat of Islamic fervor unleashed by the Iranian revolution, the Soviets in 1979 invaded Afghanistan and became caught in an unpopular and expensive war. Western Europe's successful economy put Communism on the defensive in eastern Europe. China demonstrated how a communist authoritarian nation could flourish by joining the international economy. The United States increased its pressure on the Soviets by large increases in military spending and interventions in favor of anti-marxist regimes.

B. The Great Powers and New Disputes

The United States became the sole superpower, while Russia's power dramatically declined. Other nations were unhappy with the new single-power dominance, but efforts at alliances did not change the situation. The United States pushed its political and economic model, and worked against potential threats from smaller nations. It intervened in regional conflicts, as in the Persian Gulf War of 1991 and in the Balkans. The terrorist attacks on the United States in 2001 raised new issues. The United States responded by changing the Islamic fundamentalist regime in Afghanistan.

C. Globalization

By the early 21st century, the unfolding of globalization - the increasing interconnectedness of all world parts - reflected the close of the Cold War and the lessening of international conflict, a movement to free markets, new technical developments (especially the computer), and a general acceptance of global connections. Complicating factors to globalization were lingering nationalism, an important religious surge, persisting nationalism, and terrorism.

D. A World of Religious and Ethnic Conflict

A resurgence of particular loyalties complicated globalization. Nationalism, subnational loyalties, and religious differences all helped stimulate intolerance or violence.

E. Global Warming and Other Perils

The opening of the communist world demonstrated that extreme economic devastation had occurred. Policies followed in China, southeast Asia, Brazil, and sub-Saharan Africa appeared equally dangerous. Economic development strategies designed to assist growth in many less-developed regions have failed to raise living standards or environmental damage. In 2000, the wealthiest one-fifth of humanity dominated consumption and produced the most pollution. No solutions were in sight.

F. Toward the Future

History has demonstrated that efforts to predict the future will fail, but it does allow a basis for thinking about what will occur.

II. CHAPTER REVIEW

A. In what way was the Soviet Union different after 1985?

B. Why did the Soviet Union disintegrate?

C. Compare and contrast the consequences of globalization in developed and less-developed nations.

D. Discuss the differing environmental policies in democratic and authoritarian societies.

III. VOCABULARY

A. Mikhail Gorbachev

B. Glasnost

C. Perestroika

D. Boris Yeltsin

E. Globalization

F. Multinational Corporations

MAP EXERCISES:

Map 36.1 – *Post Soviet-Union Russia* (Page 899)
A. How many new countries were created by the U.S.S.R. breakup?

Map 36.2 The Implosion of Yugoslavia (Page 905)
A. What ethnic faction retained the most territory after the Soviet breakup?

IV.　　DOCUMENT ANALYSIS: *Protests Against Globalization* (Page 914)

Document Analysis
　　Who wrote each document? (Attribution includes biographical references)

　　7.　What are the authors' points of view?

　　8.　How reliable are the documents? Why?

　　9.　What were the intents or purposes behind the documents?

　　10. Who were the intended audiences?

　　11. What are the documents' tones?

V.　　MULTIPLE-CHOICE QUESTIONS

　　1. Between the 1960s and the 1980s, approximately how many new states were admitted into the United Nations?
　　　A. ten
　　　B. twenty
　　　C. two hundred
　　　D. one hundred
　　　E. none

　　2. How long had the cold war lasted before its context began to shift after 1985?
　　　A. ten years
　　　B. forty years
　　　C. thirty years
　　　D. fifty years
　　　E. eighty years

3. A new strategic arms treaty called _____ was negotiated between the superpowers in 1979.
   A. SALT I
   B. SALT II
   C. NATO
   D. EFTA
   E. OPEC

4. What Russian leader significantly altered political, diplomatic, and economic policies in the Soviet Union after 1985?
   A. Yuri Andropov
   B. Leonid Brezhev
   C. Mikhail Gorbachev
   D. Yuri Gagarin
   E. Rudolph Nureyev

5. German reunification occurred in what year?
   A. 1991
   B. 1990
   C. 1988
   D. 1995
   E. 1955

6. In 1991, Boris Yeltsin emerged as head of what major Soviet Republic?
   A. Belarus
   B. Russia
   C. Ukraine
   D. Georgia
   E. Latvia

7. This man succeeded Yeltsin as leader of Russia.
   A. Krushchev
   B. Andropov
   C. Putin
   D. Kerensky
   E. Gorbachev

8. The Persian Gulf War of 1991 was in response to the Iraqi invasion of
   A. Israel
   B. Kuwait
   C. Syria
   D. Iran
   E. Jordan

9. The common currency of the European Union is called the
   A. dollar.
   B. dinero.
   C. peso.
   D. kroner.
   E. euro.

10. The increased interconnectedness of all parts of the world is called
    A. Gradualism.
    B. Universalism.
    C. Globalization.
    D. Spaceship Earth.
    E. Mercantilism.

VI.   ESSAY QUESTIONS

   A. In what sense can it be said that the twentieth century represents a new period in world civilizations?

   B. What trends in political organization and economic development can be identified in twentieth century world civilizations?

   C. The authors postulate several potential causal factors impacting civilization in the future, including population growth, the exhaustion of frontiers, and technological advances associated with the "postindustrial world." Evaluate the impact such factors are likely to have on the future.

PART VI REVIEW

I.   PART REVIEW

A. What contradictory impulses affect the understanding of the 20th century?

B. How significant is the 20th century in world history? Is it a period? Why?

C. How did the West's global position change during this period?

D. What countries have dominated this period?

E. What international contacts and exchanges typify the 20th century?

F. What conditions have changed and remained the same in the 20th century?

II.   VOCABULARY

A. Globalization

B. Multinational Corporations

III.   TIME LINE: *The 20th Century*

A. What major events herald the beginning of the period?

B. Why might one argue that the 20th century ended in 1989 or 1991?

C. What revolutions and major wars occurred between 1910 and 1999?

D. Based on items of the timeline, what themes dominated this period?

IV.   MAP EXERCISES

A. Map: *World Distribution of Manufacturing, 1930* (p.666)
    1. Which nations are the largest industrial powers?

    2. Which continents are most and least industrialized?

B. Map: *The World in 1995* (p.668)
    1. What nations and regions have experienced recent conflict and unrest?

    2. Based on the map and timeline, what regions seem the most violent?

V. MULTIPLE-CHOICE QUESTIONS

1. All of these themes are typical of the 20th century in world history EXCEPT:
   A. increased national sentiment.
   B. increased religious revivalism.
   C. rapid and fundamental changes.
   D. increasing cross-cultural contacts and connections.
   E. continuing dominance of the world by western powers.

2. Which of these statements about the West's 20th century position is a FACT?
   A. The western domination of the world has continued.
   B. The West's population relative to the rest of the world has declined.
   C. Fewer people immigrate to the West and the U.S. today than in 1900.
   D. European empires and colonial empires persist today.
   E. The west and the U.S.A still have a monopoly on military technologies.

3. Regarding world trade and manufacturing in the 20th century,
   A. Japan is the wealthiest nation with the largest economy.
   B. Brazil, China, and similar nations cannot compete with the western dominated global economy.
   C. the U.S.A. has the largest business and economic sector, but has many rivals.
   D. most societies now earn the bulk of their profits from international trade.
   E. the largest sector of the world economy is still agriculture.

4. The intensification of international contacts in the 20th century is largely due to
   A. technology.
   B. war.
   C. international trade.
   D. the spread of global diseases.
   E. the intensification of religious feeling.

5. Diplomatically, 20th century international relations
   A. has been dominated by the U.S., Russia, Western Europe and China.
   B. has too many actors for any one power to dominate.
   C. while important, have seen the decline of embassies and diplomatic staffs.
   D. has seen a proliferation of non-governmental organizations such as the U.N.
   E. has been dominated by the United Nations.

6. In the 20th century the role of the governments in societies around the world has
   A. increased dramatically.
   B. declined.
   C. remained similar to past traditional roles.
   D. lost many roles and functions to non-governmental organizations.
   E. had little effect on citizens.

7. In the 20th century, all of these institutions have challenged or modified the traditional dominance of religions over world societies EXCEPT:
   A. nationalism.
   B. communism.
   C. atheism.
   D. science.
   E. mass education.

8. The 20th century has seen what significant social change in most world societies?
   A. The disenfranchisement of minorities
   B. Pauperization of most workers and the middle class
   C. The elimination of social and political elites
   D. The wide-spread acceptance of differences in gender, race, ethnic, and sexual preferences
   E. The displacement of long-time systems of inequalities

9. The system of government or political ideology, which seems to have had the largest support in the 20th century has been
   A. aristocratic monarchy.
   B. nationalism.
   C. communism.
   D. popular sovereignty.
   E. theocracy.

10. All of these events have had profound effects on the development of the 20th century EXCEPT:
    A. World War I.
    B. the Agricultural Revolution.
    C. World War II.
    D. decolonization.
    E. the Cold War.

VI. ESSAY QUESTIONS

A. Compare and contrast the beginnings of the contemporary period and the Early Modern Period.

B. Compare and contrast the decline of Western influence in the 20th century with the decline of Chinese or Arabic Muslim influences in earlier periods.

C. Compare the patterns and nature of international contacts in the 20th century with contacts in the Classical, Post-Classical, or Early Modern periods.

D. Compare and contrast demographic and environmental changes in the 20th century with the shift from the Neolithic cultures to classical civilizations or the Industrial Revolution.

PART VI GEOGRAPHY: THE MAP OF THE CONTEMPORARY WORLD

The 20th-century world encompassed the globe. All continents were explored and except for the Antarctic, settled. Physical geography no longer played an important role as protection or isolation from contact. Physical geography was critical only in the sense that it helped or retarded development and population through its resource base or lack of one. The only barrier to movement or communication remained distance and time. Although civilization became truly global, strong regional alliances arose. And vast super cities spread out.

X. POLITICAL GEOGRAPHY
   A. MODERN ALLIANCES
      1. N.A.T.O.
      2. N.A.F.T.A.
      3. European Union
      4. A.S.E.A.N.
      5. Arab League
      6. O.P.E.C.
      7. C.I.S.

   B. HISTORIC ALLIANCES AND STATES
      1. Warsaw Pact Organization
      2. COMECON
      3. Triple Entente
      4. Triple Alliance
      5. Axis Powers
      6. Yugoslavia
      7. U. S. S. R.

XI. LOCATE
   A. CITIES
      1. Mexico City
      2. Shanghai
      3. Los Angeles
      4. Jakarta
      5. Singapore
      6. Hong Kong
      7. Calcutta
      8. São Paulo
      9. Lagos
      10. Cairo

   B. COUNTRIES
      1. United States
      2. Mexico
      3. Brazil
      4. United Kingdom
      5. France
      6. Germany
      7. Russia
      8. Turkey
      9. India
      10. Egypt
      11. Israel
      12. Iran
      13. Saudi Arabia
      14. Nigeria
      15. Ghana
      16. Kenya
      17. Senegal
      18. Algeria
      19. Zimbabwe
      20. South Africa
      21. Pakistan
      22. China
      23. Vietnam
      24. Japan
      25. Indonesia
      26. Koreas
      27. Taiwan
      28. Malaysia
      29. Singapore
      30. Cuba

MULTIPLE-CHOICE ANSWERS

CHAPTER 28

1. A
2. D
3. E
4. B
5. C
6. A
7. C
8. D
9. C
10. D

CHAPTER 29

1. C
2. E
3. C
4. A
5. D
6. A
7. B
8. C
9. A
10. C
11. B
12. C

CHAPTER 30

1. E
2. C
3. D
4. C
5. A
6. C
7. B
8. D
9. C
10. D

CHAPTER 31

1. C
2. D
3. B
4. A
5. A
6. B
7. D
8. B
9. C
10. B

CHAPTER 32

1. C
2. D
3. B
4. D
5. B
6. C
7. D
8. B
9. D

CHAPTER 33

1. A
2. E
3. B
4. E
5. C
6. E
7. C
8. E
9. E
10. C
11. B
12. C

CHAPTER 34

1. C
2. E
3. B
4. D
5. A
6. C
7. E
8. A
9. D
10. E
11. B
12. E
13. A
14. C
15. B
16. D
17. C

CHAPTER 35

1. Λ
2. A
3. D
4. E
5. C
6. D
7. C
8. E
9. B
10. C
11. A
12. D
13. E
14. B
15. D
16. A
17. C

CHAPTER 36

1. D
2. B
3. B
4. C
5. A
6. B
7. C
8. B
9. E
10. C

PART VI

1. E
2. B
3. C
4. A
5. D
6. A
7. C
8. E
9. D
10. B

DOCUMENT-BASED QUESTION:
CHANGE IN WOMEN'S WORLDS

DIRECTIONS

The following question is based on the accompanying documents. (The documents have been edited for the purpose of this exercise). The question is designed to test your ability to work with and understand historical documents. Write an essay that:

- Has relevant thesis and supports that thesis with evidence from the documents.

- Uses all or all but one of the documents.

- Analyzes the documents by grouping them in as many appropriate ways as possible and does not simply summarize the documents individually.

- Takes into account both the sources of the documents and the authors' points of view.

ESSAY PROMPT

How has the status of women changed over the course of history? What reasons would account for these changes?

Based on the following documents, discuss the general status of women in world history. What types of additional documentation would help explain conditions affecting women?

HISTORICAL BACKGROUND

Frequently hidden from official, male-written accounts of history, women existed in the twilight of a male-dominated world. Often legally proscribed from any role in the public world of politics, education, intellectual activities, and business, women were forced to reside within the private worlds of the family, children, and the home. Yet changes in history were paralleled and reflected in changes affecting women's place and status within society.

DOCUMENT 1

WOMEN HEADS OF STATE AND GOVERNMENT

EUROPEAN RULERS

COUNTRY	# RULERS (TYPES)	# YEARS RULED	COUNTRY	# RULERS (TYPES)	# YEARS RULED
1450 - 1815			**1815 - 2000**		
Spain	1 Queen	30	Portugal	1 Queen	11
Austria	1 Empress	40	Spain	2 Queens	36
England	3 Queens	57	Netherlands	3 Queens	110
UKGB	1 Queen	12	Denmark	1 Queen	28
Scotland	1 Queen	25	Ireland	2 Presidents	10
Portugal	1 Queen	39	Iceland	1 President	16
France	4 Regents	31	UKGB	2 Queens	112
Sweden	1 Queen	23	UKGB	1 Prime Min.	11
Russia	1 Regent	7	Norway	1 Prime Min.	10
Russia	4 Empresses	67	Eur. Union	1 President	8
			Luxembourg	2 Duchesses	71
18 leaders for 331 years			**17 leaders for 423 years**		

AFRICAN, ASIAN, PACIFIC, AND AMERICAN RULERS

COUNTRY	# RULERS (TYPES)	# YEARS RULED	COUNTRY	# RULERS (TYPES)	# YEARS RULED
1450 - 1815			**1815 - 2000**		
Japan	2 Empresses	20	Brazil	1 Regent	13
India	2 Empresses	22	China	1 Empress	35
Ethiopia	1 Regent	39	Hawaii	1 Queen	4
Cambodia	1 Queen	12	Korea	1 Empress	13
Ashante	1 Queen	50	Philippines	1 President	6
			Sri Lanka	2 Prime Min.	18
			Pakistan	1 Prime Min.	2
			Nicaragua	1 President	6
			India	1 Prime Min.	15
			Israel	1 Prime Min.	5
			Haiti	1 Prime Min.	1
			Argentina	1 President	2
			Ethiopia	2 Empresses	21
			Dominica	1 Prime Min.	15
7 leaders for 143 years			**16 leaders for 156 years**		

DOCUMENT 2

Ban Zhao, foremost female Confucian scholar of her age and official court historian to Emperor Han Hedi, from her *Lessons for Women*, c. 110 C.E.

"On the third day after the birth of a girl the ancients observed three customs: first to place the baby below the bed; second to give her a piece of broken pottery with which to play; and third to announce her birth to her ancestors as an offering. Now to lay the baby below the bed plainly indicated that she is lowly and weak, and should regard it as her primary duty to humble herself before others. To give her pieces of pottery signified that she should practice labor and consider it her primary duty to be industrious. To announce her birth before her ancestors clearly meant that she ought to esteem as her primary duty the continuation of the observance of worship in the home [produce male heirs as only a male can conduct the ceremonies to the ancestors]. These customs epitomize a women's ordinary way of life and the teachings of the traditional ceremonial rights and regulations. Let a woman modestly yield to others; let her respect others; let her put others first; herself last. Should she do something good, let her not mention it; should she do something bad, let her not deny it. Let a woman retire late to bed, but rise early to duties. Let a woman be correct in manner and upright in character in order to serve her husband."

DOCUMENT 3

Thema Khumalo, Zimbabwean guerrilla describing her role in the revolution and civil war against the white regime in Rhodesia, 1965 – 1980

"We woman also fought the war and I still feel proud of this. Even our children are proud of us because they saw that women were not the cowards they had thought we were. Instead they discovered that women are very strong. The women provided everything the freedom fighters needed. The women were very courageous and strong and fought to the end. We became used to people dying at the time and so we were ready for anything. We accepted death and even became reconciled to the idea. We became almost immune to it because a lot of our children and neighbors died. But somehow we resolved never to go backwards but to go forwards until we had won our country. And so we fought side by side with the men, falling down, getting injured and getting up again. Mothers, women are the people who fought this war and I feel proud of it. If our affairs were now to be decided on how each of us fought, I can tell you that all the homes would now belong to women. Before the war women were not seen, but now we have been noticed. Some women are even members of Parliament and have posts in the government."

DOCUMENT 4

Sor Juana Ines de la Cruz, Roman Catholic nun, late 1600s C.E., Mexico; a letter in response to a bishop who criticized her writing as inappropriate for a nun

"Afterward, when I already knew how to read and write, along with all the sewing skills and needlework that women learn, I discovered that in the city of Mexico there was a university and I deluged my mother to send me to Mexico City so that I might study and take courses. She refused; nevertheless, I found a way to read many different books. [Later] I became a nun because, given my disinclination to marriage, it was the least unreasonable and most becoming choice I could make to assure my ardently desired salvation and to have no fixed occupation which might curtail my freedom to study. I went on with the studious pursuit of reading and more reading, study and more study. Even if these studies were to be viewed as to one's credit (as I see they are indeed celebrated in men), none would be due me, since I pursue them involuntarily. If they are seen as reprehensible, for the same reason I do not think I should be blamed. Dr. Arce, in virtue and cultivation a worthy professor, decides that to lecture publicly in the classroom and to preach in a pulpit are not legitimate activities for women, but that studying, writing, and teaching privately are most edifying and useful. The interpretation of Holy Scripture should be forbidden not only to women considered so inept, but to men, who merely by virtue of being men consider themselves sages."

DOCUMENT 5

Hebrew *Book of Proverbs* 31: 10 – 31, compiled around the 6th century B.C.E.

"When one finds a worthy wife, her value is beyond pearls. Her husband, entrusting his heart to her, has an unfailing prize. She brings him good, and not evil, all the days of her life. She obtains wool and flax and makes cloth with skillful hands. Like merchant ships, she secures her provisions from afar. She rises while it is still night, and distributes food to her household. She picks out a field to purchase; out of her earnings she plants a vineyard. She is girt about with strength, and sturdy are her arms. She enjoys the success of her dealings; at night her lamp is undimmed. She puts her hands to the distaff and her fingers ply the spindle. She reaches out her hands to the poor, and extends her arms to the needy. She makes her own coverlets; fine linen and purple are her clothing. Her husband is prominent at the city gates as he sits with the elders of the land. She makes her garments and sells them and stocks the merchants with belts. She is clothed with strength and dignity and she laughs at the days to come. She opens her mouth in wisdom, and on her tongue is kindly counsel."

DOCUMENT 6

Al-Mawardi, 11th century C.E. Muslim jurist, from his discourse "On Judges"

"Nobody may be appointed to the office of judge who does not comply fully with the conditions required to make his appointment valid and his decisions effective. The first condition is that he must be a man. This condition consists of two qualities, puberty and masculinity. As for the child below puberty, he cannot be held accountable, nor can his utterances have effect against himself. As for women, they are unsuited to positions of authority, although judicial verdicts may be based on what they say. Abu Hanifa said that a woman can act as judge in matters on which it would be lawful for her to testify, but she may not act as judge in matters on which it would not be lawful for her to testify. Ibn Jarir al-Tabari, giving a divergent view, allows a woman to act as judge in all cases, but no account should be taken of an opinion which is refuted by both the consensus of the community and the word of God. "Men have authority over women because of what God has conferred on the one in preference to the other," [Quran 4:38], meaning by this, intelligence and discernment. He does not, therefore, permit women to hold authority over men."

DOCUMENT 7

Ida Husted Harper, article for the American magazine, *Independent*, 1901 C.E.

"The moment we accept that women must enter wage-earning occupations only when compelled to do so by poverty, that moment we degrade labor and lower the status of all women. As long as a woman advertised her dire necessity by going outside the home to work, she could not avoid a feeling of humiliation. The fact that only a few insignificant jobs with meager wages were permitted added further to the disgrace. However, in the rapid evolution of the last century, practically all occupations were thrown open and into these poured women of education and social standing belonging to families of ample means, barriers at once began to fall and the stigma to fail. The great organizations of women, which have been formed, admit wage earners, and frequently women engaged in business are elected to the offices. Those who insist that women of the family should confine their labors to the household wholly ignore the fact, that in the past most of women's duties have been carried on outside the house. Those who note that a century ago no women were in our factories, and now 45 percent of the employed are women, omit to state that most of the work now done in factories has been taken directly away from women of the household."

DOCUMENT 8

City of Magdeburg, German Holy Roman Empire, code of city laws, 1261 C.E.

12. If a man dies leaving a wife, she shall have no share in his property except what he has given her in court, or has appointed for her dower. She must have six witnesses, male or female, to prove her dower. If the man has made no provision for her, her children shall support her as long as she does not remarry. If her husband had sheep, the widow shall take them.

18. No one, whether man or woman, shall, on his sick-bed, give away more than three shillings worth of his property without the consent of his heirs, and the woman must have the consent of her husband.

55. When a man dies his wife shall give to his heirs his sword, his horse, saddle, and his best coat of mail. She shall also give a bed, pillow, sheet, tablecloth, two dishes, and a towel. If she does not have these things, she shall not give them, but she shall give proof for each article that she does not have it.

56. After giving the above articles the widow shall take her dower and all that belongs to her; that is, all the sheep, geese, chests, yarn, beds, pillows, cushions, table linen, bed linen, towels, cups, candlesticks, linen, women's clothing, finger rings, bracelets, headdresses, psalters, and all prayer-books, chairs, drawers, bureaus, carpets, curtains, etc., and there are many other trinkets which belong to her, such as brushes, scissors, and mirrors. But uncut cloth, and unworked gold and silver do not belong to her.

DOCUMENT 9

M. N. Srinivas, Indian anthropologist, observations on an Indian village, compiled while living in Rampura during the late 1940s C.E.

"Sex difference provided an important basis for the division of labor, and this was true for all the castes. Among the castes the kitchen was the recognized sphere of feminine activity but the extent of participation in man's traditional occupation varied from caste to caste, and even household to household. The income of a household, and the degree to which its style of life was Sanskritized, was also significant in determining whether women participated in agricultural work or not. Generally, women from the richest households and the highest castes remained confined to their homes while women from the poorest households and lowest castes worked outside for cash wages. It was the male head of the household who carried on the traditional caste occupation, be it agriculture, blacksmithing, trade or priesthood. And there was an unstated assumption that his occupation was the important one.

FOOTNOTES: CHANGES IN WOMEN'S WORLDS

1. William L. Langer, ed., *An Encyclopedia of World History: Ancient, Medieval, and Modern Chronologically Arranged*, 5th ed. (Boston: Houghton Mifflin Co., 1971), 295-660 in passim.

   Chris Cook and John Stevenson, *The Longman Handbook of Modern European History 1763-1991*, 2nd ed. (London and New York" Longman Inc., 1987, 1992), 1-29 in passim.

   Guida M. Jackson, *Women Who Ruled: A Biographical Encyclopedia* (New York: Barnes and Noble Books, 1998), in passim.

2. Alfred J. Andrea and James H. Overfield, *The Human Record: Sources of Global History*, 3rd Edition, *Volume 1: To 1700* (Boston: Houghton Mifflin Company, 1998), 147.

3. Stuart Schwartz, Linda R. Wimmer, and Robert S. Wolff, *The Global Experience: Readings in World History, volume II* (New York: Longman, 1998), 270 – 272.

4. Mark B. Rosenberg, A. Douglas Kincaid, and Kathleen Logan, *Americas: An Anthology* (New York: Oxford University Press, 1992), 180 – 181.

5. Proverbs 31: 10 – 31, The New American Bible.

6. Bernard Lewis, ed. and trans., *Islam: From the Prophet Muhammad to the Capture of Constantinople*, vol. 2, *Religion and Society* (New York: Oxford University Press, 1974), 40.

7. Helen Hemingway Benton, ed., *The Annals of America*, Volume 12, *1895 – 1904: Populism, Imperialism, and Reform* (Chicago: Encyclopedia Britannica, Inc., 1968), 394.

8. Oliver J. Thatcher and Edgar H. McNeal, eds., *A Source Book for Medieval History* (New York: Charles Scribner's, 1907), 592 – 601 in passim.

9. M. N. Srinivas, *The Remembered Village* (Berkeley, California: University of California Press, 1976), 137.

APPENDICES: ORGANIZATIONAL CHARTS

After reading your text or prior to writing any of the Advanced Placement essays, students should organize their thoughts and notes. This should involve creating an outline of the assigned reading materials or proposed essay. While the standard outline format is one method of achieving this goal, another is to use charts and paradigms.

A paradigm is a method of studying materials. One such paradigm is called P.E.R.S.I.A.N. Each of the letters in this acronym represents some aspect of history that students will study in all Advanced Placement curricula. "P" represents politics, "E" is economics, "R" is religion, "S" is social including gender, "I" is intellectual, "A" is artistic, and "N" is geography. It is a pattern or a model that students may use to organize either essays or take notes.

As you read a chapter and study any civilization, organize your reading and lecture notes along with important vocabulary around the PERSIAN paradigm. This allows you to easily review your notes or to compare civilizations, which is one type of essay students will be required to write. And example of a one-page PERSIAN chart is included below as is a similar chart comparing and contrasting two civilizations.

Change Over Time essays are variants upon the theme of compare and contrast essays. Rather than comparing two civilizations, students discuss changes and continuities in one civilization across centuries. This chart is also included.

CHART: CHANGE OVER TIME

1ST CIVILIZATION & TIME PERIOD: _____ _____
2ND CIVILIZATION & TIME PERIOD: _____ _____

	Basic Features in 1st Time Period	Basic Features in 2nd Time Period	Key Changes	Key Continuities
POLITICAL				
ECONOMIC				
RELIGIOUS				
SOCIAL				
INTELLECT OR ARTS				
GEOGRAPHY (NEAR)				

CHART: COMPARATIVE TWO CIVILIZATIONS

1ST CIVILIZATION & TIME PERIOD: _____ _____

2ND CIVILIZATION & TIME PERIOD: _____ _____

	Basic Features in 1st Civilization	Basic Features in 2nd Civilization	Key Similarities	Key Differences
POLITICAL				
ECONOMIC				
RELIGIOUS				
SOCIAL				
INTELLECT OR ARTS				
(NEAR) GEOGRAPHY				

CHART: CHARACTERISTICS OF A CIVILIZATION

POLITICAL • **Leaders, Elites** • **State Structure** • **War** • **Diplomacy, Treaties** • **Courts, Laws**	
ECONOMIC • **Type of System** • **Technology, Industry** • **Trade, Commerce** • **Capital/Money** • **Types of Businesses**	
RELIGIOUS • **Holy Books** • **Beliefs, Teachings** • **Conversion** • **Sin/Salvation** • **Deities**	
SOCIAL • **Family** • **Gender Relations** • **Social Classes** • **Inequalities** • **Life Styles**	
INTELLECTUAL, ARTS • **Art, Music** • **Writing, Literature** • **Philosophy** • **Math & Science** • **Education**	
NEAR: GEOGRAPHY • **Location** • **Physical** • **Movement** • **Human/Environment** • **Region**	

FIRST SEMESTER AP WORLD HISTORY PRACTICE EXAM
(Covering the Periods through 1450)

1. As compared with Paleolithic and Neolithic societies, the agriculture of civilizations
   A. totally replaced hunting and gathering.
   B. permitted migration.
   C. could not adapt to a wide range of climates and environments.
   D. limited human exposure to and death rates from diseases.
   E. changed man's physical environment.

2. The period of the Neolithic Revolutions and river valley civilizations ended when
   A. widespread invasions and new technologies led to the rise of large empires.
   B. various civilizations first established contacts between the regions.
   C. iron was introduced.
   D. the civilizations developed writing.
   E. epidemic diseases destroyed the first civilizations.

3. The first truly revolutionary transformation of human society was
   A. the Agricultural Revolution.
   B. the Black Death.
   C. the First Global Age.
   D. the Industrial Revolution.
   E. the Russian Revolution.

4. In most ancient and classical civilizations and societies, priests developed considerable social power and influence because they
   A. controlled agriculture.
   B. dominated government.
   C. interpreted the gods' wishes and placated the deities.
   D. owned the land.
   E. regulated trade between cities and regional centers.

5. Which of these is an example of patriarchal society in the classical world?
   A. Young men went to live with their wives' families.
   B. After marriage, a woman moved to the residence of her husband's family.
   C. Family descent and property inheritance traced through the female line.
   D. A woman could have had more than one husband.
   E. Women and men had equal legal rights as written into the first law codes.

6. Periodic nomadic invasions in the early history of Eurasia
   A. caused disruptions, but facilitated innovations and prompted synthesis.
   B. led to the collapse of civilization.
   C. were easily beaten back by the technologically advanced sedentary peoples.
   D. caused mass popular migrations throughout Eurasia.
   E. failed to upset the established political and social patterns of most regions.

7. Unlike Sumer and Egypt, the Indus Valley or Harappan civilization
   A. became a geographic center for a unified, continuous culture, lasting millennia.
   B. was secure from nomadic incursions and invasions.
   C. never developed a military social class.
   D. had a system of writing that has never been translated.
   E. developed a monotheistic religion.

8. Compared with river valley cultures in Egypt and Mesopotamia, civilization in China
   A. probably developed after civilizations in the Nile Valley and Southwest Asia.
   B. predates the rise of civilization in both Egypt and Mesopotamia.
   C. developed simultaneously with Egypt and Mesopotamia.
   D. did not rely on heavy irrigation, as year-round water was plentiful.
   E. has no verifiable historic origins and left no written records.

9. Classical China and the post-classical Muslim world are similar in that unity and cultural identity were provided by
   A. divine monarchs.
   B. shared religious ceremonies.
   C. commonalities of the spoken or written language.
   D. Buddhism.
   E. contacts through international or interregional trade.

10. In order to counterbalance feudalism and its tendency to decentralize ruling power, and in order to maintain their influence, leaders in Japan, China, and Western Europe
   A. developed the Mandate of Heaven to give them authority.
   B. created strong national armies capable of suppressing aristocratic independence.
   C. fostered common religions in which the ruler was the chief deity and head priest.
   D. encouraged widespread fear about the constant threats of nomadic invasions.
   E. owned all the land and granted nobles land tenure only for their lifetimes.

11. Peasants in Zhou China, serfs in Medieval Europe, or slaves in Aryan India
   A. were largely independent and free from interference by nobles.
   B. were free to leave their farms.
   C. had no military obligations to the state or nobles.
   D. generally lived in peaceful, well-fed communities.
   E. were burdened by obligations to the rulers and local nobles.

12. Classical differed from river valley civilizations in all of these ways EXCEPT:
   A. their societal institutions were more complex.
   B. interregional contacts, especially through trade, war, or migration, increased.
   C. government was larger and more complex.
   D. classic religions were largely monotheistic or atheistic.
   E. large empires and elaborate government institutions arose.

13. Historically, pastoral nomads
    A. lived interspersed with sedentary farmers.
    B. were rare in Africa and the Americas, but common in Central Asia.
    C. prevented contacts between the civilized centers of the world.
    D. had little lasting impact on the development of civilizations.
    E. lived on the grassy plains of the continents, where sedentary agriculture was extremely difficult.

14. In comparison to women in sedentary societies, women in nomadic, pastoral societies
    A. had more rights.
    B. belonged to paternalistic societies as strong as any sedentary societies.
    C. were treated relatively equally to their husbands and male counterparts.
    D. were valued if they could equal males in military courage and accomplishments.
    E. had fewer rights.

15. All of these actions and responses typified contacts between sedentary and nomadic peoples EXCEPT:
    A. acceptance of each other and each other's ways of life.
    B. trade.
    C. tribute payments by weak sedentary societies to strong nomadic groups.
    D. nomads served as mercenaries to some societies.
    E. raids and warfare between both groups.

16. Confucianism, Daoism, and Legalism, as well as Buddhism
    A. were officially sanctioned doctrines of the Chin and Han emperors.
    B. are religions, that developed in classical India.
    C. emphasized the needs of the individual over the welfare of the state.
    D. had little influence upon China and Chinese society until the late 900s C.E.
    E. originated as responses to societal problems during times of disruption.

17. Although they varied greatly in wealth and social status in the classical world,
    A. the commoners, especially the peasants, remained the largest group.
    B. the literate elites cooperated to limit the influence of the ruler.
    C. aristocrats owned most of the land.
    D. women had many legal rights and protections.
    E. urban artisans and merchants dominated classical societies.

18. Women in most Classical Age societies
    A. were free to choose the men they would marry.
    B. could become bureaucrats, provided they passed the state exams.
    C. were legally subordinated to fathers and husbands at all class levels.
    D. dominated the intellectual and artistic activities of many cultures.
    E. varied greatly in status, influence, and rights.

19. Rural population pressures in classical societies such as China, India, and Rome
    A. led to frequent outbreaks of disease, famine, and population declines.
    B. were mitigated by migration to unoccupied lands or clearing of forests.
    C. rarely exceeded the production and carrying capacities of the farmlands.
    D. were avoided by infanticide, high death rates, and selling children into slavery.
    E. threatened the stability of most governments.

20. Despite their material success and increased wealth, in China and Rome
    A. foreigners were prohibited from settling amongst most classical societies.
    B. merchants often ranked below peasants and had little societal influence.
    C. classical rulers were isolated from the masses and did not intervene in government.
    D. classical aristocrats and elites had no influence within the government.
    E. the educated elite were prohibited from owning land.

21. The major impact of Alexander the Great's conquests was
    A. the elimination of foreign influences from Greek culture.
    B. the establishment of the first unified government for the Eastern Mediterranean.
    C. the birth of mystery religions and the forced migration of the Jews.
    D. the spread of Greek culture throughout the Eastern Mediterranean, Southwest Asia, and into India.
    E. the destruction of regional trade and commerce.

22. In comparison to the Hindus, Persians, and Jews, religiously, the Greeks
    A. most resembled Hinduism's polytheism with its caste system.
    B. never developed a major religion.
    C. developed a compassionate system similar to Buddhism.
    D. sought universal harmony in a manner similar to Daoism.
    E. avoided portraying gods with human characteristics.

23. Much of what is called classical Greek and Chinese philosophy traced its origins to the
    A. cultural crisis and intellectual uncertainty that followed prolonged periods of war.
    B. translations and influences of other ancient classical civilizations.
    C. public speakers who argued the merits of contemporary Greek and Chinese society.
    D. inventions and discoveries of the sciences and mathematicians.
    E. civic religions of the Greek city-states and Zhou rulers.

24. Unlike Qin legalist philosophy, Roman imperial law
    A. harshly punished mistakes and rewarded success.
    B. insisted on centralization of government and absolutist rule.
    C. was intolerant of innovation.
    D. rested heavily on toleration and local autonomy.
    E. distrusted the military and military rule.

25. What sentence BEST describes both Roman and Chinese gender relations?
    A. Roman and Chinese women had numerous political rights.
    B. While subordinate to men, Roman women were considerably freer and less oppressed then were their Chinese counterparts.
    C. Both cultures were matrilocal – husbands resided with their wives' families.
    D. Over the length of the empires, women's lives improved and their rights increased.
    E. Rome and China were patriarchal societies where elite women had considerable influence.

26. Far more than classical Greece, India, or China, slavery in Rome
    A. dominated the labor markets – Rome became dependant on slavery.
    B. was hereditary.
    C. granted no rights or protections to slaves.
    D. was lenient and refused to enslave the young or the elderly.
    E. encouraged Romans to develop their technology in agriculture and industry.

27. With regard to merchants, classical civilizations in Rome, Greece, China, and India
    A. accorded them high social status.
    B. waw little use for their talents in otherwise largely agricultural societies.
    C. were ambivalent towards merchants despite their vital roles in commerce.
    D. rewarded merchant success through upward social mobility.
    E. made them state bureaucrats.

28. The major difference between Buddhism and Hinduism was
    A. Hinduism was monotheistic and Buddhism was polytheistic.
    B. Buddhism denied rebirth and reincarnation, and emphasized the importance of the real world.
    C. Hinduism supported the ruling castes, whereas Buddhism encouraged its followers to renounce the political world.
    D. Hinduism taught respect for all living things and prohibited killing.
    E. Buddhism denied the need for castes, rites, and sacrifice to achieve nirvana.

29. Although the Mayas developed similarly to other civilizations, they never
    A. developed complex religions.
    B. progressed much past Neolithic technologies.
    C. produced complex mathematics, sciences, and calendrical traditions.
    D. invented written languages.
    E. built elaborate structures.

30. When the Bantu migrated, they
    A. disrupted older, more established civilizations and states in Africa.
    B. adopted pastoral nomadism and abandoned sedentary agriculture.
    C. spread agriculture, crops, and iron technologies across much of Africa.
    D. settled largely in the Nile and Niger River valleys.
    E. were assimilated by the older civilizations into whose areas they moved.

337

31. Contacts with China introduced all of these to Japan EXCEPT:
    A. Chinese writing.
    B. the idea and position of the emperor and imperial rule.
    C. the Buddhist religion.
    D. bureaucratic government and trained officials.
    E. patriarchal and patrilineal family relationships.

32. All of these happenings must generally occur for a new period in world history to begin EXCEPT:
    A. nomadic peoples must overrun sedentary civilizations.
    B. the world map must change significantly.
    C. new types of contacts between civilized regions must develop.
    D. new patterns and parallel institutional developments will occur.
    E. new technologies may arise.

33. At the end of the Classical Age
    A. belief systems failed to survive the collapse of classical civilizations.
    B. only the Mediterranean Greco-Roman civilization experienced upheavals.
    C. the Huns (Hsiung-Nu) destroyed all great Eurasian classical civilizations.
    D. there was a religious upsurge as a result of social and economic problems.
    E. trade ceased to be important.

34. In comparison with the end of classical civilizations in China and India, the collapse of the Roman Empire was
    A. milder, and the recovery that followed was quicker.
    B. more severe and extensive than elsewhere.
    C. largely due to internal political, economic, and social decay.
    D. caused exclusively by Germanic and Hunnic invasions.
    E. also saw the collapse of the institutions associated with the Christian Church.

35. In contrast to Mahayana Buddhism, as Christianity evolved and spread, it
    A. was intolerant of other faiths.
    B. did not emphasize missionary activities.
    C. discouraged converts.
    D. failed to set up a hierarchy and formal church organizations.
    E. encouraged the use of icons and holy images.

36. All of these developments characterize the Post-classical age EXCEPT the:
    A. expanding influence of the Arabs and Islam.
    B. domination of the Atlantic and Mediterranean by Christian Europeans.
    C. spread of civilization to new regions such as West Africa and Southeast Asia.
    D. widespread shift in basic belief systems such as Christianity and Islam.
    E. development of a world network for trade, ideas, and diseases.

37. The leading civilization during the Post-classical Era (450-1450 C.E.) was
    A. the Christian West.
    B. the Byzantine Empire.
    C. India.
    D. a collection of sea-based trading states, such as Venice and the Swahili states.
    E. Islam.

38. One of the strengths of Islam that made it a successful universalizing faith similar to Christianity and Buddhism was its
    A. use of a common language, such as Arabic, Latin, or Pali, to unite all members.
    B. insistence that there was only one God.
    C. support for merchants and commercial values.
    D. egalitarianism that transcended previous loyalties, ethnicities, or allegiances.
    E. condemnation of violence as incompatible with faith.

39. The Pillar of Islam that helped create the first trans-regional civilization was
    A. profession of faith.
    B. charity and almsgiving to help the Muslim community.
    C. the pilgrimage by the faithful to Mecca.
    D. fasting during Ramadan.
    E. the Holy War (Jihad) against unbelievers.

40. Initially, Islam, with regard to women and gender roles
    A. retained Bedouin matrilineal traditions and greatly strengthened the position of women in society.
    B. adopted Christian attitudes towards women.
    C. secluded women and took away most of their property rights.
    D. introduced a harsh patriarchal system.
    E. greatly strengthened the position of women.

41. Unlike merchants in classical civilizations, Muslim traders
    A. had little influence within society.
    B. often ran the governments of the Muslim states.
    C. acquired great wealth and were protected and encouraged by Muslim states.
    D. could not legally change their social status.
    E. were ranked socially behind peasants and farmers.

42. Mameluks
    A. were Turkish-speaking slave armies used by Muslims.
    B. were the last great Central Asian nomads to disrupt Eurasian civilizations.
    C. broke from the Sunni Muslims over who should be the rightful leader.
    D. overran Spain and established a brilliant Arabo-Hispanic civilization.
    E. were non-Muslim boys forcibly converted to Islam and employed as farmers.

43. The Seljuks
    A. conquered the Abbasid Caliphate and Byzantine Empire.
    B. favored the Shia sect and became its protector.
    C. settled in the lands of modern Turkey and became the Abbasids' protector.
    D. were unable to stop the Crusades or end Crusader control of Jerusalem.
    E. became a sect of Islam devoted to learning, mysticism, and medicine.

44. The impact of the Crusades
    A. disrupted the Muslim world.
    B. had little effect on the military capabilities of the Europeans.
    C. led to the collapse of the Abbasid caliphate.
    D. was greater on the Europeans because it brought Europe into contact with Muslim civilizations and their accomplishments.
    E. encouraged mass European migrations to the lands of the Eastern Mediterranean.

45. Contacts between Hindus and Muslims led to
    A. the seclusion of Hindu women.
    B. the absorption by the Muslims of many Hindu social practices.
    C. constant warfare between the two groups.
    D. mass conversion of Hindus to Islam.
    E. decreased trade opportunities.

46. Unlike the Americas, sub-Saharan Africa
    A. never developed a classical civilization.
    B. was never totally isolated from other civilizations.
    C. had little popular migration or trade.
    D. developed its indigenous civilizations later.
    E. had no extensive river systems or grasslands.

47. Sub-Saharan African societies are similar to Latin American Indian societies in that both
    A. built classical civilizations without cultural diffusion from other civilizations.
    B. developed in mountainous environments.
    C. originated complex mathematics and scientific traditions.
    D. are so numerous that it is impossible to generalize about them.
    E. were devastated by contacts with Europeans and Arabs, which led to mass epidemics and the death of whole indigenous populations.

48. Prior to the 15th century C.E., Islam was spread through West and East Africa as well as Southeast Asia by
    A. merchants who established Muslim families and traditions.
    B. Jihad or holy war.
    C. mass conversions ordered by the rulers and monarchs.
    D. wandering Sufi mystics.
    E. migration to the areas by large groups of Muslims.

49. The slave trade from West Africa to the Muslim world
    A. was abolished once the inhabitants converted to Islam.
    B. consisted only of slave porters to the Muslim traders.
    C. was introduced by the Muslims.
    D. rivaled the Trans-Atlantic slave trade in numbers and brutality.
    E. preferred male slaves for administration and military occupations.

50. As had Hammurabi's Code (Mesopotamia), Justinian's Code (Byzantine)
    A. dealt primarily with church law and religious issues.
    B. led to internal disruptions and faced harsh opposition.
    C. became the basic unified law code for states, which existed after its original creator.
    D. greatly influenced the laws of Islam.
    E. deviated sharply from previous legal traditions when it sought to create a new tradition.

51. Within the Byzantine state, as had been the case with government in most of the dynasties of China, the chief power and influence was
    A. emperors and their trained bureaucrats.
    B. the Church and clergy.
    C. large aristocratic landowners.
    D. the military.
    E. merchants and artisans.

52. Unlike monarchs in western Europe, but like the caliphs, the Byzantine emperor
    A. held political but not religious power.
    B. headed both church and state; there was no separation of power.
    C. were considered divine.
    D. were uninterested in running the daily affairs of government and left all but ceremonial duties to their advisors.
    E. was the head of the military but not the government.

53. When scholars began to study Greek classics, most early West European intellectuals and scholastics, like their Muslim counterparts
    A. rejected Christianity or Islam when it conflicted with classical learning.
    B. found that Aristotle and Plato stressed the importance of faith and God.
    C. doubted the accuracy and validity of classical learning.
    D. readily accepted Greek ideas and integrated them into their theologies.
    E. found the Greek notion of reason troubling because it questioned faith.

54. Manorialism in Medieval Europe was characterized by all of these conditions EXCEPT:
    A. most peasants were serfs.
    B. manors and peasants depended on merchants for most necessities.
    C. peasants were obligated to give their lord a portion of their produce.
    D. the lords protected the peasants.
    E. levels of production and technology were low and limited.

55. European serfs differed from slaves in that
    A. serfs were largely commercialized artisans, while slaves were agricultural.
    B. serfs were ethnically Europeans, while slaves were Muslims, pagans, and Africans.
    C. serfs existed only in Russia.
    D. serfs could serve in the military, while slaves could not.
    E. slaves frequently were better educated and lived in towns.

56. As happened in the Fertile Crescent, India, and China, the fall of civilizations in the Americas was often due to
    A. migrating nomadic invaders.
    B. crop collapse.
    C. famine and diseases.
    D. civil war.
    E. environmental disasters.

57. Neo-Confucianism
    A. blended Buddhism and Daoism with traditional Confucian doctrine.
    B. abandoned the emphasis on classical learning and test-taking.
    C. warmly encouraged the merchant and commercial activities.
    D. emphasized tradition, authority, and harmony at the expense of innovation.
    E. borrowed and utilized legalist ideas to run the Song state.

58. Both footbinding in China and the harem and veil in Islam
    A. ended with the spread of Buddhism to Confucian and Muslim areas.
    B. were condemned by the Confucian scholar-gentry.
    C. were rejected by their societies' religious establishments.
    D. originated in Hindu lands and spread to Chinese and Muslim lands.
    E. symbolized the increasing subordination of women to men.

59. Tang military expansion into central Asia
    A. led to constant warfare between the Chinese and the Muslims.
    B. promoted renewed commercial contacts between China and West Asia.
    C. eliminated nomadic invasions.
    D. obtained land to settle large Chinese population surpluses.
    E. was easily defeated by the Turks and other pastoral nomads.

60. The only indigenous aspect of Japanese culture during the Heian era was
    A. Mahayana Buddhism.
    B. the imperial administration.
    C. written characters.
    D. Shinto.
    E. court etiquette and protocol.

61. The group that most directly challenged Chinese influences in Japan and Vietnam during the Post-Classical era was
    A. the merchants.
    B. Buddhist monks and priests.
    C. aristocrats and local provincial administrators.
    D. the emperor.
    E. the imperial bureaucracy.

62. The typical pattern for relations between China and its neighbors during the post-classical period was
    A. military occupation by the Chinese armies.
    B. for states to acknowledge Chinese superiority, pay tribute, but remain independent.
    C. incorporation of these states as provinces in the Chinese empire.
    D. to form equal alliances as partners against nomadic invaders.
    E. to maintain no formal relations or treaties with neighboring states.

63. Although the Mongols were often brutal, they were
    A. no less violent than Europeans, Muslims, or the Chinese of the day.
    B. unwilling to destroy art works and buildings.
    C. devoted to non-violence.
    D. apt to leave enemies alive and revolting cities unpunished.
    E. tolerant of religious differences and supportive of trade.

64. Pastoral nomads from the Central Asian steppe who had threatened sedentary civilizations throughout world history included all of these EXCEPT:
    A. Indo-Europeans.
    B. Hsiung-nu (Huns).
    C. Bantu.
    D. Scythians.
    E. Turks.

65. The greatest long-term demographic impact of the Mongol unification of much of Central Eurasia was the
    A. new technologies introduced.
    B. facilitation of trade.
    C. conversion of the Mongols to Christianity.
    D. destruction of old states and the rise of new ones.
    E. spread of the Black Death from China to Europe and the Muslim world.

66. The transformation that most immediately weakened the power and influence of pastoral nomads over sedentary civilization was due to
    A. introduction of better organized sedentary states.
    B. increased centralization of sedentary governments.
    C. the devastation to nomadic populations caused by the Black Death.
    D. newer technologies, especially weapons, used by sedentary civilizations.
    E. settling of farmers on the traditional lands of the nomads.

67. Besides the Italian city-states, the geographic region or state in West Europe MOST supportive of change at the end of the post-classical era was
    A. the Holy Roman Empire (Germany and Low Countries).
    B. France.
    C. England.
    D. the Iberian Peninsula (Spain and Portugal).
    E. Russia.

68. The major barrier to Western European expansion prior to the 15ᵗʰ century C.E. was
    A. the low level of European technology.
    B. the lack of interest by West European rulers for acquiring territory.
    C. the overwhelming power of Muslim and Mongol states.
    D. the fact that religious civil wars divided Western Europe and made overseas expansion impossible.
    E. lack of popular interest and public funds to support expansion.

69. The Ming Chinese naval expeditions of the early 15ᵗʰ century C.E.
    A. were followed by the Chinese conquest of Southeast Asia.
    B. were stopped by Muslim navies in the Indian Ocean.
    C. ended because they challenged Confucian values and typical expenditures.
    D. led to a renewed Chinese interest in scientific and geographic exploration.
    E. stimulated trade between China and Africa.

70. All of these events led to the weakening or end of Medieval Western European institutions EXCEPT:
    A. the Bubonic Plague.
    B. political and theological attacks on the Roman Catholic church.
    C. the rise of national monarchies.
    D. the rise of non-aristocratic armies loyal to national monarchs.
    E. the Ottoman Turk invasion of Western Europe.

ANSWER KEY TO 1ST AP WORLD HISTORY SEMESTER EXAM

1.	E	42.	A
2.	B	43.	C
3.	A	44.	D
4.	C	45.	B
5.	B	46.	B
6.	A	47.	D
7.	D	48.	A
8.	A	49.	E
9.	C	50.	C
10.	B	51.	A
11.	E	52.	B
12.	D	53.	E
13.	E	54.	B
14.	B	55.	C
15.	A	56.	A
16.	E	57.	D
17.	A	58.	E
18.	C	59.	B
19.	D	60.	D
20.	B	61.	C
21.	D	62.	B
22.	B	63.	E
23.	A	64.	C
24.	C	65.	E
25.	B	66.	D
26.	A	67.	D
27.	C	68.	A
28.	E	69.	C
29.	B	70.	E
30.	C		
31.	E		
32.	A		
33.	D		
34.	B		
35.	A		
36.	B		
37.	E		
38.	D		
39.	C		
40.	E		
41.	C		

SECOND SEMESTER AP WORLD HISTORY PRACTICE EXAM
(Covering the Periods from 1450 to the Present)

1. A major feature of the early modern globalization of international trade was the
   A. dominance of trade by the Muslims.
   B. intentional isolation of countries from participating in international trade.
   C. unequal commercial relationships and the dependence of many states on Europe.
   D. decline of the luxury trade.
   E. decrease of unfree labor, such as slavery and serfdom.

2. The major development between 1450 and 1750 was the rise of
   A. the first truly global world trade network.
   B. empires ruling transcontinental land masses.
   C. mass migrations of peoples.
   D. capitalism as the dominant economic ideology.
   E. an almost instantaneous global communication network.

3. Fundamental to the European acquisition of colonies between 1450 and 1750 was
   A. the superiority of European military technologies against the Muslim states.
   B. the lack of immunity amongst world populations to European diseases.
   C. European maritime technologies.
   D. lack of opposition.
   E. European overpopulation, which allowed large armies and provided willing settlers.

4. All world labor systems during the Early Modern period can be characterized as
   A. increasingly slave-oriented.
   B. increasingly serf, sharecropper, or tenant farmer associated.
   C. increasingly capitalist, with wages paid for work.
   D. largely unfree.
   E. machine-based and electrically powered.

5. The Columbian exchanges involved all of these global movements EXCEPT:
   A. European diseases devastated the Americas.
   B. American foodstuffs and crops spread around the world.
   C. Africans were forcibly transported to the Americas.
   D. Europeans transplanted their crops, animals, and economic systems to the Americas.
   E. Indian populations were resettled to the Pacific islands and African lands.

6. The Renaissance was largely influenced and financed by
   A. the Roman Catholic Church.
   B. the urban environment and commercial economy.
   C. medieval institutions.
   D. the popular culture and the lifestyles of the masses.
   E. scientists and the Scientific Revolution.

7. Renaissance humanism would have been most comfortable with the values and ideas of which world belief system?
   A. Christianity
   B. Buddhism
   C. Confucianism
   D. Hellenism
   E. Hinduism

8. The fragmentation of Christianity during the Reformations into Catholic and Protestant sects most closely resembles
   A. Sunni-Shia divisions within Islam over political leadership of the Muslim community.
   B. Buddha's founding of Buddhism out of Hindu traditions.
   C. the expulsion of the Christians from Judaism around 70 C.E.
   D. the transformation of religions from polytheism to monotheism.
   E. the absorption of Muslim ideas by Hinduism following contacts between the two religions.

9. Western European monarchs, as did the Japanese Tokugawa shoguns, employed all of these methods or groups to win "absolute" control of their states EXCEPT:
   A. increasing royal revenues through new taxes and supporting mercantilism.
   B. allowing representative assemblies to make and to pass laws.
   C. limiting the rights of medieval parliaments and diets.
   D. creating a professional army.
   E. recruiting trained bureaucrats from the middle, non-aristocratic (urban) classes.

10. The main reason European conquerors and navigators were able to sail and continue to explore, and the reason the Ming Chinese fleets in the Indian Ocean failed was
    A. the Europeans had superior military technologies and the Chinese did not.
    B. Europe encountered no opposition, while the Chinese did.
    C. European governments supported and encouraged overseas expeditions; the Ming did not.
    D. Europe was wealthier than were the Chinese.
    E. China had a smaller population base than Europe and could not afford to send people abroad.

11. European nations acquired their first colonies in the Americas
    A. following the conquests by military, gold seeking adventurers.
    B. when merchants bought islands and landholdings from the inhabitants.
    C. through missionary activities to convert the inhabitants.
    D. through intermarriage between reigning royal families.
    E. peacefully.

12. In Africa during the Early Modern period, Europeans
    A. controlled the slave trade.
    B. settled widely in West Africa.
    C. exported gold and raw minerals.
    D. started the slave trade.
    E. had to negotiate with African kings, who controlled the slave trade.

13. All of Russia's reforms under Peter the Great were largely attempts to
    A. preserve Russian cultural identity from Western influences.
    B. protect the serfs from the harsh rule of the boyars.
    C. please his wife, who was Italian.
    D. undermine the power of the Russian Orthodox clergy.
    E. modernize the state and strengthen the army in order to conquer desired lands.

14. Modernization and westernization in Russia under Peter the Great and Catherine the Great did not include
    A. military reforms.
    B. liberalizing state policies and tolerating democratic ideas.
    C. educational reforms.
    D. improvements in the conditions of upper-class women.
    E. internal economic and industrial changes.

15. In comparison with American slaves, Russian serfs
    A. had fewer rights.
    B. were largely skilled laborers working in export industries.
    C. grew mostly cotton, sugar, and tobacco.
    D. could neither be owned nor sold.
    E. produced only for a domestic, local economy.

16. The greatest source of social unrest in early modern Russia was
    A. noble opposition to westernization.
    B. the clergy and religious opposition to the non-Christian minorities.
    C. the lack of real reform, especially rights for the serfs.
    D. rapid growth of towns and factories.
    E. caused by intellectuals and radicals opposed to the tsars' autocracy.

17. All of these Iberian traits influenced Spain and Portugal colonial patterns and society in the Americas EXCEPT:
    A. local political and religious autonomy.
    B. land grants to provincial nobles.
    C. the use of serfs.
    D. patriarchal family structures.
    E. an alliance between church and state.

18. The Spanish assimilation of the American peoples and the replacement of Indian by Spanish cultures were facilitated by
    A. the enslavement of Indians.
    B. the demographic decline of Indian populations caused by European diseases.
    C. the use of superior weapons.
    D. the utilization of European technologies.
    E. the introduction of the institutions of government and law.

19. The export of silver from the Americas led to all of these outcomes EXCEPT:
    A. payment for Spain's religious and dynastic wars.
    B. a sharp inflation in Western Europe.
    C. exchange of silver for Chinese luxuries Europeans desired.
    D. the increasing impoverishment and bankruptcy of Spain.
    E. the discouragement of foreign rivals and pirates.

20. Within the Spanish American Empire, the Roman Catholic Church
    A. administered the state bureaucracy.
    B. administered the state judicial system.
    C. supported the state, influenced cultural life, and defended Indian rights.
    D. was the largest landholder.
    E. had no major role because the kings feared their influence amongst the Indians and the poor.

21. Under the doctrine of mercantilism, Spain and Portugal encouraged their Latin American colonies to
    A. permit foreign merchants to trade within the empires.
    B. allow the free settlement of English colonists within the New World.
    C. practice free trade.
    D. buy manufactured goods only from the mother country.
    E. become self-sufficient.

22. What event was most directly responsible for the rise of the gunpowder empires in Turkey, Iran, and India and similar states in Tsarist Russia and Ming China?
    A. Gunpowder and military technologies spread.
    B. The Mongol Empire and its khanates collapsed.
    C. Western European merchants arrived in the area.
    D. Eurasian trade revived.
    E. Steppe nomads established all five states.

23. The Ottoman, Safavid, and Mughal empires possessed all of these shared characteristics EXCEPT:
    A. all originated in Turkish nomadic cultures of the steppe.
    B. all were Muslim led.
    C. all were based on conquest and the use of military technologies.
    D. all began with absolutist rulers and efficient bureaucracies.
    E. all ruled predominantly Muslim populations.

24. With regard to the West Europeans and their institutions and technologies, the Ottomans and Safavids
    A. ignored and looked down upon all things Europeans, which later hurt them.
    B. borrowed freely and heavily any useful idea, tool, or institution.
    C. were clearly superior to the Europeans in all respects.
    D. heavily influenced West European political culture and military traditions.
    E. had no contacts because they had no trade with West Europeans.

25. Which of these statements about women in India during the Mughal Empire is TRUE?
    A. child-bride marriages were ended.
    B. seclusion (purdah) of upper class Hindu and Muslim women began.
    C. widow remarriage was ended.
    D. the practice of sati (widow burning) ended.
    E. the birth of girls was seen as an unlucky event.

26. In the beginning of the early Modern Age, the relationship between Europeans in Africa and Africans was
    A. one of mutual respect.
    B. an inferior status, with Europeans predominating.
    C. often one of relative equality in which no one power was dominant.
    D. dominated by superior European technology.
    E. contentious and led to constant warfare.

27. The European slave trade out of Africa arose and expanded when
    A. Europeans began to supply Muslim slave markets in the Middle East.
    B. Europe conquered the coasts of West Africa.
    C. gold was discovered in Iberia, necessitating greater numbers of laborers.
    D. sugar plantations were established on the Atlantic islands and in the Americas.
    E. Spain and Portugal launched their crusades against Muslim states in Africa.

28. Slavery in the United States differed from slavery and the slave trade to the rest of the Americas in all of the following ways EXCEPT:
    A. the slave trade to the United States was abolished after 1807.
    B. the U. S. supported its need for slaves with domestic breeding and internal trade.
    C. American plantations grew cotton and tobacco instead of sugar.
    D. the total slave population in the United States grew.
    E. the death rate of slaves due to brutality was higher in the United States.

29. The Trans-Atlantic slave trade differed from the Trans-Saharan slave trade to the Muslim world in that
    A. the Trans-Atlantic was less brutal than the Trans-Saharan slave trade.
    B. the Trans-Saharan slave trade included women for domestic work.
    C. the Atlantic route transported whole families to the Americas whereas the Trans-Saharan trade broke families up.
    D. the trade to the Muslim world ended before the Trans-Atlantic trade began.
    E. more people were transported across the Sahara than across the Atlantic.

30. Ashante, Benin, and Dahomey are comparable to the empires of the Mughals, Safavids, and Ottomans in that they all:
    A. established absolutist, centralized governments and institutions that resisted European penetration.
    B. relied on firearms to establish and to maintain their states.
    C. defeated the Portuguese.
    D. were Muslim states.
    E. expelled European merchants.

31. The Portuguese were able to control trade in Asian waters because
    A. they had endless supplies of gold and silver to buy goods.
    B. states in the area granted Portuguese merchants a trade monopoly.
    C. they had superior weapons and controlled trade through force.
    D. the Chinese had withdrawn from trade in Asia.
    E. the Portuguese captains allied with the Mughals, who controlled the area.

32. During the Ming Dynasty, the true power of China resided with
    A. prosperous peasants.
    B. merchants in port cities who administered foreign trade missions.
    C. the cunuch bureaucrats in the capital city.
    D. rural landlord families with relatives in the imperial bureaucracy.
    E. aristocrats and nobles.

33. The period 1750 – 1914 is characterized by
    A. the rise of civilizations.
    B. the rise of classical religions.
    C. the rise of trans-regional civilizations.
    D. the first global connections.
    E. growing European imperialism.

34. European and many North American areas were transformed during the period 1750 – 1914 by
    A. Colonialism.
    B. the Industrial Revolution and technology.
    C. world war.
    D. global trade.
    E. the great religions.

35. The region that had resisted European penetration from 1450 – 1750, and was mostly carved up into colonies was
    A. Africa.
    B. South America.
    C. North America.
    D. East Asia.
    E. Southwest Asia.

36. The demographic transition of 1750–1914 included all these characteristics EXCEPT:
    A. declining birthrates in industrial nations.
    B. decreased death rates due to public health measures.
    C. the spread of new food plants around the world.
    D. Europe's percentage of the total world population declined.
    E. high birthrates in Africa, Latin America, and Asia.

37. During the 19th century, mass immigration was generally
    A. from less developed countries to industrialized nations.
    B. surpassed by numbers from the slave trade.
    C. from Mexico and Central America to the United States.
    D. from China and India to coastal areas.
    E. religious in nature.

38. All of these were forces for change in Western Europe during the period 1750 – 1914 EXCEPT:
    A. the ideas of the Enlightenment.
    B. the increasing wealth and success of the business classes.
    C. religious innovation.
    D. the population pressures caused by a demographic shift.
    E. industrialization and mechanization.

39. Which statement is a FACT about the worldwide influence of the American Revolution and early American government?
    A. the Americans abolished slavery and helped enforce the ban on slave trade.
    B. the American government modeled its constitution after France.
    C. Americans adopted mercantilism and established tariffs against European nations.
    D. Americans received no support from Europe in their struggle for independence.
    E. the American Revolution and Constitution impacted the later French, Haitian, and Latin American revolutionaries and their ideas.

40. The older European loyalty to the Church and God was often replaced after the French Revolution by
    A. devotion to the Pope.
    B. support of the king and national rulers.
    C. allegiance to local leaders.
    D. nationalism and loyalty to the nation-state.
    E. allegiance to strong military leaders.

41. The social questions, demands for reform, and the need for monies to support the construction of railroads in Western Europe during the 19th century led to
    A. the expansion of and increasing intervention by governments in society.
    B. increasing radicalization of a majority of workers and peasants.
    C. numerous violent, socialist revolutions.
    D. the decrease in support for socialism, Marxism, or revisionist socialism.
    E. the bankruptcy of many governments.

42. The European educated colonial peoples tended to
    A. ally with their European rulers, but nevertheless became the leaders of future independence movements.
    B. side with traditional ruling elites in the colonies against the colonizers.
    C. immigrate to the mother countries, which owned the colonies.
    D. favor the peasants and poor people of their colonies.
    E. became merchants and businessmen.

43. The most likely reason for the success of European colonial acquisitions during the 19th century would be
    A. the enthusiasm by European Christian clergy to convert "the heathens."
    B. superior European military and transportation technologies.
    C. the epidemic amongst most native populations that preceded European arrival.
    D. lack of resistance to the Europeans.
    E. the successes in European agricultural technologies.

44. Haiti's independence differed from other Latin American movements in that
    A. the British landed troops to assist with the movement for independence.
    B. the United States supported the Haitians in their revolution with supplies.
    C. it began as a slave revolt against slave owners and led to independence.
    D. France and Napoleon welcomed and recognized Haiti's independence.
    E. Spain supported the movement for independence.

45. Leaders of Latin American independence revolts were generally
    A. monarchists, who wanted monarchs to govern their states.
    B. radicals, who supported the ideas of the French Jacobins.
    C. liberals, who wanted universal male suffrage.
    D. moderates, who wanted some democratic institutions but feared the masses.
    E. conservative republicans, who favored the church and rich landowners.

46. Socially, after independence, Latin America nations
    A. emancipated women and granted them rights denied during colonial times.
    B. ended legal systems of discrimination, but strong social barriers persisted.
    C. granted Indians rights to reclaim their lost lands.
    D. prohibited educational opportunities for women and Indians.
    E. saw increased conflict between the old landed elite and the commercial middle classes.

47. All of these led to increased American (United States) interest in Central America and the Caribbean EXCEPT:
    A. the American acquisition of Puerto Rico following the Spanish-American War.
    B. the desire for Latin American imports, especially coffee, sugar, and oil.
    C. investments in Mexico, Central America, and Caribbean economies.
    D. the desire to build a canal between the Pacific Ocean and Caribbean Sea.
    E. the suppression of the slave trade and slavery in the region.

48. The decline of the Ottoman Empire in the 18th and 19th centuries can be traced to all of these reasons EXCEPT:

A. sultans who were weak or inept rulers.
B. frequent defeat of the Ottoman Empire and annexations of its land.
C. religious divisions within Islam.
D. decline in the productivity of peasants and artisans.
E. Christian and non-Turkish populations, who resented Turkish rule.

49. In the last decades of the 19th century, the Chinese and Ottoman inability to reform or modernize was largely due to

A. foreign pressures not to modernize at all.
B. constant rebellions and peasant revolts.
C. the lack of a prosperous merchant class.
D. elites, who would do nothing to limit their authority.
E. the lack of an educated elite willing to lead or propose reforms.

50. 19th century ruling elites in Russia embraced which philosophy and ideas?

A. Autocratic government, Orthodox religion, and extreme nationalism
B. Liberalism, including the emancipation of serfs and British style democracy
C. Socialism with land reform for the peasants and protections for workers
D. Bolshevism, or a worker-led revolution and abolition of private property
E. Constitutional monarchy with an elected parliament and limitations on the ruler's powers.

51. Industrially and socially, 19th century Russia was most transformed by

A. The emancipation of the serfs, which furnished millions of workers.
B. The construction of railroads, which opened markets, jobs, and movement.
C. Compulsory education for women and the peasants.
D. The state's support of free enterprise, free trade, and entrepreneurship.
E. The government's land reform policy giving the peasants land and money.

52. Which of these statements is a fact about the policies of the Meiji restoration?

A. Political power was centralized and the Emperor's authority was restored.
B. Feudalism was retained, although it was limited.
C. The samurai retained some of its rights and privileges.
D. The samurai and educated Confucian elite staffed the state bureaucracy.
E. The Diet obtained rights and powers similar to British parliament.

53. Japan avoided the fates of Qing China and the Ottoman Empire by

A. closing its country to foreign influences.
B. accepting the United States as a protector to balance European influences.
C. defeating American, British, and other European expeditions to Japan.
D. reforming, modernization, selective westernization, and industrialization.
E. relying on its samurai, bushido, and Shinto traditions.

54. All of these themes are typical of the 20th century in world history EXCEPT:
    A. increased national sentiment.
    B. increased religious revivalism.
    C. rapid and fundamental changes.
    D. increasing cross-cultural contacts and connections.
    E. continuing dominance of the world by western powers.

55. Which of these statements about the West's 20th century position is a FACT?
    A. The western domination of the world has continued.
    B. The West's population relative to the rest of the world has declined.
    C. Fewer people immigrate to the West and the USA today than in 1900.
    D. European empires and colonial empires persist today.
    E. The West and the USA still have a monopoly on military technologies.

56. Regarding world trade and manufacturing in the 20th century,
    A. Japan is the wealthiest nation with the largest economy.
    B. Brazil, China, and similar nations cannot compete with the western-dominated global economy.
    C. The USA has the largest business and economic sector, but has many rivals.
    D. most societies now earn the bulk of their profits from international trade.
    E. the largest sector of the world economy is still agriculture.

57. The intensification of international contacts in the 20th century is largely due to
    A. technology.
    B. war.
    C. international trade.
    D. the spread of global diseases.
    E. the intensification of religious feeling.

58. Which of the following statements about the effects of World War I and the Great Depression on world governments is a FACT?
    A. Both made it likely governments were more responsive to the needs of the governed.
    B. Both made it easier for the military to dominate the government.
    C. Both supported the rise of totalitarian dictatorships.
    D. Both encouraged the growth of democracy and representative governments.
    E. Both led to the unprecedented growth of governments and their intervention in society.

59. The immediate result of World War I was
    A. the rise of the United States as a great power.
    B. the beginning of European decolonization.
    C. the rise of Japan to great power status.
    D. the Great Depression.
    E. the collapse of all European empires.

60. After World War II, the increase in internationalism was best represented by
    A. the rise to prominence of the USA and USSR.
    B. the victory of the communists in the Chinese Civil War.
    C. the United Nations and its organizations and activities.
    D. the willing breakup of the colonial empires by the European powers.
    E. the United States' end of its isolationism in international affairs.

61. The central thread in Western culture after 1920 has been the
    A. conflict and tension especially in the arts.
    B. dynamism of scientific research and faith that science can solve anything.
    C. continuing importance of religion in everyday life.
    D. collective understanding or responsibility.
    E. inability to change or absorb foreign or new elements.

62. All of these descriptions form the pattern of 20th century revolutions EXCEPT:
    A. they occurred in societies undergoing significant changes.
    B. different groups existed, each with divergent demands for their nations.
    C. groups with strong ideological and religious outlooks dominated them.
    D. they occurred in states with strong governments.
    E. winning groups all developed authoritarian institutions and policies.

63. In the 20th century, Soviet and Western European lifestyles were similar in all these ways EXCEPT:
    A. living standards improved and extensive health care services developed.
    B. the emphasis on consumerism and the development of a consumer society.
    C. the pace of work and its increasing supervision.
    D. leisure activities, including movies and sports.
    E. the division on class lines between better educated elites and bureaucrats on one hand, and workers and peasants on the other.

64. The chief stimulus for the collapse of Western colonial rule and influence in the Pacific Rim was
    A. due to the communist victory in the Chinese civil war in 1945.
    B. due to the British grant of independence to India in 1947.
    C. caused by the initial Japanese defeat of the western colonial powers.
    D. the American insistence during World War II that Europe grant its colonies independence.
    E. the Russian invasion of Asian colonial territories in World War II.

65. The relationship between business and government in Japan, Korea, and Taiwan in the later half of the 20th century is BEST described as a(n)
    A. communist-style command economy.
    B. socialist-capitalist mix of private property and public welfare.
    C. separated by American style constitutions.
    D. cooperative – the government encourages and protects businesses in an almost mercantilist manner.
    E. antagonistic towards each other.

66. The major Latin American social or cultural change between 1914 and 1945 was
    A. the rise of a political influential middle class and activist worker movements.
    B. the increasing "Indianization" of Latin American countries and cultures.
    C. the enfranchisement of minorities and women.
    D. the immigration of millions of Africans to Latin America.
    E. the spread of the Pentecostal Christians throughout Latin America.

67. In 20th century Latin America and Africa, the military was typically
    A. small and usually ineffective.
    B. liberal and reform-minded.
    C. anti-religious and in favor of a secular society.
    D. democratic but involved in politics.
    E. socially conservative, elitist, and authoritarian.

68. World War I directly threatened continued European colonialism for all of these reasons EXCEPT:
    A. the war helped develop colonial enterprises and industries to support the war effort.
    B. the myth of European invincibility and superiority was destroyed on the battlefields.
    C. colonial powers increasingly gave native troops and officers real opportunities for the first time.
    D. the British and French defeat in World War I led directly to the first grants of independence for some of the colonies.
    E. it was hard to speak of equal rights and defending democracy while having colonies.

69. What statement BEST characterizes the role of women in African and Asian nationalist movements?
    A. women were often the leaders of political movements.
    B. women's involvement in national independence movements was paralleled by a campaign for women's rights within their own society.
    C. women remained largely secluded and uninterested in the movements.
    D. while women participated, it was often in secondary roles.
    E. only elite, upper-class women participated in independence movements.

70. Most problems affecting the modern states in post-colonial Africa and Asia can be traced to
    A. industrialization.
    B. continuing neo-colonialism.
    C. overpopulation.
    D. linguistic, cultural, and religious differences.
    E. international warfare.

MULTIPLE-CHOICE ANSWERS

1.	C	44.	C
2.	A	45.	D
3.	C	46.	B
4.	D	47.	E
5.	E	48.	C
6.	B	49.	D
7.	D	50.	A
8.	A	51.	B
9.	B	52.	A
10.	C	53.	D
11.	A	54.	E
12.	E	55.	B
13.	E	56.	C
14.	B	57.	A
15.	D	58.	E
16.	C	59.	A
17.	A	60.	C
18.	B	61.	B
19.	E	62.	D
20.	C	63.	B
21.	D	64.	C
22.	B	65.	D
23.	E	66.	A
24.	A	67.	E
25.	E	68.	D
26.	C	69.	B
27.	D	70.	C
28.	E		
29.	B		
30.	B		
31.	C		
32.	D		
33.	E		
34.	B		
35.	A		
36.	C		
37.	A		
38.	C		
39.	E		
40.	D		
41.	A		
42.	A		
43.	B		

MAPS FOR ADVANCED PLACEMENT WORLD HISTORY

FIRST RIVER VALLEY CIVILIZATIONS

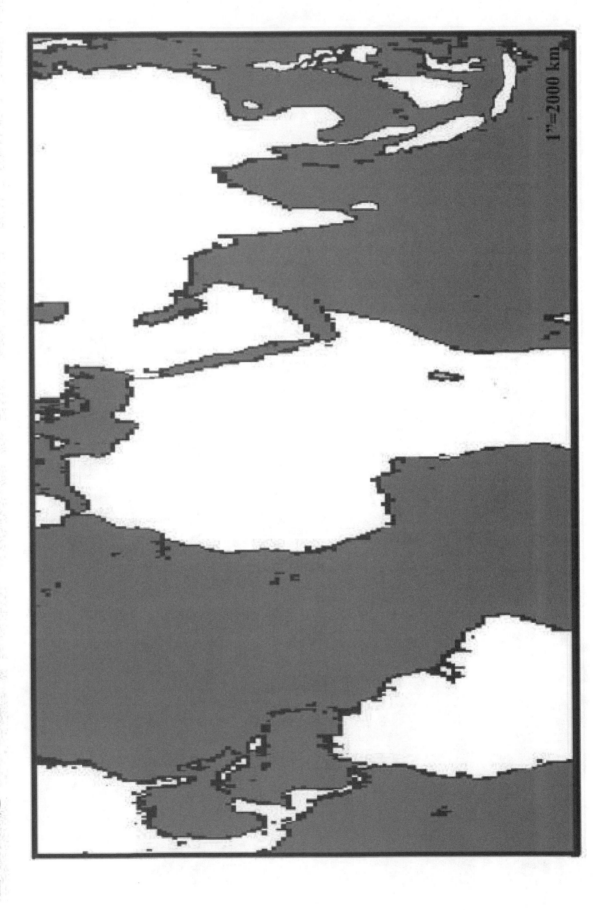

1"=2000 km

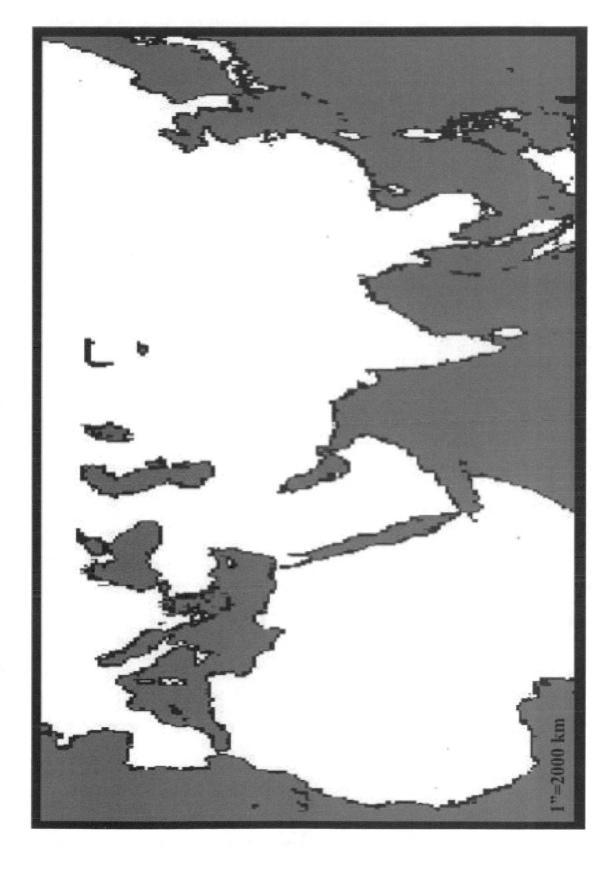

AFRO-EURASIAN REGION

1"=2000 km

SOUTH WEST ASIAN REGION

1"=800 km

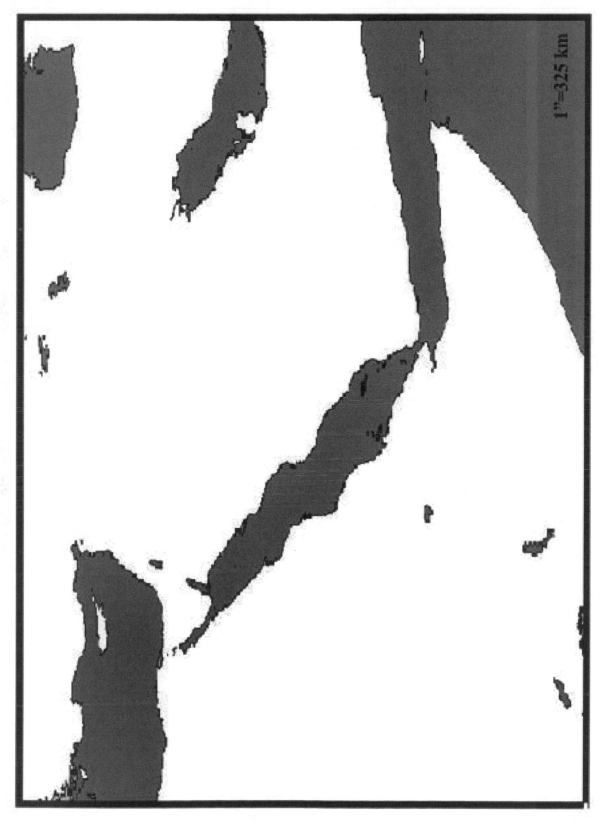

RED SEA REGION

1"=325 km

EASTERN MEDITERRANEAN REGION

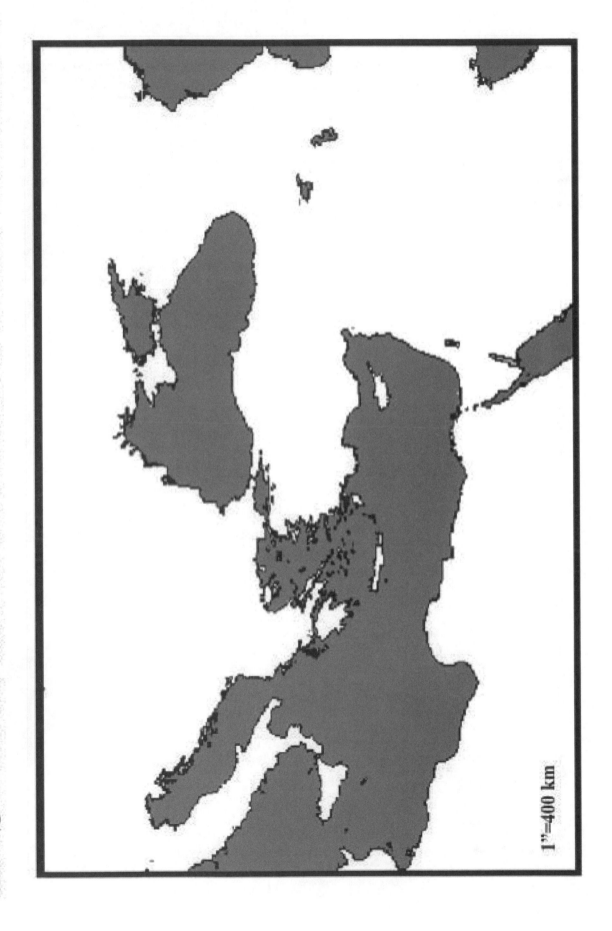

1"=400 km

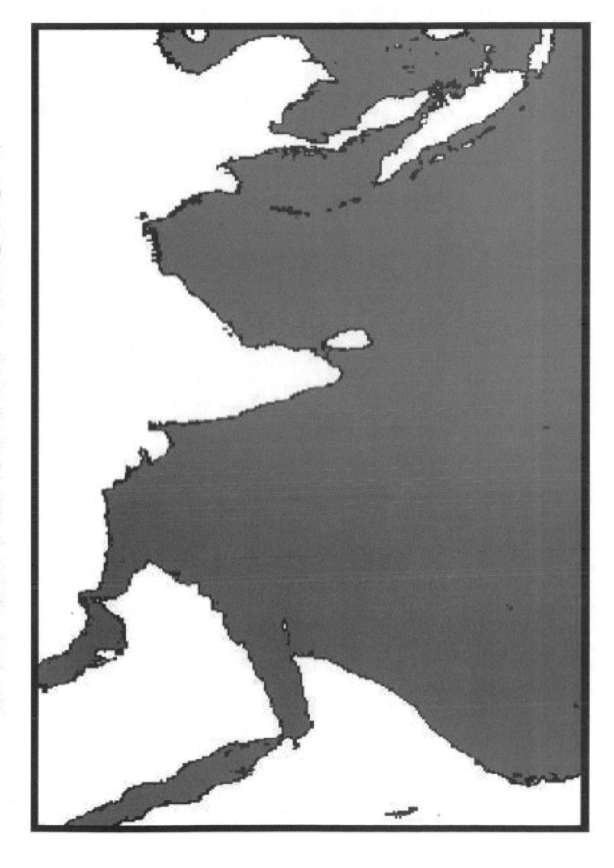

INDIAN OCEAN REGION

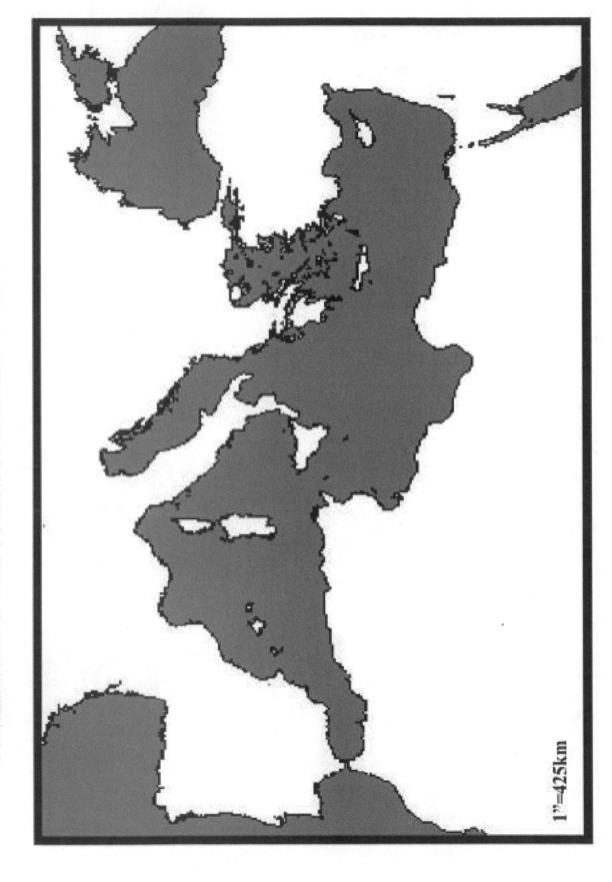

MEDITERRANEAN REGION

1"=425km

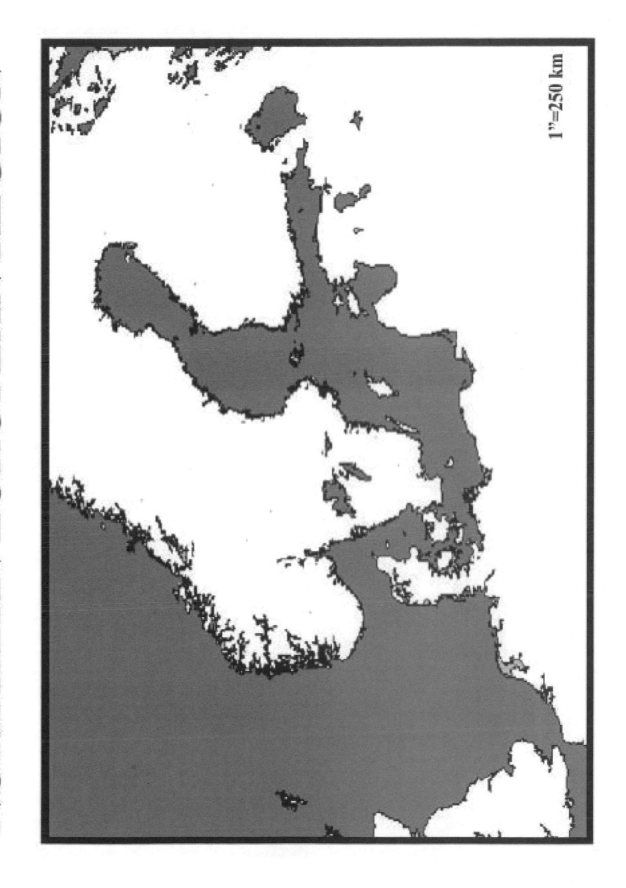

NORTHERN EUROPEAN REGION

1"=250 km

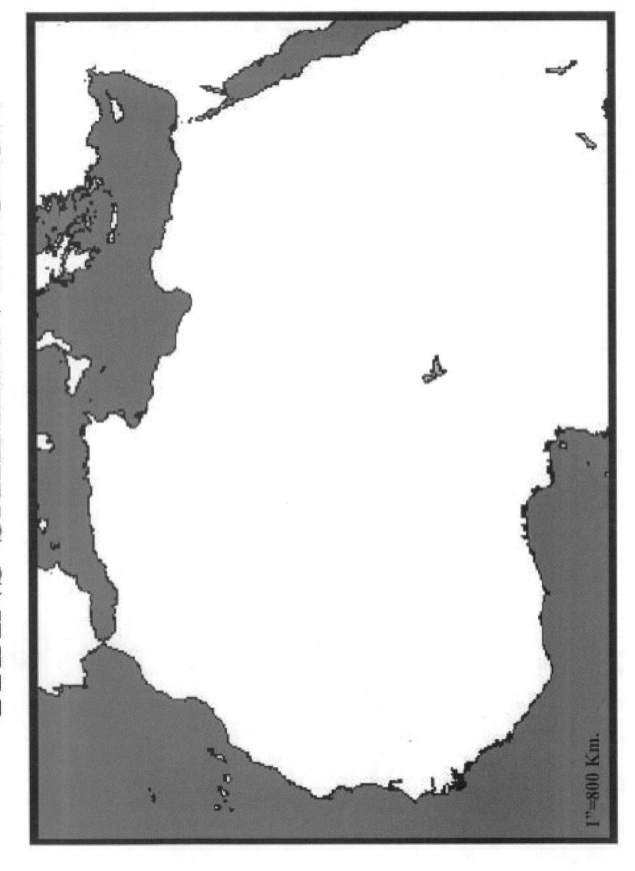

TRANS-SAHARAN REGION

1"=800 Km.

SUB-SAHARAN REGIONS

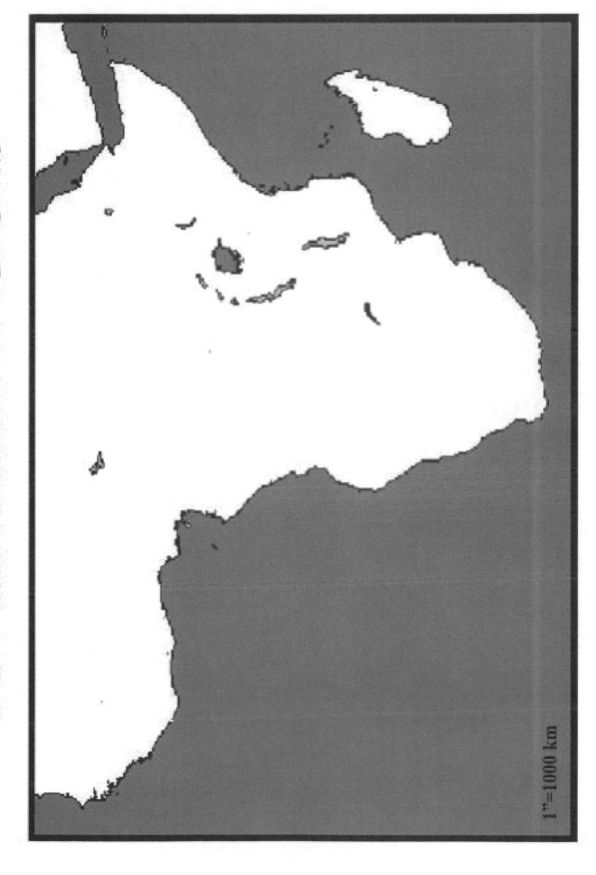

1"=1000 km

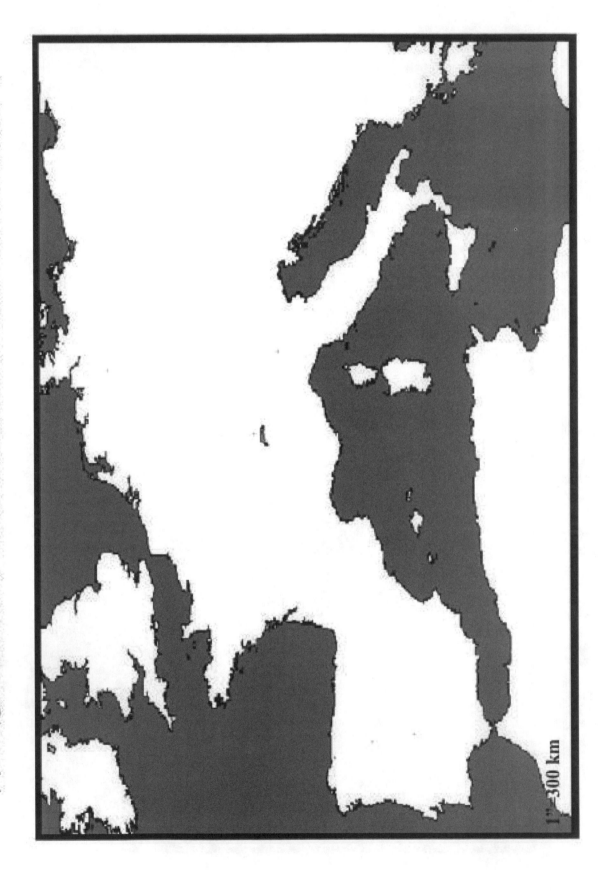

WESTERN EUROPEAN REGION

1"=300 km

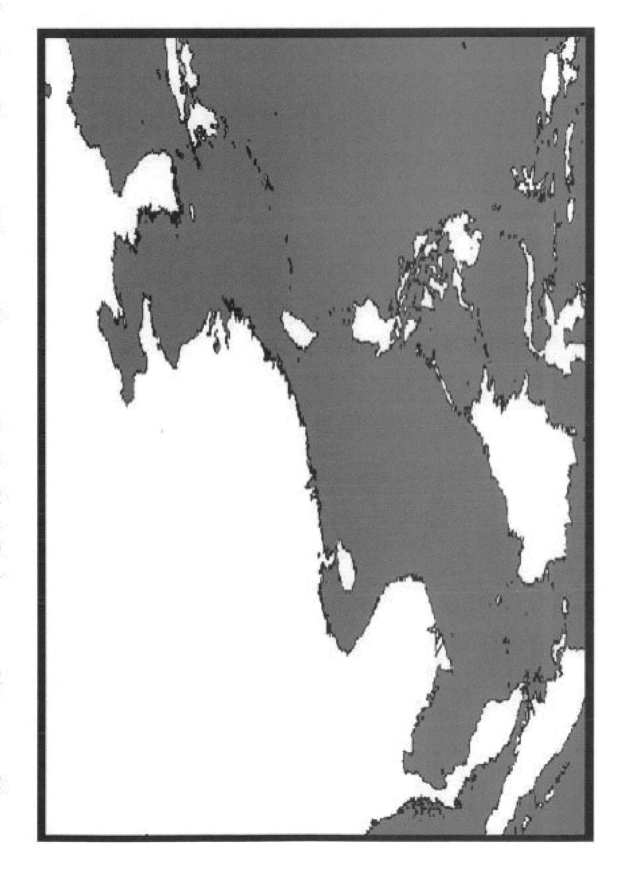

EAST ASIAN & SOUTH SEAS REGION

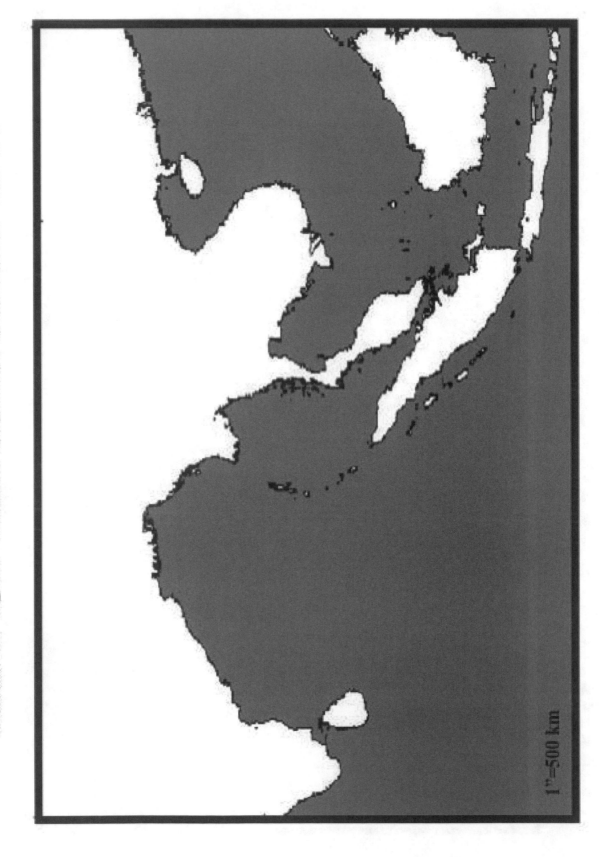

BAY OF BENGAL REGION

1"=500 km

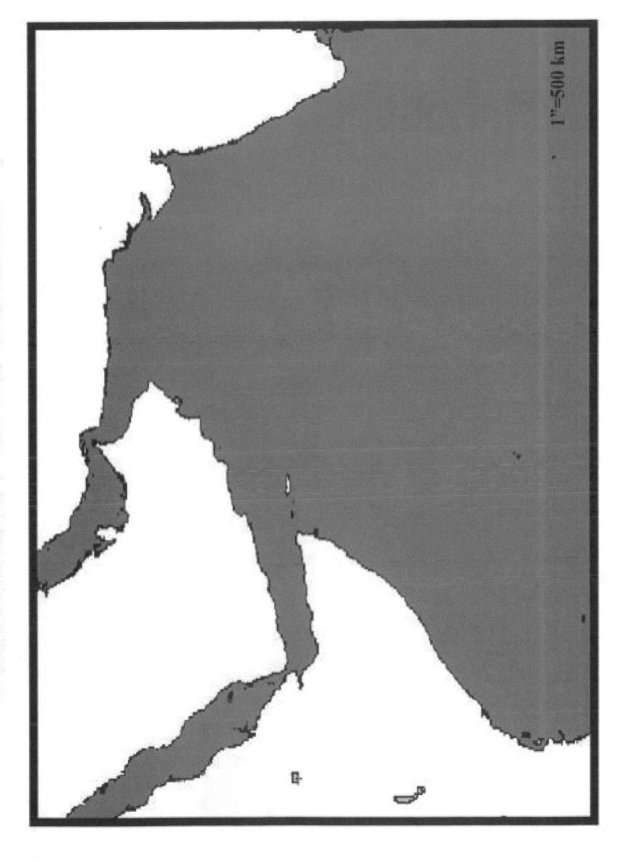

ARABIAN SEA REGION

1"=500 km

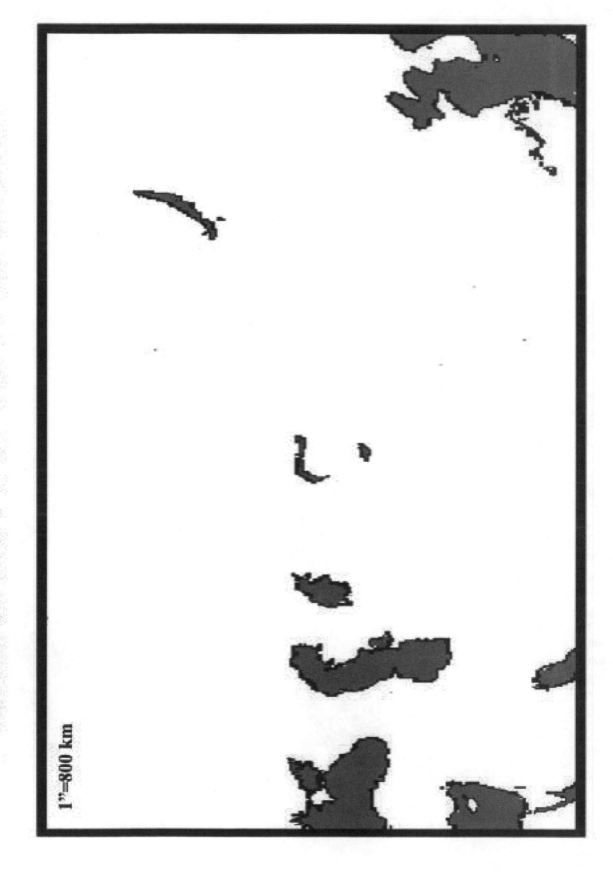

EURASIAN STEPPE REGION

1"=800 km

MESO-AMERICA & ANDEAN REGIONS

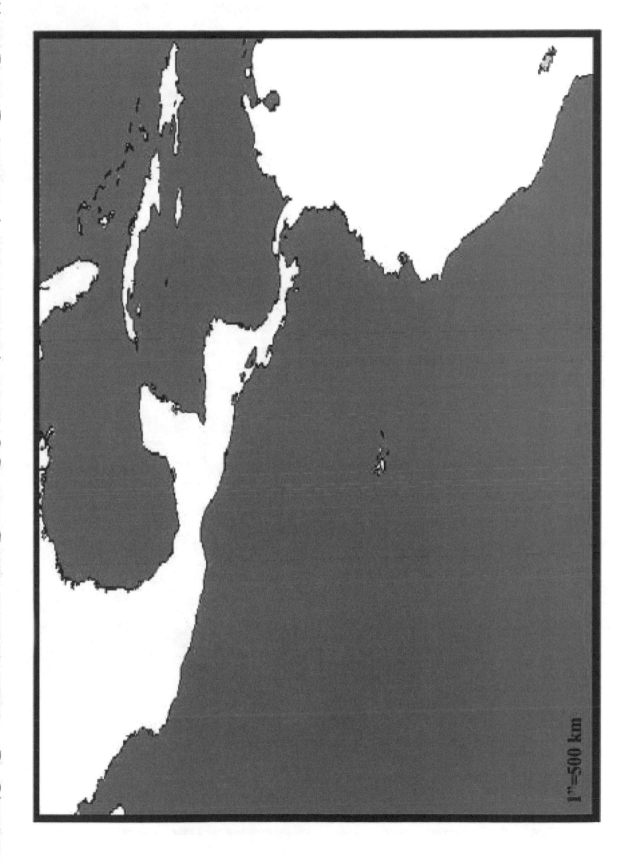

1"=500 km

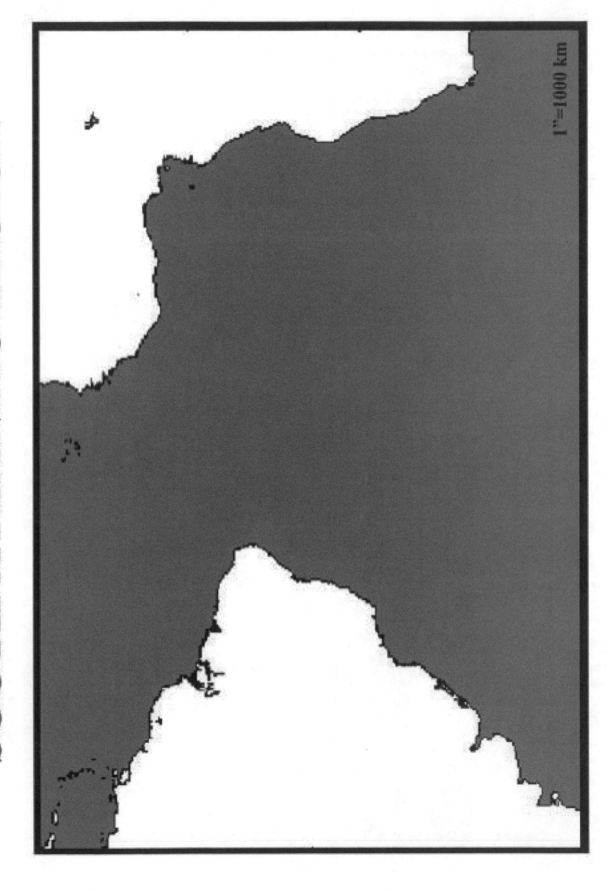

SOUTH ATLANTIC REGION

1"=1000 km

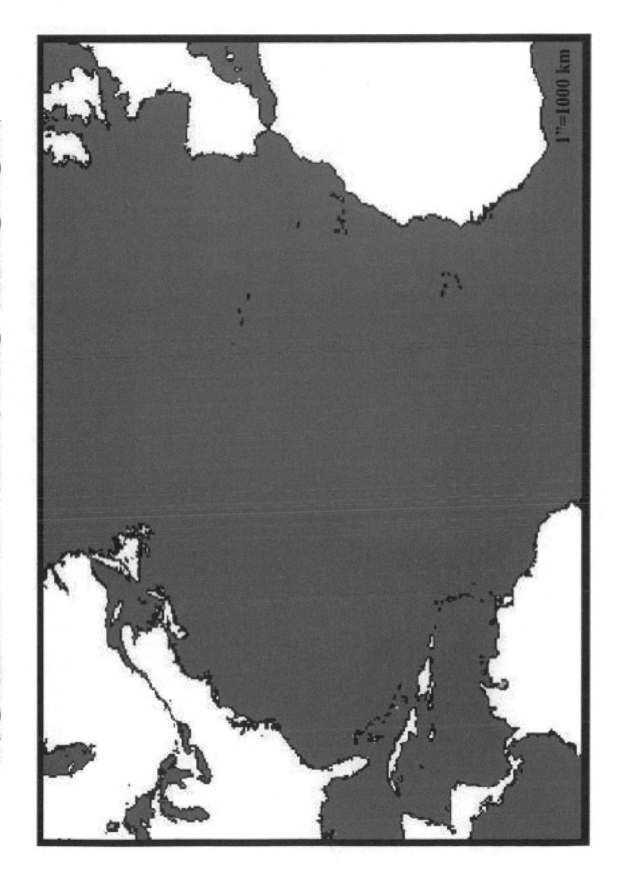

NORTH ATLANTIC REGION

1"=1000 km

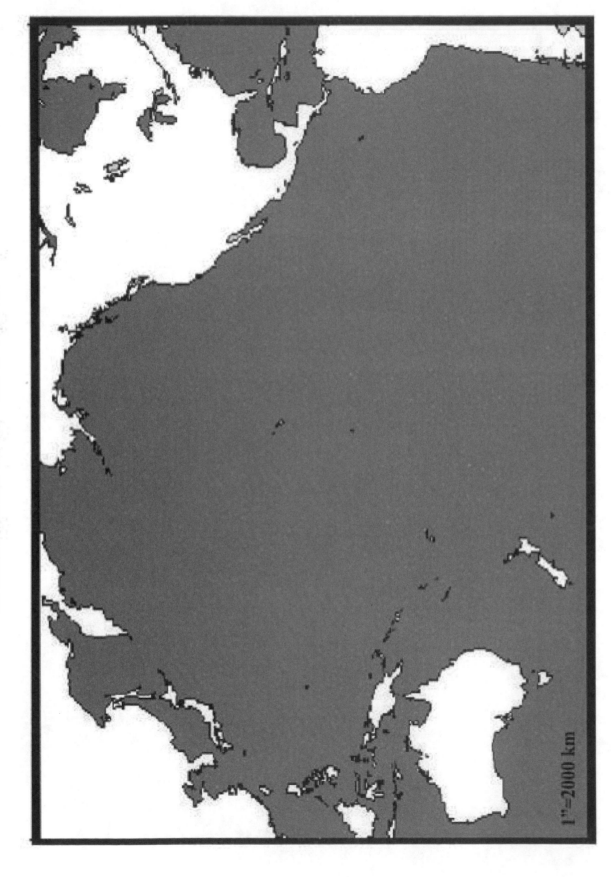

PACIFIC BASIN

1"=2000 km